The First Book of

WordPerfect® 5.1
Bestseller Edition

The First Book of

WordPerfect® 5.1
Bestseller Edition

Kate Barnes

SAMS

A Division of Prentice Hall Computer Publishing

11711 North College, Carmel, Indiana 46032 USA

To Jeff and "the girls."
May you live happily ever after.

International Standard Book Number: 0-672-27413-2
Library of Congress Catalog Card Number: 92-60384

95 94 93 92   8 7 6 5 4 3

Interpretation of the printing code: the rightmost number of the first series of numbers is the year of the book's printing; the rightmost number of the second series of numbers is the number of the book's printing. For example, a printing code of 92-1 shows that the first printing of the book occurred in 1992.

Screen reproductions in this book were created by means of the program Collage Plus from Inner Media, Inc., Hollis, NH.

Printed in the United States of America

 The text in this book is printed on recycled paper.

Publisher
Richard K. Swadley

Associate Publisher
Marie Butler-Knight

Managing Editor
Elizabeth Keaffaber

Product Development Manager
Lisa A. Bucki

Development Editor
Faithe Wempen

Production Editors
Lisa C. Hoffman
Annalise DiPaolo

Manuscript Editor
Kathy Huggler

Copy Editor
Audra Gable

Cover Designer
Tim Amrhein

Designer
Michele Laseau

Indexers
Jeanne Clark
Johnna VanHoose

Production Team
Claudia Bell, Scott Boucher, Paula Carroll, Brad Chinn, Christine Cook, Joelynn Gifford, Kate Godfrey, Tim Groeling, Denny Hager, Carla Hall-Batton, Carrie Keesling, Bob LaRoche, Laurie Lee, Matthew Morrill, Linda Quigley, Caroline Roop, Linda Seifert, Sandra Shay, Dennis Sheehan, Kevin Spear, Angie Trzepacz, Sue Vandewalle, Mary Beth Wakefield, Corinne Walls, Kelli Widdifield, Allan Wimmer, Phil Worthington, Christine Young

Special thanks to C. Herbert Feltner for assuring the technical accuracy of this book.

Contents

6   Changing Margins   97

7   How to Print Your Work   113

8   Giving Characters a New Look   129

Introduction

The *First Book of WordPerfect 5.1* has helped almost 100,000 people learn WordPerfect quickly. Now, this Bestseller Edition is available, featuring expanded topics and more help.

Popular word processors usually have hundreds of features for you to learn to use. This is more than the average user needs or wants, and for the beginning user, the sheer bulk can be intimidating.

What the *First Book of WordPerfect 5.1 Bestseller Edition* does is glean only the "most used" features. It focuses on those features you'll need to use in the great majority of your work. This way, you save time and eliminate the frustration of trying to sort out what you need from what you don't need.

The approach is meant to be simple. Such aids as Quick Steps to operations, overviews, everyday examples, and plentiful screen illustrations are designed for the beginning user. It's a simple, short book to make your learning of WordPerfect short and simple.

Conventions Used in This Book

Read "In This Chapter" at the beginning of each chapter for a brief idea of what you'll learn in the chapter. The most important procedures are summarized at the beginning of every chapter too, so if you're in a hurry, you don't need to wade through any text to find what you need.

Throughout the chapter, tables, notes, tips, cautions, FYIdeas and steps make learning easy. At the end of the chapter, read "What's Next?" to explore a few advanced features related to the chapter subject.

Once you have learned WordPerfect, you may need an occasional reminder. The tear-out quick reference card repeats the Quick Steps from the book in handy, take-along form. The inside back cover of the book summarizes the WordPerfect codes that you may encounter most often.

Icons

Several special icons are used in this book:

The generous number of *Quick Steps* give you the at-a-glance steps to quickly perform an operation. These numbered steps describe both the actions you perform and the result of those actions. The inside front cover provides a list of Quick Steps for fast reference.

TIPS: offer hints and shortcuts for using the program more effectively.

NOTES: point out additional features and provide background information you need to understand special terms.

CAUTIONS: alert you to potential pitfalls and help solve common problems.

FYIdeas describe practical ways that you can use Word-Perfect at work and at home, to create projects and documents you may not have even thought of!

Entering Commands

WordPerfect allows you to enter commands via menus or keypresses. The instructions in this book cover both options (along with details on the use of the mouse). Work with whatever approach is most comfortable for you. Keystrokes to be made in combination are separated by a hyphen (-) and in this book, are represented by small key cap illustrations meant to replicate the common keyboard key appearance. For example, ⇧Shift-F9 indicates you should press ⇧Shift and F9 simultaneously.

When an operation is described as follows:

"Press ⇧Shift-F8 and select 1 - Line, or choose Line from the **L**ayout menu"

it means that there are two different methods of accomplishing the same thing. The first method would be to hold down the ⇧Shift key and press F8, and then press 1 or L to select the Line option. (When a letter is bold, as is the **L** in **L**ine, it means you can type that letter to select the command.) The second method would be to pull down the **L**ayout menu (you'll learn how to do this later in the book) and select the Line option from it. (Again, the bold letter in the command indicates that you can choose it by typing that letter.)

Acknowledgments

Many thanks to the continued excellent support from the staff at Prentice Hall Computer Publishing. Special thanks to Marie Butler-Knight, Faithe Wempen, Lisa Hoffman, Kathy Huggler, Annalise DiPaolo, and Audra Gable.

Trademark Acknowledgments

All terms mentioned in this book that are known to be trademarks or service marks are listed below. In addition, terms suspected of being trademarks or service marks have been appropriately capitalized. Sams cannot attest to the accuracy of this information. Use of a term in this book should not be regarded as affecting the validity of any trademark or service mark.

Lotus and 1-2-3 are registered trademarks of Lotus Development Corporation.

WordPerfect is a registered trademark of WordPerfect Corporation.

MS-DOS is a registered trademark of Microsoft Corporation.

In This Chapter

Start WordPerfect for Windows

1. Type **cd\wp51** and press `⏎Enter`
2. Type **wp** and press `⏎Enter`

Set Up the Mouse

1. Press `⇧Shift`-`F1` or from the **F**ile menu, select Setup.
2. Select 1 - Mouse
3. Select 1 - Type
4. Use the arrow keys to highlight your mouse type.
5. Press `⏎Enter`

Use a Pull-Down Menu

1. Press `Alt` or click the right mouse button.
2. *Keyboard:* Use the arrow keys to highlight a selection, then press `⏎Enter`

   or

   Mouse: Click on a selection with the left mouse button.

   To use a key combination (for example `Alt` `F4`), press both key simultaneously.

Get Help

1. Press `F3` or select Help from the main menu.

Getting Started with WordPerfect 5.1

Welcome to the quick and easy way to learn WordPerfect. If you're not sure how to get started, this chapter will provide some help. In it, you'll learn how to start WordPerfect, how to move around and enter commands, and how to use the on-line Help feature.

TIP: If you're a newcomer to Computers (or want to review the basics) take a look at Appendix A, Getting Ready to Use WordPerfect. If WordPerfect has not been installed on your computer, refer to Appendix B, Installing WordPerfect for instructions.

Starting WordPerfect

Once WordPerfect is installed, you are ready to begin using the program.

On a floppy-drive system, make sure the computer is turned on and the WordPerfect disk is in drive A. From the A: prompt, type wp (for WordPerfect).

From a hard disk, type wp at the C: prompt. Or, go to the WordPerfect directory by typing in the change directory (CD) command, followed by the path to the directory, and press ↵Enter. For example, you would type this command line if you used the Basic installation:

```
cd\wp51
```

The advantage to starting from the WP51 directory is that you won't have to change the directory later when you save and retrieve files.

The opening screen shown in Figure 1.1 appears, followed by the WordPerfect document screen shown in Figure 1.2. Don't be alarmed at the blank appearance. This chapter will show you how to access WordPerfect's menu system and how to speed up your work with mouse techniques and keyboard shortcuts.

The Mouse

If the only type of mouse that draws your attention is the furry variety, you can skip this section. It covers setting up and using the mechanical type of mouse with WordPerfect.

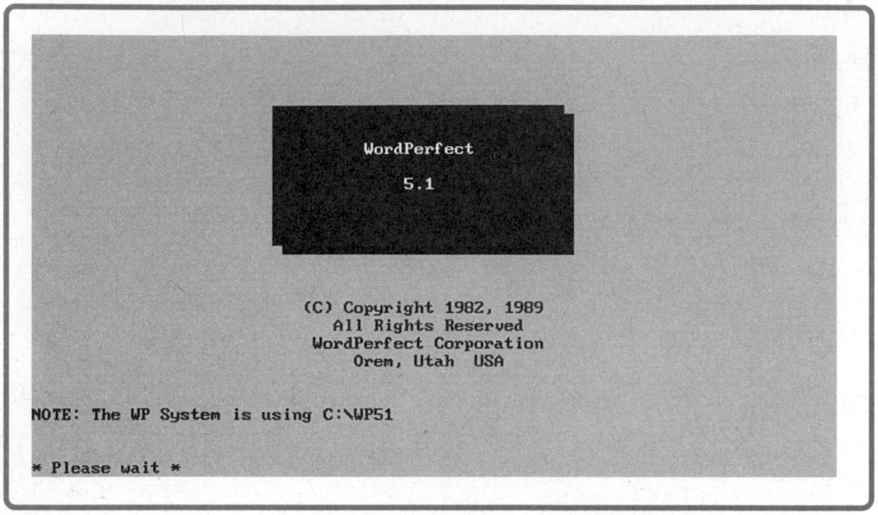

Figure 1.1

The WordPerfect opening screen.

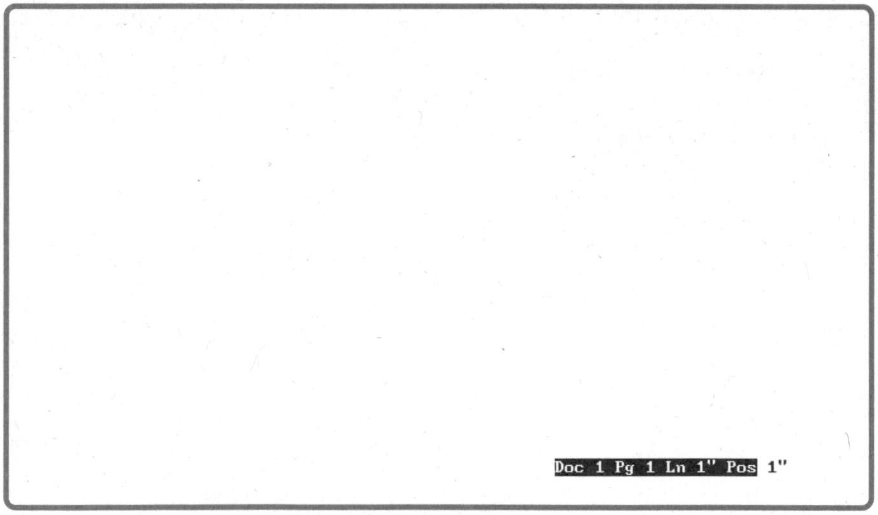

```
            WordPerfect

               5.1



         (C) Copyright 1982, 1989
            All Rights Reserved
         WordPerfect Corporation
            Orem, Utah  USA

NOTE: The WP System is using C:\WP51

* Please wait *
```

Figure 1.2

The WordPerfect document screen.

```



                                                    Doc 1 Pg 1 Ln 1" Pos 1"
```

Setting Up the Mouse

Before you can use your mouse, you must introduce it to WordPerfect by type and connection. (Ask your mouse dealer to help you if you don't know the settings to make.)

To set up the mouse, follow these steps:

1. Press ⬆Shift-F1 (Setup) or select Setup from the File menu. The Setup menu appears.

2. Select 1 - Mouse (or Mouse from the menu). The Setup: Mouse menu appears.

3. Select 1 - Type. The Setup: Mouse Type menu, shown in Figure 1.3, appears.

Figure 1.3

The Setup: Mouse Type menu.

```
Setup: Mouse Type

Appoint MousePen (PS/2)
Appoint MousePen (Serial)
CH Products Roller Mouse (PS/2)
CH Products Roller Mouse (Serial)
IBM PS/2 Mouse
Imsi Mouse, 2 button (Serial)
Imsi Mouse, 3 button (Serial)
Kensington Expert Mouse (PS/2)
Kensington Expert Mouse (Serial)
Keytronic Mouse (Bus)
Keytronic Mouse (Serial)
Logitech Mouse (Bus)
Logitech Mouse (PS/2)
Logitech Mouse (Serial)
Logitech MouseMan (Bus)
Logitech MouseMan (PS/2)
Logitech MouseMan (Serial)
Logitech TrackMan (Serial)
Microsoft Mouse (Bus)
Microsoft Mouse (Serial)
Mouse Driver (MOUSE.COM)

1 Select; 2 Auto-select; 3 Other Disk; 1 Name Search: 1
```

4. Use ↑ and ↓ to highlight the type of mouse you are using. When it is highlighted, press ↵Enter

5. If you selected a serial mouse type, check the 2 - Port setting, which refers to where the mouse is attached to your computer, to see if it is correct. Otherwise, skip to step 8.

> **TIP:** A serial mouse is, by definition, connected to one of your COM ports. Most computers only have two: COM1 and COM2. To determine which one your mouse is hooked up to, just look at the back of your computer; the COM ports are usually marked. Failing this, you can either call your dealer or determine the right one by trial-and-error.

6. If the port listed is incorrect, select 2 - Port . Use the arrow keys to highlight a new setting and press ⏎Enter

7. Press F7 (Exit) to return to the WordPerfect document screen.

You know the mouse is properly set up when the pointer moves across the screen as you move the mouse on your desk. If it doesn't work, you might try this setup process again and select a different mouse type or port.

Using a Mouse

The mouse pointer marks your place on the screen. To use a mouse, simply move it across your desk. The roller on the bottom of the mouse causes the pointer to move across the screen. If you run out of desk space, just pick up the mouse and reposition it on the desk; the pointer position will remain unchanged on your screen.

Table 1.1 explains the basic mouse actions and the special terms used to describe them.

Table 1.1
Mouse Terms.

Term	Mouse Action
Point	Place the mouse marker on a spot.
Click	Press a button once.
Double click	Press a button twice quickly.
Drag	Press a button and hold it down while moving the mouse.

You can use the mouse to move about the screen, as described in Table 1.2. You can also use the mouse to make menu selections and choose Yes/No options. You'll learn about these uses in the section titled "Using the Menu."

Table 1.2
Moving with the Mouse.

Screen Movement	Mouse Action
Move the cursor to a spot	Point to the spot and press the left button.
Move to parts of the document that are off the screen	Press and hold the right button, drag the mouse to the edge of the screen; release the button to stop the screen movement.

Making WordPerfect Selections

When you work with WordPerfect, you usually have two options for selecting WordPerfect functions. You can:

▲ Make a menu selection from the main menu (with the keyboard or a mouse).

▲ Press a function key alone or in combination with the Alt, Ctrl, or ⇧Shift keys.

Since the main menu provides an easy way for a beginner to access commands without memorizing function keys, we'll start our discussion there.

The Main Menu

When you first enter WordPerfect, the document screen resembles a blank stare. Most new users quite rightly don't know what to make of it. To get WordPerfect to give you a hint about what to do, you need to set up and use the menu system.

A menu on a computer screen is similar to a menu in a restaurant. Each offers a choice of options, but once you pick a selection on a computer menu, you are often presented with other options. For example, Figure 1.4 shows the initial menu, called the *main menu*. If you select File, the options for handling a file appear. The File menu is shown in Figure 1.5. The menus that appear from the main menu are called *pull-down* menus, since the effect is that they are pulled down from the first selection. Notice that from the File menu, you can print, exit WordPerfect, or select any other option related to file handling.

Displaying the Main Menu

In WordPerfect's initial setting, the main menu does not appear. You'll probably want to change this so that the main menu always appears. You can later change back if you like.

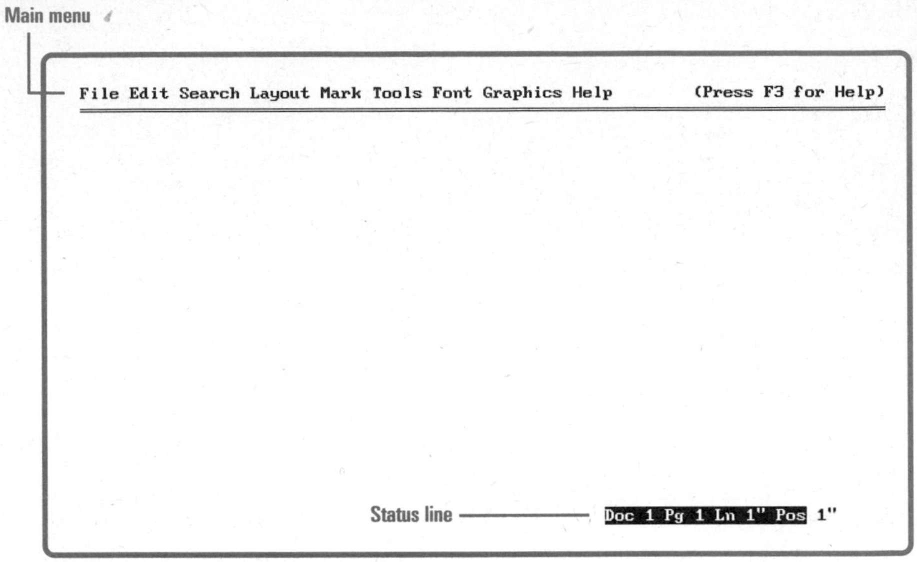

Figure 1.4

The WordPerfect main menu.

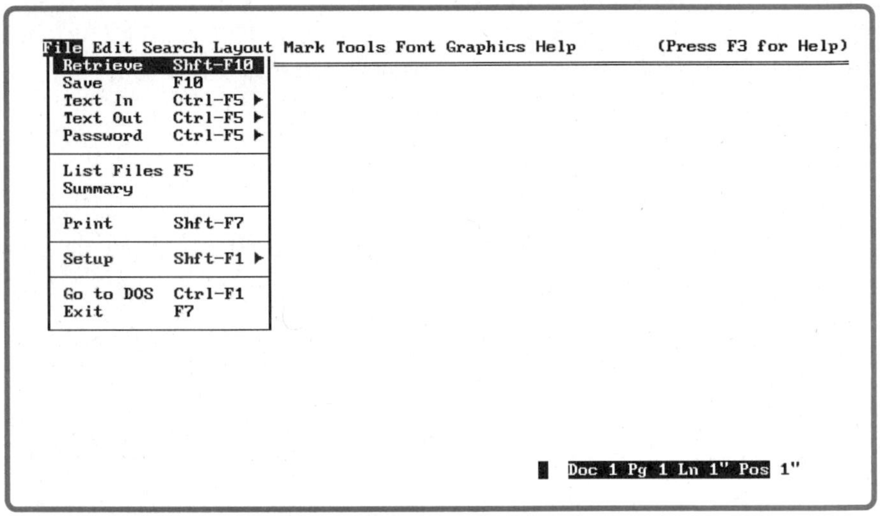

Main menu

```
  File Edit Search Layout Mark Tools Font Graphics Help        (Press F3 for Help)
  ────────────────────────────────────────────────────────────────────────────




                                                 Status line ─────────  Doc 1 Pg 1 Ln 1" Pos 1"
```

Figure 1.5

The File menu (a pull-down menu).

```
  File Edit Search Layout Mark Tools Font Graphics Help        (Press F3 for Help)
 ┌─────────────────┐───────────────────────────────────────────────────────────
 │ Retrieve  Shft-F10 │
 │ Save      F10      │
 │ Text In   Ctrl-F5 ▶│
 │ Text Out  Ctrl-F5 ▶│
 │ Password  Ctrl-F5 ▶│
 ├─────────────────┤
 │ List Files F5     │
 │ Summary           │
 ├─────────────────┤
 │ Print     Shft-F7 │
 ├─────────────────┤
 │ Setup     Shft-F1 ▶│
 ├─────────────────┤
 │ Go to DOS Ctrl-F1 │
 │ Exit      F7      │
 └─────────────────┘
                                                  ▮  Doc 1 Pg 1 Ln 1" Pos 1"
```

> **TIP:** If you are a beginner, set up and use the main menu. Menu actions are grouped logically. If you are unsure of the keys to press to perform a function, look through the menus. Even sophisticated word processing users will hunt for commands as they become familiar with a new word processing system. Then, once you are more familiar with WordPerfect, you may want to begin using the key combinations to speed up your work.

In the next section, you'll learn more about using WordPerfect's menus. For now, just follow these steps to set up the main menu to be displayed all the time.

> **NOTE:** The ⌐Alt⌐-⌐F1⌐ key combination used to access the Setup menu in these steps is an example of a keyboard shortcut, which you'll learn about later in this chapter.

1. Press ⌐⇧Shift⌐-⌐F1⌐ (Setup). The Setup menu shown in Figure 1.6 appears.

2. Press ⌐2⌐ or ⌐D⌐ to select 2 - Display. The Setup: Display menu, shown in Figure 1.7 appears.

3. Press ⌐4⌐ or ⌐M⌐ to select 4 - Menu Options. The Setup: Menu Options menu appears.

4. Type ⌐4⌐ or ⌐A⌐ to select Alt Key Selects Pull-Down Menu, then press ⌐Y⌐ for Yes. This sets up WordPerfect so that pressing the ⌐Alt⌐ key activates the main menu.

5. Press ⌐7⌐ or ⌐S⌐ to select Menu Bar Separator Line, then press ⌐Y⌐ for Yes. This creates a line that divides the main menu from the document, making it easier to distinguish the two.

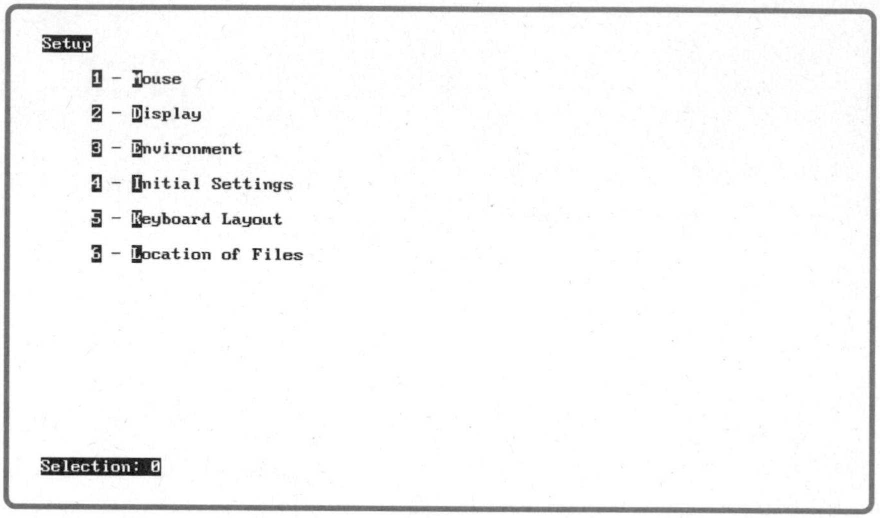

Figure 1.6

The Setup menu.

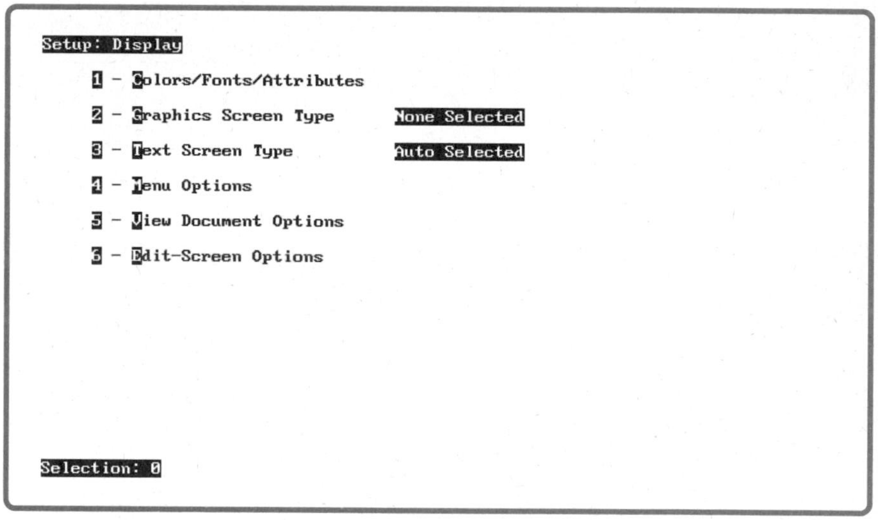

```
Setup
    1 - Mouse
    2 - Display
    3 - Environment
    4 - Initial Settings
    5 - Keyboard Layout
    6 - Location of Files




Selection: 0
```

Figure 1.7

The Setup: Display menu.

```
Setup: Display
    1 - Colors/Fonts/Attributes
    2 - Graphics Screen Type     None Selected
    3 - Text Screen Type         Auto Selected
    4 - Menu Options
    5 - View Document Options
    6 - Edit-Screen Options




Selection: 0
```

6. Press 8 or V to select Menu Bar Remains Visible, then press Y for Yes. This allows the main menu to remain visible every time you use WordPerfect. At this point, Yes should appear for each option.

7. Press F7 to return to the WordPerfect document screen. The main menu appears according to your settings.

Using the Main Menu

In the preceding procedure, you accessed the Setup menu by pressing a key combination (Alt - F1). As you'll learn later in this chapter, pressing the Alt key in conjunction with different function keys opens different menus. (The Ctrl and ⇧Shift keys work this way too.)

But working with function keys is only a part of the Alt key's duties—because in the preceding example we set up the Alt key to access WordPerfect's main menu. Follow these Quick Steps to learn how to access the main menu with the Alt key.

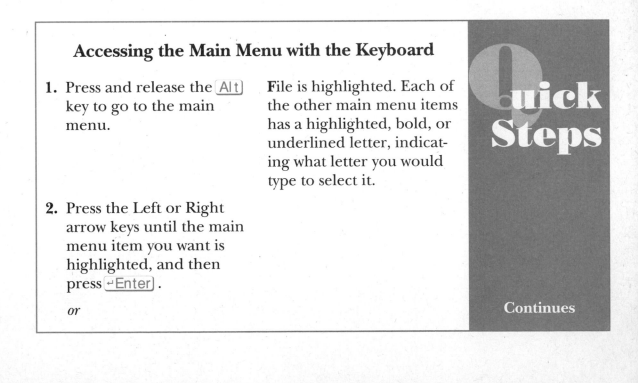

Accessing the Main Menu with the Keyboard

1. Press and release the Alt key to go to the main menu.

   File is highlighted. Each of the other main menu items has a highlighted, bold, or underlined letter, indicating what letter you would type to select it.

2. Press the Left or Right arrow keys until the main menu item you want is highlighted, and then press ↵Enter .

   or

Quick
Steps

Continues

Continued

Press the bold or under-lined letter of the menu selection to select it.

The selected pull-down menu appears. Each option on the pull-down menu has a bold or underlined letter, just like the items on the main menu.

3. Use ↑ ↓ to choose the desired option, then press ↵Enter to select it.

   or

   Press the bold or under-lined letter of the item to select it.

4. Provide additional infor-mation on any submenus that might appear.

5. When you're finished, press Esc to return to the previous level of the menu structure, or press F7 to return to the WordPerfect document screen.

If you have a mouse, you can use it to open and use the main menu. (Or, you may prefer to stick with the Alt method—whatever seems best to you.) The following steps show how to select main menu items using the mouse.

Accessing the Main Menu with a Mouse

1. Move the mouse on your desk until the pointer is over the menu selection you want.

    The mouse pointer appears as a small rectangle on your screen.

2. Click the left mouse button to pull down the menu.

    The menu appears. For example, if you clicked on File, the File menu would appear, as shown in Figure 1.5.

3. To make menu selections, point at the item and click the left mouse button.

4. Provide additional information on any submenus that might appear.

5. When you're finished, click the right mouse button.

Quick Steps

TIP: Double-clicking the left mouse button is the same as clicking the left mouse button and then pressing Enter. If you often find yourself clicking the left button and then pressing Enter, you can save steps by double-clicking. If you click the right mouse button with the menu displayed, the menu will disappear. Click the button again to make the menu visible again.

As you can see, the main menu can be accessed in many different ways. Table 1.3 summarizes the ways to use the main menu.

Table 1.3
Using Menus.

Action Desired	How to Perform
To access the main menu line	Press Alt or click the right mouse button.
To pull down a menu	▲ Highlight with the Left or Right arrow keys and press ↵Enter.
	▲ Press the highlighted, bold, or underlined letter of the menu.
	▲ Point with the mouse and click the left button.
To leave a menu	Press Esc or click the right mouse button.
Select Yes or No response	Point to the response and click. Press Y for Yes or N for No.

Using Keyboard Shortcuts

As you've seen, the keyboard can be used to select commands from the main menu. But keyboard shortcuts are also available, via the function keys, which circumvent the sometimes lengthy route through several menus to a particular feature. For example, to block some text you could press Alt to go to the main menu, press $\boxed{E}$ for the **E**dit menu, then $\boxed{B}$ for **B**lock. Or, you could simply use the keyboard shortcut $\boxed{Alt}$-$\boxed{F4}$.

Keyboard shortcuts primarily involve function keys (the "F" keys—$\boxed{F1}$, $\boxed{F2}$, etc.). When using a keyboard shortcut, you might press a function key alone or in conjunction with one or more other keys (usually some combination of $\boxed{Ctrl}$, $\boxed{⇧Shift}$, or $\boxed{Alt}$). To use a key combination, such as $\boxed{Alt}$-$\boxed{F4}$, just hold down the keys simultaneously.

CAUTION: If you have your $\boxed{Alt}$ key set up to access the main menu, as we set it up earlier in the chapter, be careful when using a key combination that involves the $\boxed{Alt}$ key. If you press the $\boxed{Alt}$ key but not the accompanying function key, the main menu will be activated, and you will have to press $\boxed{Alt}$ to return to normal mode.

After you are familiar with the keyboard shortcuts, you may find that you don't use the $\boxed{Alt}$ key to activate the main menu anymore. If this happens, you can reenter the Setup menu and turn off the Alt Key Selects Pull-Down Menu feature, to avoid this potential annoyance.

The Keyboard Template

The quickest way to perform an operation or command is with a key combination. But how do you remember all those combinations? Each function key has a separate operation for it by itself, with the $\boxed{⇧Shift}$ key, with the $\boxed{Ctrl}$ key, and with the $\boxed{Alt}$ key—in total, more than 40 commands.

Luckily, WordPerfect comes with a keyboard template. The template fits on your keyboard, and provides a quick reference of all the function key combinations and their meanings.

If you lose your template, or find yourself on someone else's computer without one, don't lose hope! WordPerfect's on-line Help feature can show you the template. See the "Help!" section later in this chapter.

Let's look at a couple of template examples. Take a look at the operations under F7 on your template. It looks something like this:

Ctrl	Footnote
Alt	Columns/Table
Shift	Print
	Exit
	F7

Starting at the bottom of the template:

▲ To exit a document, just press F7 .

▲ To print a document, press ⇧Shift - F7 .

▲ To open the Columns/Table menu, press Alt - F7 .

▲ To open the Footnote menu, press Ctrl - F7 .

The template is color coded to make it easier to read each line across and identify which key to press.

Don't be intimidated by the number of key options on the template. Use this book to get started, and you will learn the most useful functions first. Concentrate on learning key combinations for the functions you use most. The more you use them, the more the key combinations will become second nature to you.

Moving the Cursor

The *cursor* is the insertion point for any text you type. You can move it around the screen, and use it to designate where you want certain commands to take effect. By default, it appears as a blinking underline.

Some keyboard actions allow you to move the cursor quickly. These are called *quick movement keys*. Table 1.4 summarizes the quick movement keys. You will probably want to refer to this table frequently as you begin working in WordPerfect.

Move	Keys to Press
One character left	←
One character right	→
Left a word	Ctrl with ← (Word Left)
Right a word	Ctrl with → (Word Right)
Beginning of a line	Home, then ←
End of a line	Home, then →
Up a single line	↑
Down a single line	↓
Top of the screen	Home, then ↑
Bottom of the screen	Home, then ↓
First line on previous page	PgUp
First line on next page	PgDn
Up a paragraph	Ctrl-↑
Down a paragraph	Ctrl-↓

Table 1.4
Quick Movement Keys.

continues

Table 1.4
continued

Move	Keys to Press
Beginning of document (after WordPerfect codes)	[Home], [Home], [↑]
Beginning of document (before codes)	[Home], [Home], [Home], [↑]
End of document (after WordPerfect codes)	[Home], [Home], [↓] or [Home], [Home], [Home], [↓]
To a character or page number you type in	[Ctrl]-[Home]

Look back at the document screen in Figure 1.4. Notice the status line on the last line of the screen. On the right, this appears:

```
Doc 1 Pg 1 Ln 1" Pos 1"
```

This information indicates which of two possible WordPerfect documents you are working with. Then, information about your cursor position appears. Shown are the page (Pg) number, the line (Ln) position in inches from the top of your page, and the position (Pos) in inches from the left of the page. Messages about WordPerfect operations also appear at the bottom of your screen. So, keep an eye on what's happening down there.

Help!

WordPerfect can answer your cry of Help! Just select Help from the main menu. You have three options from which to choose:

▲ *Help:* An introductory Help screen. From this screen, press any function key for information about it, or press any letter to access the Help index. You can also press F3 to see the template from here.

> **NOTE:** Pressing F3 at WordPerfect's document screen, unless you are executing a command or using a feature, will take you directly to this introductory help screen. If you're in the middle of something, pressing F3 will take you to a Help screen that deals with the topic at hand. This is called *context-sensitive help.* To leave Help, press ⏎Enter

▲ *Index:* An index, the same one accessed through the introductory Help screen described above. It includes keys, features, and keystrokes.

▲ *Template:* This illustrates the template for the function keys on an IBM keyboard.

> **TIP:** If you have don't have your template and would like a printout of the one presented by the Help screen, press ⇧Shift-PrtSc. The resulting printout will not be pretty—it will contain all sorts of odd characters in place of the graphic lines—but it will include all template commands in a readable form.

Take some time to play with the Help feature. It can answer your questions and save you some frustrating moments.

What's Next?

Now that you've learned a bit about the WordPerfect keyboard and mouse procedures, you may want to try the following "extras." Remember, if you get lost at any time, press F3 for Help.

Customizing Mouse Settings

Using WordPerfect with the keyboard and mouse becomes easier with time. Once you are an expert with the mouse, you may want to alter the speed of your mouse response, to make it more or less sensitive to movement. Follow these steps:

1. Select ⬆Shift-F1 (Setup) or select Setup from the **File** menu.

2. Select 1 - Mouse (or Mouse from the menu).

3. Select and change any of the mouse settings:

   ▲ *Double Click Interval:* Determines the maximum amount of time between the two clicks of a double-click. If you exceed this time between your clicks in a double-click, WordPerfect will consider your action to be two single clicks.

   ▲ *Submenu Delay Time:* Determines how long your cursor rests on the name of a pull-down menu before it opens.

   ▲ *Acceleration Factor:* Determines how far the mouse pointer moves in response to mouse movement. The smaller the acceleration factor, the less responsive the mouse pointer will be (that is, the less distance it will move).

▲ *Left-Handed Mouse:* Allows you to set up the mouse for use with your left hand. If you select Yes, operations normally performed with the left mouse button are performed with the right, and vice versa.

▲ *Assisted Mouse Pointer Movement:* When set to Yes, automatically moves the mouse pointer to a menu whenever one is open.

4. When you are finished, press F7 to return to the document screen. If you made changes, test the mouse to make sure the new settings are right for you.

Setting Selection Letter Format

When using the keyboard, one way to make menu selections is to type the letter that is bold or underlined (often appearing in reverse video colors). (You may need to adjust your screen to see which letter is bold.) If the Setup: Menu Options menu appears with a letter in each selection clearly brighter (bold), you may leave the other options on this menu "as is." For example, the "M" in 1 - Menu Letter Display should be bold. Alternatively, you can underline all the letters that are bold. Figure 1.8 illustrates the main menu and the **F**ile menu with the letters underlined (which appear as reverse video) just to give you an idea of this look.

To change the appearance of letters, select and change the setting for each of these options on the Setup: Menu Options menu (accessed by pressing ⇧Shift-F1, then selecting 2 - Display, 4 - Menu Options):

1 - Menu Letter Display: To change letter appearance on full-screen menus like the Setup: Menu Options menu.

2 - Pull-Down Letter Display: To change letter appearance on the pull-down menus from the WordPerfect menu.

5 - Menu Bar Letter Display: Affects the letter appearance on the main WordPerfect menu.

Once you make any of these selections, this message appears:

`1 Size; 2 Appearance; 3 Normal:`

Select 2 - Appearance and this message appears:

`1 Bold 2 Undln 3 Dbl Und 4 Italc 5 Outln 6 Shadw`
`7 Sm Cap 8 Redln 9 Stkout`

Select an option according to the appearance you want.

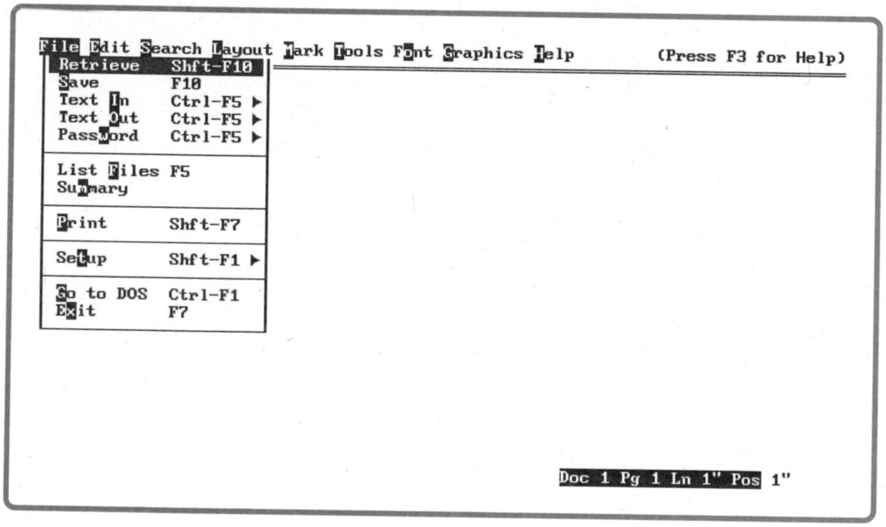

Figure 1.8

Menu letters underlined (appearing as reverse video).

In This Chapter

Creating a New Document

•

Document Codes

•

Insert versus Typeover Mode

•

Controlling Hyphenation

Turning on Reveal Codes

1. Press [Alt]-[F3] or select Reveal Codes on the **Edit** menu.
2. Repeat step 1 to remove the Reveal Codes screen.

Toggling Between Insert and Typeover Modes

1. Press the [Ins] key to toggle between insert and typeover modes.

Turning On Automatic Hyphenation

1. Press [⇧Shift]-[F8] (Format) and choose 1 Line (or select Line from the **Layout** menu).
2. Select 1 - Hyphenation, then enter [Y] or [N] to set your hyphenation choice.

Starting a New Document

Now that WordPerfect is set up and ready to go, you can start entering a document. This chapter covers how to create a new document and how to enter codes to control the appearance of text in the document. Unless you never make a mistake, you'll find an opportunity to use the typeover and insert modes to edit your work. Finally, if you like text to be hyphenated as you type, you'll appreciate learning how to use WordPerfect's automatic hyphenation feature.

Creating a New Document File

Once you are in the WordPerfect document screen, creating a new document file is easy. The cursor appears in the upper left corner of the screen. As you type, the characters appear on-screen at the cursor.

Do not press ⏎Enter until you reach the end of a paragraph. Just continue typing and the text will move automatically to the next line. This is called *word wrapping*. Then, when you later edit the text, the lines of text within the paragraph will readjust automatically to fit within the margins.

To get a feel for entering text, type in the following example. [Enter] at the end of a line indicates that you should press ⏎Enter. [Tab] indicates that you should press Tab. When you are done, your screen should look like Figure 2.1.

```
Mr. David Randolph [Enter]
Vice President [Enter]
Bennington Corporation [Enter]
45 Superstition Highway [Enter]
Phoenix, Arizona 85251 [Enter]
[Enter]
Dear Mr. Randolph: [Enter]
[Enter]

[Tab] I am interested in pursuing a career with
the Bennington Corporation.
```

Figure 2.1

Sample text entered onto a blank document screen.

```
File Edit Search Layout Mark Tools Font Graphics Help      (Press F3 for Help)
Mr. David Randolph
Vice President
Bennington Corporation
45 Superstition Highway
Phoenix, Arizona 85251

Dear Mr. Randolph:

     I am interested in pursuing a career with the Bennington
Corporation._




                                              Doc 1 Pg 1 Ln 2.5" Pos 2.2"
```

Cursor

Codes in Your Document

When you create a document, as you saw in entering the example text, you not only type letters and numbers, but you also press special keys, like ⏎Enter and Tab↹, that affect the text.

Some word processing programs put codes on the screen to symbolize such actions, but having all those codes among your text can get confusing. WordPerfect hides its codes, leaving your text pretty much in a "what you see is what you get" state. You can see the codes through the Reveal Codes screen. Handling the codes in this way provides two major benefits:

▲ There are no confusing symbols on your screen.

▲ Longer codes (instead of cryptic symbols) can be used, which fully explain the action taken.

To see the codes, press Alt-F3 (Reveal Codes) or select Reveal Codes from the **Edit** menu. The Reveal Codes screen appears on the bottom half of your screen. It not only shows the text in the document but also each code entered.

Let's look at an example. The address entered for a letter, along with the Reveal Codes screen, is shown in Figure 2.2. When the Reveal Codes screen is active, the regular document text is shown at the top of the screen. The same text—along with the codes—appears at the bottom of the screen. Notice these codes:

```
[HRt]
[Tab]
[SRt]
```

The [HRt] code stands for a *hard return*. This shows each place you have pressed the Return or Enter key. The [Tab] code shows where the Tab key was pressed. The [SRt] code stands for a *soft return*. This code is automatically entered by WordPerfect and shows where each line wraps around.

Figure 2.2

Address and Reveal Codes screen.

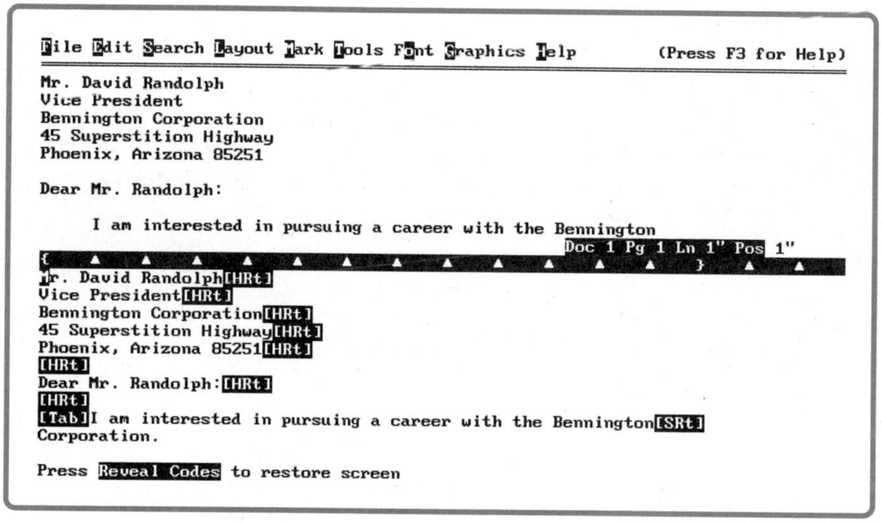

```
File Edit Search Layout Mark Tools Font Graphics Help        (Press F3 for Help)

Mr. David Randolph
Vice President
Bennington Corporation
45 Superstition Highway
Phoenix, Arizona 85251

Dear Mr. Randolph:

    I am interested in pursuing a career with the Bennington
                                        Doc 1 Pg 1 Ln 1" Pos 1"
{   ▲   ▲   ▲   ▲   ▲   ▲   ▲   ▲   ▲   ▲   ▲   }   ▲   ▲
Mr. David Randolph[HRt]
Vice President[HRt]
Bennington Corporation[HRt]
45 Superstition Highway[HRt]
Phoenix, Arizona 85251[HRt]
[HRt]
Dear Mr. Randolph:[HRt]
[HRt]
[Tab]I am interested in pursuing a career with the Bennington[SRt]
Corporation.

Press Reveal Codes to restore screen
```

It's a good idea to use Reveal Codes when you want to insert, move, or copy text. This way, you can make sure the codes are handled properly along with the text. Reveal Codes is also helpful in tracking down formatting problems. If your text looks odd, you may have entered a code inadvertently. Just check the Reveal Codes screen and remove any unwanted codes.

Although codes appear to be made up of individual characters, each is really a single entity. Therefore, you cannot edit codes the same way that you edit regular text. You can, however, insert and delete codes very easily.

▲ To insert a code, move the cursor to the desired location, and then perform the action. The action's code appears. For example, to insert a [HRt] code at the cursor location, just press ↵Enter.

▲ To delete a code, move the cursor to the code and press the ⌊Del⌋ (Delete) key.

To close the Reveal Codes screen, press ⌊Alt⌋-⌊F3⌋ again or select Reveal Codes from the Edit menu.

Some common WordPerfect codes that you might encounter are shown in Table 2.1.

Table 2.1
Common Codes.

Code	What it represents
[Bold]	Bold text
[Center]	Centered text
[Col Def]	Column definition
[Col Off]	Column feature turned off
[Col On]	Column feature turned on
[Dec Tab]	Decimal-aligned tab
[Font]	Base font style
[Footer]	Footer text
[Header]	Header text
[HPg]	Hard page break
[HRt]	Hard return
[Hyph Off]	Hyphen Off
[Hyph On]	Hyphen On
[Indent]	Indent (with arrow included for the direction)
[Just]	Justification
[L/R Mar]	Left and right margins
[Ln Spacing]	Line spacing
[Paper Sz/Typ]	Paper size and type
[Pg Num]	New page number

continues

Table 2.1
continued

Code	What it represents
[Pg Numbering]	Page numbering
[SRt]	Soft return
[Subscpt]	Subscript
[Superscpt]	Superscript
[T/B Mar]	Top and bottom margins
[TAB]	Hard left-aligned tab
[Und]	Underline

Insert and Typeover Text

When you type in text, it is inserted among existing text. This is commonly called working in *insert mode*. It is WordPerfect's default mode. In insert mode, the text to the right of your cursor moves right to make room for the new text. For example, in the sample letter shown in Figure 2.3, the phrase As I mentioned in our conversation today, was inserted after the tab and before the beginning of the existing sentence. That sentence moved to the right and wrapped around automatically.

WordPerfect also allows you to type over existing text rather than inserting text. You may go into *typeover mode*, which means any characters you type will replace existing characters. Take a look at the letter in Figure 2.4. The word mentioned in As I mentioned was typed over with the word discussed. Notice that the word Typeover appears in the bottom left corner of the screen.

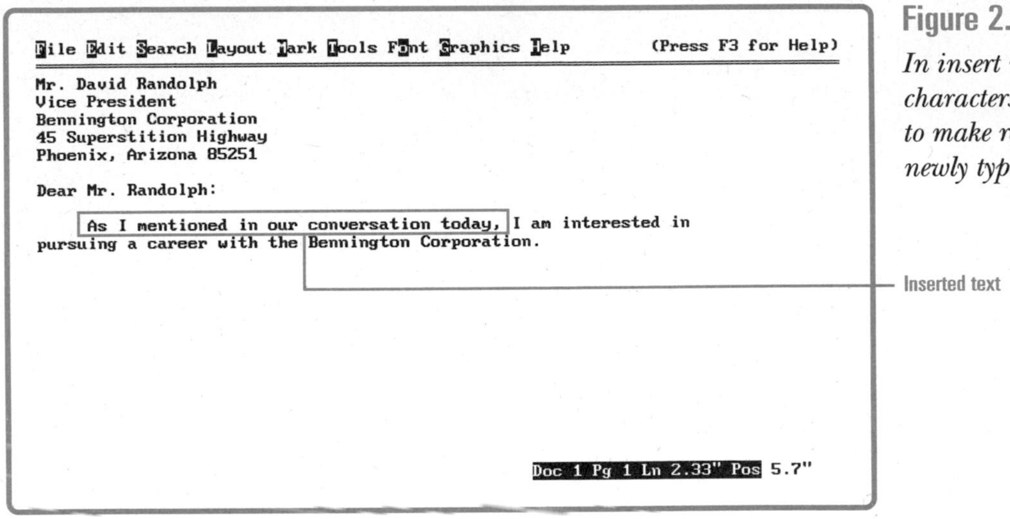

Figure 2.3

In insert mode, old characters move over to make room for newly typed ones.

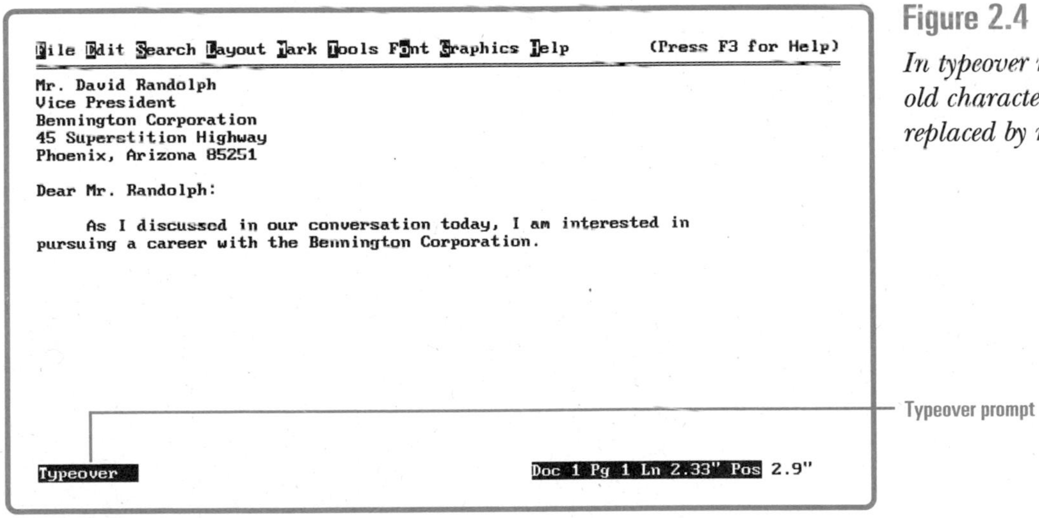

Inserted text

Figure 2.4

In typeover mode, old characters are replaced by new ones.

Typeover prompt

To switch between insert mode and typeover mode, just press the Ins key (marked Ins on most computers). This key is called a *toggle* key since pressing it toggles you between one option and another.

> **TIP:** Text that you type will never replace a code, even in typeover mode. The code will simply move over, just as text does in insert mode.

Picking a Mode

Pick either insert or typeover mode as your "primary" mode of work. That way, if you begin typing within existing text and are paying more attention to your keyboard or reference material than the screen, you are less likely to be surprised. The mode that does the least damage if used inadvertently is insert mode, because you have added text that can be deleted. If you accidentally enter text over existing text with typeover mode, you "delete" text you may not be able to replace.

Hyphenation

Some WordPerfect users like hyphenating words at the end of a line for more of an even right edge. Other users don't care and regard hyphenation as unnecessary. If you like hyphenating words, read on.

WordPerfect is smart enough to automatically hyphenate words for you; simply turn hyphenation on. To do this, follow these Quick Steps.

Turning On Hyphenation

1. Place your cursor where you want hyphenation to begin.

2. Press ⬆Shift-F8 (Format) and then select 1 Line. Or select Line from the Layout menu.

   The Format: Line menu appears.

3. Select 1 - Hyphenation.

4. Press Y to turn hyphenation on, or N to turn it off.

5. Press F7 (Exit) to return to the document window.

   The code [Hyph On] is placed in your text at the cursor location (or [Hyph Off], if you're turning it off).

The text you enter following the code will be hyphenated at the end of a line if appropriate. If you later edit the text so the hyphenated words do not appear at the end of a line, the hyphenation stays in place but does not appear on your screen. This hyphen is called a *soft hyphen* because it only appears when the word is at the end of a line. You can always view the soft hyphen through the Reveal Codes screen.

Figure 2.5 shows our letter with hyphenation on. Notice that the Reveal Codes screen shows the [Hyph On] code before Mr. David Randolph. Also notice that the word very was added and the word interested was hyphenated at the end of the line.

Figure 2.5

WordPerfect's automatic hyphenation feature places soft hyphens where appropriate.

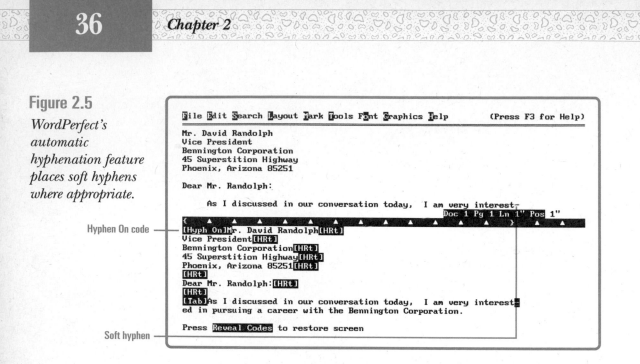

Hyphen On code ——

Soft hyphen ——

To stop automatic hyphenation for new text you enter, turn it off by typing N for Hyphenation on the Format: Line menu, or you can delete the [Hyph On] code. When you do this, the hyphens in place do not disappear. You can delete hyphens already in place. (Use the Reveal Codes screen to find each hyphen.)

If WordPerfect hyphenates a word that you don't want hyphenated, you can cancel the hyphenation. Place your cursor on the beginning of the word. Press Home and type in a slash. the code [/] appears in your document. Now delete the hyphen.

CAUTION: You can type in a hyphen with the hyphen (or minus) key. The hyphen will be in place even if you edit your document, however, and it may no longer be at the end of a line. This is not good. A preferable course is to use a soft hyphen (like the one WordPerfect inserts) which will "disappear" when the word is no longer at the end of a line. To do this, hold down Ctrl and press Del. The hyphen only appears on your screen when the word is at the end of a line.

What's Next?

In this chapter, you've learned about some WordPerfect features upon which many others are built. Becoming familiar with the basics of codes, hyphenation, and text insertion will pave the way for the specific features you'll learn about in upcoming chapters.

Now that you're familiar with the basics, you may want to investigate a more advanced option: the Hyphenation Zone.

Setting a Hyphenation Zone

When you set hyphenation from the Format: Line menu, you may have seen another hyphenation option: 2 - Hyphenation Zone. The hyphenation zone is rarely used by beginning WordPerfect users (or many advanced users for that matter). It is a difficult concept; I'll try to explain it here as simply as possible.

The *hyphenation zone* is the area WordPerfect uses to identify the valid region where a hyphen can occur. If you want more hyphens and a smoother right edge in your text, or fewer hyphens and a more ragged edge, you can change the hyphenation zone.

To change the hyphenation zone, press ⇧Shift-F8 and select 1 - Line (or select Line from the Layout menu). From the Format: Line menu, select 2 - Hyphenation Zone. You will see that you may control the left or right hyphenation zone. The length of the zone is expressed as a percent of the total line length measured from the left or right margin.

For a more ragged edge and fewer hyphens, increase the hyphenation zone percentage. For a smoother edge and more hyphens, reduce the hyphenation zone percentage. To determine the settings best for you, experiment with printing the result for the type style you'll use.

Check your *WordPerfect Reference* for more information about changing the settings.

In This Chapter

Ways to Delete Text

▲ Press the ⟨✦Backspace⟩ or ⟨Del⟩ key to delete a character.

▲ Block the text, then press ⟨Del⟩.

▲ Press ⟨Ctrl⟩-⟨F4⟩ (Move) or choose Select from the **Edit** menu, and then choose 1 Sentence, 2 Paragraph, or 3 Page.

Cancel a Deletion

1. Press ⟨F1⟩ (Cancel) or select Undelete from the **Edit** menu.

2. Select 1 Restore, or select 2 Previous Deletion to view other recent deletions.

Block Text to be Manipulated

▲ *With the keyboard:* position the cursor, press ⟨Alt⟩-⟨F4⟩ (Block) or select Block from the **Edit** menu, and complete block highlight by moving the cursor.

▲ *With the mouse:* press the left mouse button, hold it down, and drag it across the text to block.

Ways to Move or Copy a Sentence, Paragraph, or Page

1. Move the cursor to the text to be moved or copied.

2. Press ⟨Ctrl⟩-⟨F4⟩ (Move) or choose Select from the **Edit** menu.

3. Choose 1 Sentence, 2 Paragraph, or 3 Page (or 1 Block if it appears), then 1 Move or 2 Copy.

Retrieving Text

1. Place the cursor in the spot for the text.

2. Press ⟨Ctrl⟩-⟨F4⟩ (Move) or choose Select from the **Edit** menu.

3. Select 4 Retrieve.

Deleting, Copying, and Moving Text

We're only human . . . we all make mistakes. Whether you make a mistake or just change your mind, it is easy to delete, move, or copy text to omit or rearrange the text. You may also want to place text in another document for safekeeping for another time and later retrieve it for use in a document.

Deleting Text

One way to get rid of text one character at a time is to press the ⟨◆Backspace⟩ key; the character, space, or code to the left of the cursor is deleted as the cursor moves left. Figure 3.1 shows the "before" and "after" of pressing it. Notice that the cursor is after the ZIP code. After pressing the key once, the last number of the ZIP code is deleted and the number 2 can be entered to complete the ZIP code. On many computers, you can hold down the ⟨◆Backspace⟩ key to continue deleting text until you release the key.

Figure 3.1a

*Before pressing
the Backspace
key.*

```
File Edit Search Layout Mark Tools Font Graphics Help        (Press F3 for Help)

Mr. David Randolph
Vice President
Bennington Corporation
45 Superstition Highway
Phoenix, Arizona 85251_

Dear Mr. Randolph:

     As I discussed in our conversation today,  I am very interest-
ed in pursuing a career with the Bennington Corporation.




Cursor






                                        Doc 1 Pg 1 Ln 1.67" Pos 3.2"
```

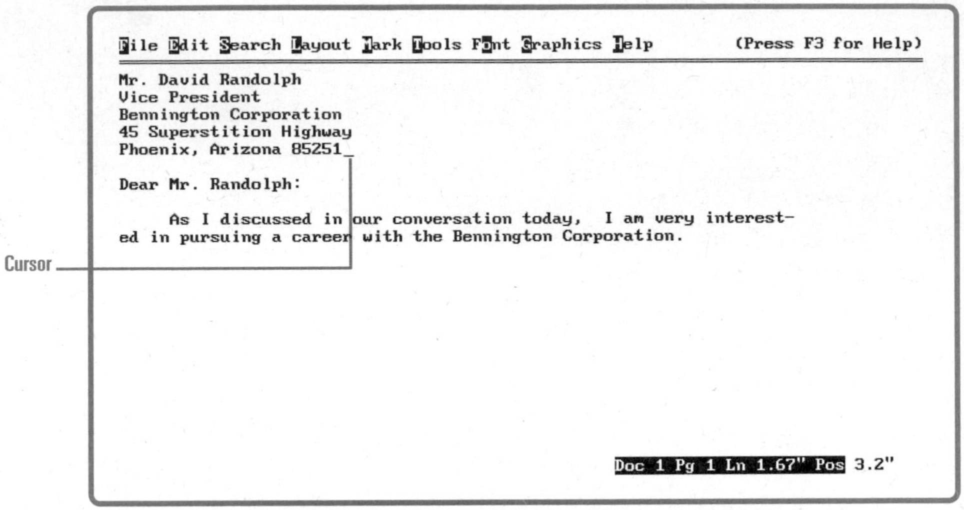

Figure 3.1b

*After pressing
the Backspace
key.*

```
File Edit Search Layout Mark Tools Font Graphics Help        (Press F3 for Help)

Mr. David Randolph
Vice President
Bennington Corporation
45 Superstition Highway
Phoenix, Arizona 8525_

Dear Mr. Randolph:

     As I discussed in our conversation today,  I am very interest-
ed in pursuing a career with the Bennington Corporation.







                                        Doc 1 Pg 1 Ln 1.67" Pos 3.1"
```

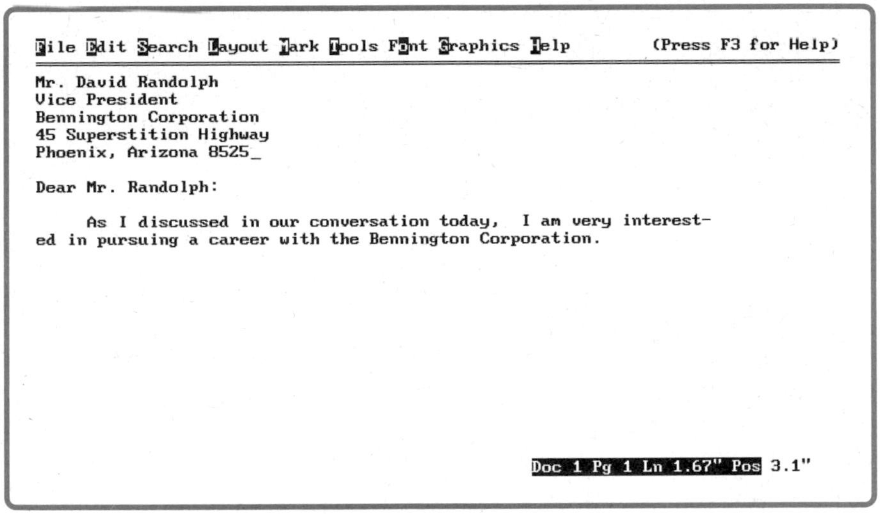

Another way to delete text is to use the Delete key, marked
Del on many keyboards. When you press Del, the character,
space, or code at the cursor is deleted and all remaining text on
the page moves one position to the left. Figure 3.2 illustrates text
before and after Delete is pressed. The cursor is in the space

before the i in in our conversation today. Delete is pressed repeatedly until the rest of the phrase is deleted. Notice that the cursor remains in the same screen position. The text moves left and wraps around.

> **TIP:** When you delete text, it is removed from the document. Because text in WordPerfect may contain codes as well as text and spaces, it is a good idea to turn on Reveal Codes (Alt - F3) when you delete. This way you can be assured that you're deleting precisely the text, spaces, or codes you want to delete.

As with the Backspace key, holding down Del on most keyboards repeats the delete. Your cursor stays in position and the text to the right of the cursor moves to the left as you delete one character at a time.

> **TIP:** To delete a word at the cursor, press Ctrl - Backspace. To delete from the cursor to the end of a line, press Ctrl - End.

Deleting a Sentence, Paragraph, or Page

You may delete a sentence, a paragraph, or a page quickly with WordPerfect. The key to use is a little misleading because it is called *Move*. Bear with me—soon you will see the delete option behind this key.

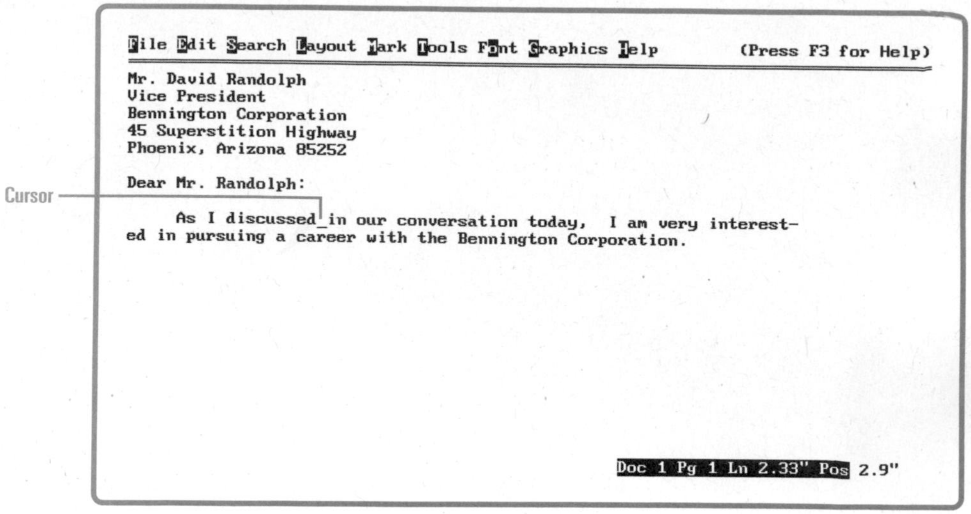

Figure 3.2a

Before pressing the Delete key.

```
File Edit Search Layout Mark Tools Font Graphics Help        (Press F3 for Help)

Mr. David Randolph
Vice President
Bennington Corporation
45 Superstition Highway
Phoenix, Arizona 85252

Dear Mr. Randolph:

    As I discussed_in our conversation today,  I am very interest-
ed in pursuing a career with the Bennington Corporation.




                                                  Doc 1 Pg 1 Ln 2.33" Pos 2.9"
```

Cursor

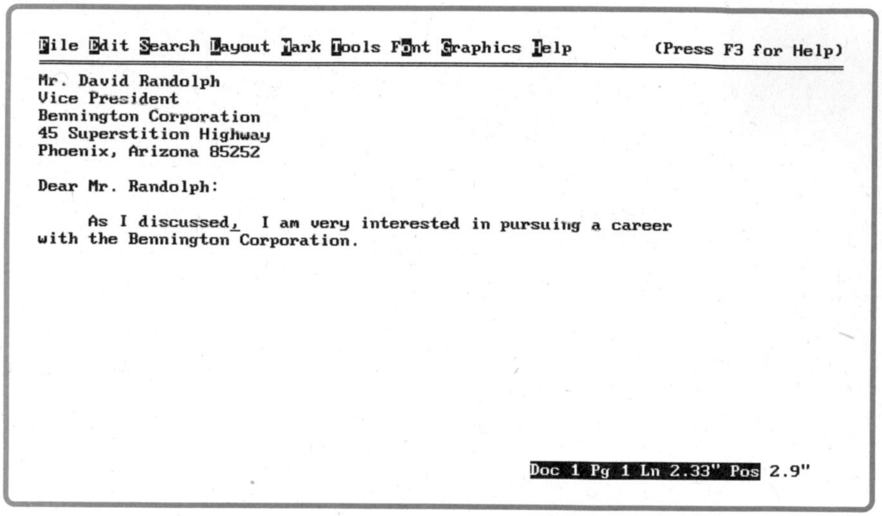

Figure 3.2b

After pressing the Delete key.

```
File Edit Search Layout Mark Tools Font Graphics Help        (Press F3 for Help)

Mr. David Randolph
Vice President
Bennington Corporation
45 Superstition Highway
Phoenix, Arizona 85252

Dear Mr. Randolph:

    As I discussed,  I am very interested in pursuing a career
with the Bennington Corporation.




                                                  Doc 1 Pg 1 Ln 2.33" Pos 2.9"
```

Put your cursor anywhere on the sentence, paragraph, or page you wish to delete. For example, suppose you want to delete David Randolph's title from Figure 3.2. You would position the cursor somewhere on the Vice President line. Then you press Ctrl - F4 (Move) or choose Select from the Edit menu. You will see this prompt:

```
Move: 1 Sentence; 2 Paragraph; 3 Page; 4 Retrieve:
```

Enter the number that identifies the amount of text you want to delete. For our example, you would press ②, because the title line is a paragraph.

TIP: Each hard return signifies the end of a paragraph. It is easier to see where paragraph breaks occur if you turn on Reveal Codes (Alt-F3).

When you select 1 Sentence, the entire sentence is highlighted, as shown in Figure 3.3. This prompt appears:

```
1 Move; 2 Copy; 3 Delete; 4 Append:
```

Press ③ or Ⅾ to choose 3 Delete. The highlighted text and spaces are deleted.

```
File Edit Search Layout Mark Tools Font Graphics Help        (Press F3 for Help)
Mr. David Randolph
Vice President
Bennington Corporation
45 Superstition Highway
Phoenix, Arizona 85252

Dear Mr. Randolph:

     As I discussed,  I am very interested in pursuing a career
with the Bennington Corporation.




 1 Move; 2 Copy; 3 Delete; 4 Append: 3
```

Figure 3.3

Deleting a sentence.

The following Quick Steps summarize the process.

Deleting a Sentence, Paragraph, or Page

1. Put the cursor on a sentence, paragraph, or page to delete.

Your cursor marks the text.

2. Press Ctrl-F4 (Move) or choose Select from the **E**dit menu.

A prompt appears from which you can choose sentence, paragraph, page, or append.

3. Select 1 Sentence, 2 Paragraph, or 3 Page.

The sentence, paragraph, or page is highlighted. A prompt appears from which you can choose to move, copy, delete, or append.

4. Select 3 Delete.

The text is deleted.

Blocking Text

To delete, cut, or copy larger blocks of text, you'll need to *block* the text. Blocking text marks the characters, spaces, and codes you want to manipulate. Blocking text is also used to perform other functions such as centering a large amount of text. You can block text using the keyboard or with a mouse.

Once you have blocked the text, you must immediately perform the delete, move, or copy action.

> **TIP:** Always use the Reveal Codes space when you are blocking text that may involve codes. That way you won't miss important formatting in your selection.

Blocking is Important

Many WordPerfect functions can be performed on blocked text. Delete and copy were used as examples earlier in this chapter, but there are many more. These include, but are by no means limited to:

▲ Character size and appearance

▲ Spell checking

▲ Printing

▲ Saving

▲ Searching

▲ Replacing

▲ Line spacing

▲ Indenting

You can use blocking whenever you want to perform a given action on a block of text, no matter what that action is.

The following Quick Steps detail how to block text with your keyboard.

Quick Steps

Blocking Text with the Keyboard

1. Put the cursor on the first character, space, or code in the block.

   The cursor is in the position you choose.

2. Press `Alt`-`F4` (Block) or select **B**lock from the **E**dit menu.

   `Block On` blinks in the lower left corner of the screen.

3. Move the cursor to the last character of the block of text.

   The text is highlighted. For example, Figure 3.4 shows the Reveal Codes screen when `Vice President` is blocked. Notice the code `[Block]` appears before `Vice President`.

4. Perform the delete, copy, or move.

   The text in the block is altered and `Block On` disappears. If you are deleting, a prompt appears; if not, you're finished.

5. If you are deleting, the `Delete Block? (Y/N)` prompt appears. Press `Y` to delete.

   The block is deleted (see Figure 3.5).

Note that in Figure 3.5, where Vice President was deleted, the code was deleted as well as the text since the cursor was after the return code at the end of the line.

If you press `Alt`-`F4` to block text, then decide you don't want to block text, just press `Alt`-`F4` again. `Block on` stops flashing and you may continue with other activities.

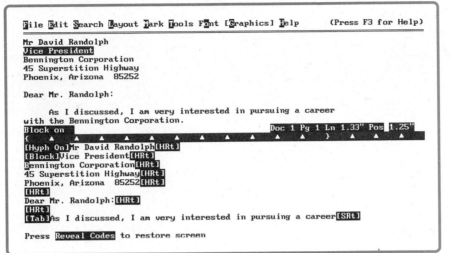

Figure 3.4

Blocked text.

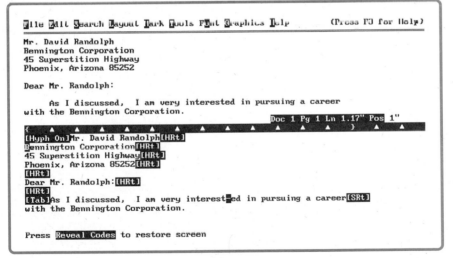

Figure 3.5

Result of deleting a block of text.

Table 3.1 lists other options to quickly block text once [Alt]-[F4] is pressed.

Table 3.1
*Other Keyboard
Blocking
Techniques.*

Press	To block
⇧Shift-→ or ←	One character at a time
⇧Shift-↑ or ↓	A line at a time
⇧Shift-End	To the end of a line after codes
⇧Shift-Home, Home	To the beginning of a line before codes
⇧Shift-PgUp or PgDn, then continue pressing PgUp or PgDn	To the top or bottom of the screen, then screen by screen
⇧Shift-Alt-PgUp or PgDn	To the first line of the previous or next page
⇧Shift-Ctrl-→ or ←	One word at a time
⇧Shift-Ctrl-↑ or ↓	One paragraph at a time
⇧Shift-Ctrl-Home	To the beginning of a document after codes
Home, Home, ↑	To the beginning of a document before codes
Home, Home, Home, ↑	To the end of a page after codes

TIP: If you make a block and want to get out of it (that is, get rid of the highlight and continue with other work), press Esc or click outside the blocked area. The block disappears.

A new feature in WordPerfect 5.1 is the ability to block text with a mouse. It's as easy as point-drag-release. The following Quick Steps detail how to block text using your mouse.

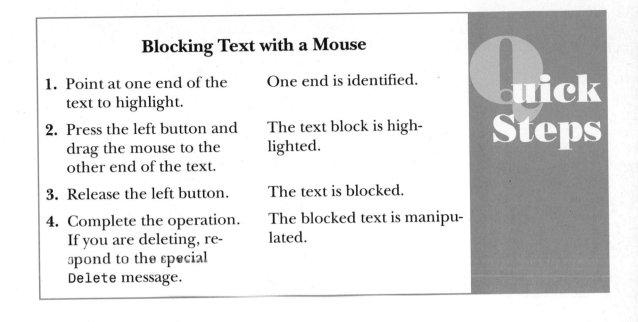

Blocking Text with a Mouse

1. Point at one end of the text to highlight.

   One end is identified.

2. Press the left button and drag the mouse to the other end of the text.

   The text block is high-lighted.

3. Release the left button.

   The text is blocked.

4. Complete the operation. If you are deleting, respond to the special Delete message.

   The blocked text is manipu-lated.

Canceling Deletions (Undelete)

With WordPerfect, you can afford an "oops" when you delete, as long as you restore the text before making three other deletions. WordPerfect stores the most recent three deletions pretty much without regard to how small or large the deletion.

To undo a deletion, follow these steps:

1. Place your cursor where you want the text to be restored.

2. Press F1 (Cancel) or select Undelete from the Edit menu. When you cancel, you may select among the last

three deletions and restore your selection. This message appears:

```
Undelete: 1 Restore; 2 Previous Deletion:
```

3. Continue to press 2 until the deletion you wish to restore appears. Then, press 1 to insert that deleted text.

If you happen to foil WordPerfect and make an unusually large deletion, WordPerfect will warn you:

```
Delete without saving for Undelete?(Y/N)
```

This message means you can go ahead and make your deletion, but it won't be available to be undeleted through F1 (Cancel) or Undelete from the Edit menu.

Quick and Dirty Copying

Some WordPerfect users like to employ the F1 (Cancel) option as a "quick and dirty" way to move or copy text. For example:

1. Delete the text you want to move or copy.

2. Position the cursor in the first location to move or copy to. (If you are copying, you will copy the text back into its original position.)

3. Press F1 (Cancel) to cancel the delete.

4. Identify the text you want and restore it.

Because a deletion is stored even after you have restored it, you may repeat a restoration as often as you like. This gives the effect of copying the text.

Moving Text

You can move a sentence, paragraph, page, or block of text at a time. When you move text, it is removed from the location you are moving from and is inserted in the location you are moving to. Figure 3.6 shows how text looks before and after the move: the last sentence and the second sentence have been transposed.

In this example, a sentence was moved. To move an unusual amount of text (not a complete sentence, paragraph, page), you can block the text with Alt-F4 (Block) or select Block from the Edit menu before starting the move procedure.

The quickest way to move blocked text is to select Move from the Edit menu. Then, press ↵Enter to insert the document at your cursor location.

A slower method of moving text gives you the flexibility of either blocking or moving the text by sentence, paragraph, or page. To begin the move, press Ctrl-F4 (Move) or choose Select from the Edit menu. If you are moving a sentence, paragraph, or page, a prompt for Sentence, Paragraph, and Page appears. If you are moving a block, a Rectangle (a vertical block), or Block prompt is available so you can select the type of text you are moving. This prompt appears:

```
1 Move; 2 Copy; 3 Delete; 4 Append:
```

Select 1 Move. The highlighted text disappears from the screen. This prompt appears:

```
Move cursor; press Enter to retrieve
```

Place your cursor on the character before which the text should be inserted. (It's okay to edit text along the way; just don't press Enter until you are ready to retrieve the moved text.) Press ↵Enter.

Figure 3.6a

Text before a move operation.

```
 File  Edit  Search  Layout  Mark  Tools  Font  Graphics  Help      (Press F3 for Help)
─────────────────────────────────────────────────────────────────────────────────────
Mr. David Randolph
Bennington Corporation
45 Superstition Highway
Phoenix, Arizona 85252

Dear Mr. Randolph:

      As I discussed,  I am very interested in pursuing a career
with the Bennington Corporation.  I look forward to speaking with
you further on June 8th.  My complete resume is attached.




                                                    Doc 1 Pg 1 Ln 1" Pos 1"
```

This text is moved ...

Figure 3.6b

Text after a move operation.

```
 File  Edit  Search  Layout  Mark  Tools  Font  Graphics  Help      (Press F3 for Help)
─────────────────────────────────────────────────────────────────────────────────────
Mr. David Randolph
Bennington Corporation
45 Superstition Highway
Phoenix, Arizona 85252

Dear Mr. Randolph:

      As I discussed,  I am very interested in pursuing a career
with the Bennington Corporation.  My complete resume is attached.
I look forward to speaking with you further on June 8th.




                                                    Doc 1 Pg 1 Ln 2.67" Pos 1"
```

... to this new location.

The following Quick Steps detail how to move text whether it is blocked or not.

Moving Text (Blocked or Not)

1. Block the text with `Alt`-`F4` (Block) or select **Block** from the **Edit** menu if necessary.

   The blocked text is highlighted.

2. Press `Ctrl`-`F4` (Move) or choose **Select** from the **Edit** menu.

   Prompts appear according to the amount of text you are moving.

3. Select **S**entence, **Para**graph, or **Page** (or **Block** if it appears).

   A prompt with the Move option appears.

4. Select 1 Move.

   The highlighted text disappears. A prompt appears.

5. Put the cursor where the text should go and press `↵Enter`.

   The text is moved.

Copying Text

You can copy a sentence, a paragraph, a page, or a block of text. When text is copied, the original remains in place. A copy is stored by WordPerfect for you to retrieve at another spot in the document. Figure 3.7 illustrates a copy operation. From the inside address, 45 Superstition Highway was copied into the sentence that has been added to the body of the letter.

Figure 3.7

Copying text.

```
File Edit Search Layout Mark Tools Font Graphics Help       (Press F3 for Help)
Mr. David Randolph
Bennington Corporation
45 Superstition Highway
Phoenix, Arizona 85252

Dear Mr. Randolph:

     As I discussed,  I am very interested in pursuing a career
with the Bennington Corporation.  My complete resume is attached.
I look forward to speaking with you further on June 8th.  I'll meet
you at your corporate office location at 45 Superstition Highway.




                                         Doc 1 Pg 1 Ln 2.83" Pos 1"
```

This information was copied from the address.

The process for copying text is very similar to moving text. If you want to copy a block of text, highlight it with Alt - F4 (Block). Select **C**opy from the **E**dit menu. With your cursor in the location where you want the text copied to, press ↵Enter .

Like the move feature, you can copy by block, sentence, paragraph, or page with a longer process. Follow the next Quick Steps.

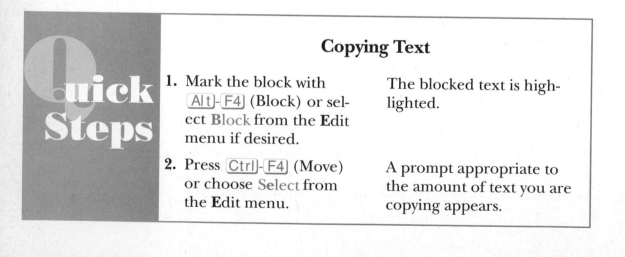

Quick **Steps**

Copying Text

1. Mark the block with Alt - F4 (Block) or select **B**lock from the **E**dit menu if desired.

   The blocked text is highlighted.

2. Press Ctrl - F4 (Move) or choose **S**elect from the **E**dit menu.

   A prompt appropriate to the amount of text you are copying appears.

3. Select from Sentence, Paragraph, or Page (or Block if it appears).

   The copy prompt appears.

4. Select 2 Copy.

   The highlighted text remains on the screen.

5. Put the cursor in the spot to insert text and press ↵Enter.

   The text is copied.

CAUTION: The results of copying, deleting, or moving rectangles can be surprising. Whenever you work with copying or moving text and you are unsure of the outcome, save your work first with F10 (Save Text). Then, if the outcome isn't as you expected, your original document is available. Chapter 4, "Saving and Closing a Document," covers the ways to save a document.

Hidden Uses for Copying

There are several "hidden uses" for copying. Copy to reduce mistakes, to repeat a line of text for a particular effect, or to streamline formats represented by codes.

Copying is handy when you want to make sure you don't introduce mistakes when existing information is repeated in a document. For example, it is easy to incorrectly enter an address, account numbers, or an unusual proper name. Assuming the first occurrence of the text is correct, copy that occurrence to ensure the other occurrences are

Continues

Continued

correct as well. Just enter the first occurrence of the text, then copy the text as needed.

Copying can also be useful to repeat a particular line of text. For example, if you are making a sign-in sheet for a meeting, create a line with tabs and underlines for the necessary information (such as name, phone number, and so on). Then copy that line to add a second line. Next, copy two lines to make four lines and so on until you create a complete page of underlines for the sign-in sheet. This approach saves you the tedium of setting up the tabs and underlines in each line and ensures all lines are the same length.

Finally, save time and use copying to repeat format or other settings held in codes. For example, you may have created a particular tab setting, then changed to a new tab setting later in the document. If you want to go back to the original tab setting later, just copy the `[Tab Set:]` code to the desired spot.

Retrieving Text

WordPerfect stores only the most recent text you moved or copied so that it can be retrieved. However, you may retrieve that text as many times as you want (or until you move or copy other text to the same storage area).

To retrieve the last text moved or copied, place your cursor on the character before which the text should be inserted. Press Ctrl-F4 (Move) and this prompt appears:

```
Move: 1 Sentence; 2 Paragraph; 3 Page; 4 Retrieve:
```

Select 4 Retrieve and this prompt appears:

```
Retrieve: 1 Block; 2 Tabular Column; 3 Rectangle:
```

Select 1 Block for regular text. The last text moved or copied is inserted to the left of the character marked by the cursor.

A quicker way to retrieve text is to use the Edit menu. Select Paste. The Retrieve prompt appears and you may select 1 Block for regular text.

Appending Text

Sometimes you may want to add text to the end of a file on a disk. This is called *appending*. For example, you might add the example letter to a file containing all letters sent to this company.

To append a block of text, you block the text first. Whether working with a block of text or not, begin the append by pressing Ctrl-F4 (Move). If you are appending a block, this prompt appears:

```
Move: 1 Block; 2 Tabular Column; 3 Rectangle:
```

Otherwise, this prompt appears:

```
Move: 1 Sentence: 2 Paragraph; 3 Page; 4 Retrieve:
```

Select the desired option, depending on what you are appending. This prompt appears:

```
1 Move; 2 Copy; 3 Delete; 4 Append:
```

Select 4 Append and this prompt appears:

```
Append to:
```

Type in the drive designation, the path if necessary, and the name of the document file to which you want to append the text. Press ⏎Enter and the portion of the document to append is added to the end of the named document.

If you are blocking text, you can use the pull-down menu shortcut. Just block the text with Alt-F4 (Block). Then, from the Edit menu, select Append. Select to File, type the file path and name, and press ⏎Enter.

> **TIP:** If the document file name you enter doesn't exist, WordPerfect creates it. This is a slick way to create a new document to hold your appended work.

Using Append to Combine Work

A common use of append is to combine the work of several authors held in multiple documents. For instance, three people may be working on a common report. With a little up-front planning, each of the three can leave out special formatting and just concentrate on developing the raw information. Then, append the text into one document with appropriate formatting and move around as needed.

What's Next?

In this chapter, you learned how to place text in another document along with how to retrieve text from a second document. In addition, features you will use often were covered, including delete, copy, and move.

When it comes to moving, the chapter covered how to move text in sentence and paragraph form. However, you may also want to move text in a rectangular shape you specify. For example, you may create text in a table-like format and want to move just the second column. Read on to learn more about this helpful alternative.

Working with Rectangular Shapes

You may have noticed the Ctrl-F4 (Move) options of working with rectangular shapes or columns separated by tabs.

To do this, follow these steps:

1. Block the text from the start and end points with Alt-F4 (Block) or by dragging the mouse. (Characters outside the rectangle or column may be highlighted.)

2. Press Ctrl-F4 (Move) and select 2 Tabular Column or 3 Rectangle.

   or

   Choose Select from the Edit menu, and then select Tabular Column or Rectangle. Continue to move or copy the blocked text as desired.

For more information about copying or moving rectangles or columns, see *The WordPerfect Bible* by Susan Baake Kelly.

In This Chapter

Saving a Document

•

Exiting WordPerfect

•

Using Passwords

•

Using WordPerfect's Automatic Backup

Ways to Save Your Work

▲ Press F10 (Save Text) or select Save from the **File** menu.

▲ Press F7 (Exit) or select Exit from the **File** menu.

Rules for Saving

▲ Get in the habit of periodically saving your work.

▲ Name a document to save using up to eight characters (optionally followed by a period and a three-character extension).

Exiting WordPerfect

▲ Press F7 (Exit) or select Exit from the **File** menu and follow the prompts.

Adding or Removing a Password

1. Press Ctrl-F5, then 2 - Password or select Password from the **File** menu.

2. Select 1 Add/Change or 2 Remove and complete the operation.

Saving and Closing a Document

Once you have learned how to create a document, you will want to protect your document. The best way is to know how to save all or part of the document and exit WordPerfect correctly. Another protection you will learn about is how to use a password to limit access to your document by others. A final protection for your documents includes the automatic backup features of WordPerfect.

Why You Must Save Your Work

We're so used to paper documents that it can be hard to adjust to using documents in another form. Imagining the contents of a file drawer of paper stored on a slim disk is difficult for many. The common way to make the transition from paper to magnetic media is to use both until disk storage alone feels comfortable. Even if you make paper copies of everything, you still have to develop the good habit of routinely saving your work. Over time, your need for security in paper will diminish.

Save your work or lose it. While dramatic, this states a plain fact. As you work on a document, it is stored in RAM, which is only available as long as there is power to the computer. When the power is cut off (maybe accidentally), the data in RAM is lost. Saving a document to a disk is mandatory to ensure the document will be available to you when you need it. Because accidents happen to disks, too, saving a document to more than one disk is your insurance that the document will be available even if one disk is lost or damaged.

Nearly every computer user can tell you a story of working for hours or days on an important document and then having the worst happen—the document is lost. Usually, a new computer user will exercise sloppy saving habits until a significant piece of work is lost. The loss may be the result of a loose power cord or an electrical voltage drop, and so on. The pain of losing the work then causes the user to pay greater attention to saving. Avoid the one-act tragedy. Always take time to save your work.

Good Saving Habits

Develop these good habits:

▲ Periodically save your work as you go. That way, if the power to your computer fails, you will have a recent, complete version of your work. How often to save? Any time you have entered edits that are significant (and that you wouldn't want to lose), save your work. For some, this is every 15 minutes. For others, it is every hour. A good rule is: *when in doubt, save it.*

▲ Always save more than one copy of your document on more than one disk. Disks can be damaged or lost.

▲ Use WordPerfect automatic *backup* options. WordPerfect has options which automatically make copies of your most recent edits as you work. Using this function will give you additional options for recovering your work if an accident happens.

How to perform each of these good saving habits is covered in detail in the remainder of this chapter.

Naming a Document

When you save a document, the document must have a unique name so that you and WordPerfect can find it again.

Names may be up to eight characters long. If you enter a name longer than eight characters, WordPerfect automatically cuts off the characters beyond eight. The eight-character name may be followed by a period and an extension of three characters, however. For example, a document might be named MYDOC123 with an extension of WPP. Its full name is MYDOC123.WPP.

When naming a document, you may use:

▲ Letters A through Z

▲ Numbers 0 through 9

▲ Many characters such as: ! @ # $ % ^ & ( ) - _ '

Some symbols, though, will result in an `Invalid` message or `File creation error` message. An asterisk, for example, will provoke such a message. If you get such a message, omit any unusual symbols and try again. Also, do not use a period in the name because it will be mistaken for the divider between the name and the extension.

Each document must have a unique name. You can store the same document under more than one name. It's a good idea to give a document a name that suggests the use of the document. Here are some examples:

LETDAVE1.WPP: The first letter to Dave.

LETDAVE2.WPP: The second letter to Dave.

IBBRPTV1.WPP: IBB Report, Version 1.

ME020892.WPP: Memo of 2/8/92.

When it comes to using file extensions:

▲ Always use one.

▲ Use the same extension for all WordPerfect documents you create.

By using an extension unique to only your WordPerfect documents, you will be able to identify WordPerfect documents when they are stored on a disk with documents created with other software. For example, a disk might contain these documents:

WPCHAP1.WPP: .WPP is used for a WordPerfect document.

LETJACK.DOC: .DOC is used for a Microsoft Word document.

CH1FIGS.WK1: .WK1 is used for a Lotus 1-2-3 document.

Because consistent extensions are used, it is clear which software to use to view each document. If inconsistent extensions are used, you might have to try the document with several software programs just to figure out what the document is all about.

It's recommended that you use .WPP as your WordPerfect extension since (to my knowledge) this is not automatically assigned by any other popular software package. Don't use .DOC because several other word processors use that extension.

Saving Your Work

Save your work as you go. Save every time you have performed edits you would hate to lose. Most users save their work every 15 minutes or so. Here's how to do it.

From the document, press F10 (Save Text) or select Save from the File menu. A message like the one shown in Figure 4.1 appears.

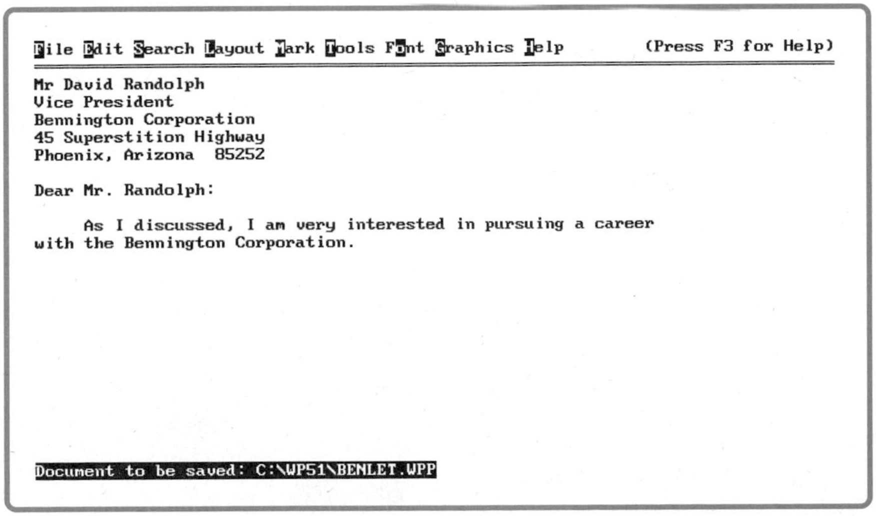

```
 File  Edit  Search  Layout  Mark  Tools  Font  Graphics  Help        (Press F3 for Help)

 Mr David Randolph
 Vice President
 Bennington Corporation
 45 Superstition Highway
 Phoenix, Arizona  85252

 Dear Mr. Randolph:

      As I discussed, I am very interested in pursuing a career
 with the Bennington Corporation.






 Document to be saved: C:\WP51\BENLET.WPP
```

Figure 4.1

Prompt to save a document.

(The drive, path, and document name only appear if the document has already been saved or retrieved.) Type in the drive, path, and document name, if needed, and press ⏎Enter.

In this example, to save the letter to the Bennington Corporation, we use drive C, WP51 as the directory for WordPerfect version 5.1, DOC as the document subdirectory, and BENLET.WPP as the document name.

> **CAUTION:** If you do not specify a drive and directory when you enter the document file name, your document will be saved to the drive and directory currently active (the default)—usually drive C and the WordPerfect directory. In this case, your document files will be mixed in with the program files and may be difficult to locate later. It is better to set up a separate directory, or a subdirectory within the WordPerfect directory, and use that directory to store your files. As you accumulate more document files, you may want to organize them into multiple directories, with a separate directory for different projects or clients. Consult your DOS manual to learn how to create directories of your own.

If this is the first time you are saving the document, this message appears as the document is saved:

```
Saving C:\WP51\DOC\BENLET.WPP
```

You're done! If the document had already existed on disk, this message would have appeared:

```
Replace: C:\WP51\DOC\BENLET.WPP? No (Yes)
```

Notice that No appears without parentheses around it; that means it's the default.

> **TIP:** The *default* is the choice that will be made if you do not specify otherwise—that is, if you just press Enter.

Select No if you want to specify a new name (and then do so), or select Yes to replace the "old" version on disk. A similar message to this one appears as the document is saved:

```
Saving C:\WP51\DOC\BENLET.WPP
```

The following Quick Steps summarize the process of saving a document.

Saving a Document

1. Press F10 (Save Text) or select Save on the File menu.

   A prompt appears for the document name.

2. Type the drive, path, and document name as necessary and press Enter. If a Replace message appears, press Y.

   The document is saved.

Creative Uses of Save

If you need multiple versions of the same document, use F10 (Save Text) or Save from the File menu to create them. Simply give each version a related name. For example, if you are working on a budget report and want to save three different versions each with a different organization, you

Continues

Continued

could name them BRPTVER1.WPP, BRPTVER2.WPP, and BRPTVER3.WPP. It is also useful to save a document under a related name if you believe you may want to go back to an earlier version.

You can also use Save to create a backup of a file. To do this, save the same document to multiple locations. For example, you may want to save to a floppy disk as well as to your hard disk. First, save to your hard disk with F10 (Save Text) or Save from the File menu. Then, use F10 (Save Text) or Save from the File menu again, this time entering the path for the floppy disk drive. In effect, you have just created a floppy disk backup of the file on the hard disk.

Saving and Closing the Document

Instead of saving the document and continuing, you may save the document, and then:

▲ Close the document and exit WordPerfect;

or

▲ Close the document and work with a different document.

From the document, press F7 (Exit) or select Exit from the File menu. This message appears:

```
Save document? Yes (No)
```

Press Y to save the document. A message like this appears:

```
Document to be saved: C:\WP51\DOC\BENLET.WPP
```

If the document has not been named, the drive, path, and name area will be blank. If necessary, type in these, and press ⏎Enter. If this is the first time you are saving the document, this message appears as the document is saved:

```
Saving C:\WP51\DOC\BENLET.WPP
```

If the document already exists on disk, this message appears:

```
Replace: C:\WP51\DOC\BENLET.WPP? No (Yes)
```

If you get the Replace message, press Y for Yes to replace the "old" version on disk. This message appears as the document is saved:

```
Saving C:\WP51\DOC\BENLET.WPP
```

Once the document is saved, a message like this appears:

```
Exit WP? No (Yes)
```

Press N for No to keep working in WordPerfect. Or press Y for Yes to exit WordPerfect. If you press N, the document is cleared from the screen and a blank screen is available for your use. If you press Y, you are returned to the operating system prompt (such as C>). From the prompt, you may use other software or turn off the computer.

The following Quick Steps summarize how to save and close a document.

> **CAUTION:** *Never* turn off the computer while in WordPerfect. This can damage your document or WordPerfect software. Always use F7 (Exit) or Exit from the **F**ile menu to leave WordPerfect. Only turn off your computer if you are at the operating system prompt.

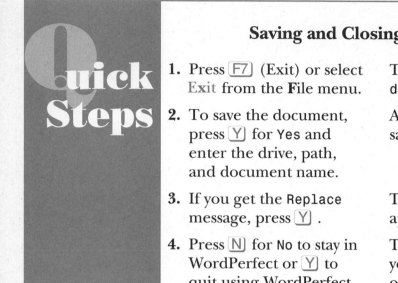

Saving and Closing a Document

1. Press F7 (Exit) or select Exit from the File menu.

This message appears: Save document? Yes (No)

2. To save the document, press Y for Yes and enter the drive, path, and document name.

A Saving or Replace message appears.

3. If you get the Replace message, press Y .

The Saving message appears.

4. Press N for No to stay in WordPerfect or Y to quit using WordPerfect.

The document is cleared or you are returned to the operating system prompt.

Exiting Without Saving a Document

Occasionally, you may not want to save a document. For example, you may want to lose the edits made since your last save, or you may not have changed the document. Skipping the save step saves time. But use it only if you want to lose any edits made since the last save.

You can use F7 (Exit) or select Exit from the File menu to leave a document without saving it. You are then given a choice of either exiting WordPerfect or continuing to work in WordPerfect (with the existing document cleared).

The Quick Steps which follow describe how to exit but not save a document.

Closing a Document Without Saving

1. From the document, press F7 (Exit) or select Exit from the File menu.

   This message appears: Save document? Yes (No)

2. To skip saving the document, press N for No.

   A message like this appears: Exit WP? No (Yes)

3. Press N to clear the document and continue working in WordPerfect. Or press Y for Yes to quit using WordPerfect.

   If you press N to keep working in WordPerfect, the document is cleared. If you press Y, you are returned to the operating system prompt (such as C>).

CAUTION: Remember, to avoid damaging your document or WordPerfect software, always use F7 (Exit) or select Exit from the File menu to leave WordPerfect and return to the operating system prompt before turning off the computer.

Saving Part of a Document

You may save just a part of a document if you wish. This is useful when you want to delete the rest of the document. It is also useful when you want to place part of a document in a new document with a unique name. The result is to create a new document made up of a portion of the existing document. Follow these steps:

1. Use Alt - F4 (Block) or **Block** from the **E**dit menu to block the part of the document you want to save, as described in Chapter 3.

2. Press F10 (Save Text) or select Save from the **File** menu. This message appears:

   ```
   Blockname:
   ```

3. Type in the name of the document, including any extension, and press ↵Enter. (Include the drive and path designation, if necessary.)

The blocked portion of the document is saved under the new name and you are returned to your document.

Saving with a Password

A *password* is a word you need to type in before a document can be used. You can attach a password to a document to help keep the document confidential. Password protection is especially useful if your documents contain sensitive personnel, sales, or strategic planning information.

> **CAUTION:** Only use a password if you are prepared to remember or record it, so you can later access the file. If you write down the password, keep it in a safe place. Don't use an obvious password such as your last name or the name of your pet.

To add a password, the document must be open on-screen. Follow these steps:

1. Press Ctrl-F5, choose 2 Password, then choose 1 Add/Change.

   or

   Select Password from the File menu, then choose Add/Change.

2. Enter the password and press ↵Enter.

3. As instructed, retype the password (to make sure it is correct) and press ↵Enter.

4. To make the password effective, save the document.

As with adding a password, to remove a password the document must be open on-screen. To remove a password from an open document, follow these steps:

1. Press Ctrl-F5, choose 2 Password, then choose 2 Remove.

   or

   Select Password from the File menu, then choose Remove.

2. Save the document to complete the omission of the password.

Using WordPerfect's Automatic Backup Options

Using F10 (Save Text) or Save from the File menu saves the complete document to the drive, directory, and document name identified. But, to effectively protect your documents, you must remember to periodically use Save. To provide additional protection for the forgetful, WordPerfect has an automatic backup option. (You will still want to use Save often in order to save your entire document.) WordPerfect also has an automatic backup option for the last saved document.

Setting up and using the automatic backup options is a little complex, so you may want to go slowly in this part. The two automatic backup options serve very different functions:

▲ *Timed Document Backup:* The document on your screen is saved at the time intervals you specify. It is saved in a file called WP{WP}BK.1 (or WP{WP}BK.2 if you have a second document on the screen). Saving takes a few seconds. When you exit WordPerfect properly, the WP{WP}BK files are deleted. If the power is accidentally cut off, the WP{WP}BK files remain on your disk. When you start WordPerfect, you can rename and load the appropriate WP{WP}BK file to see how much WordPerfect saved for you.

▲ *Original Document Backup:* When you save a document using F10 (Save Text) or Save from the File menu or F7 (Exit) or Exit from the File menu, the last disk version of the document is saved rather than replaced with the new version. The older version is placed in a file called FILENAME.BK! where "filename" is the actual name of the document file. This option has nothing to

do with saving your document as you work. It only pre-serves the "last saved" version of the document. Since this option gives you two versions of each document (the current and the last saved version), more space is con-sumed on your disk than when you save only one version.

Setting Up the Backup Options

To set up automatic backup options, follow these Quick Steps:

Backup Options Setup

1. Press ⇧Shift-F1 (Setup) or select Setup from the File menu.

   The Setup menu in Figure 4.2 appears.

2. Select 3 - Environment, then 1- Backup Options.

   The Setup: Backup screen in Figure 4.3 appears.

3. Press 1 to set the timed backup.

   Your cursor goes to the Timed Document Backup field.

4. Press Y for Yes.

   The field value appears as Yes, and your cursor moves to the Minutes Between Backups field.

5. Enter the number of minutes between back-ups (15 is suggested) and press ↵Enter.

   The number of minutes appears and your cursor goes back to the Selection: field at the bottom of the screen.

Quick Steps

Continues

Continued	6. Press 2 to set the original document backup option.	Your cursor goes to the Original Document Backup field.
	7. Press Y for Yes.	Yes is entered, and your cursor goes back to the Selection: field.
	8. To go back to your document, press F7 (Exit).	You are returned to the document screen.

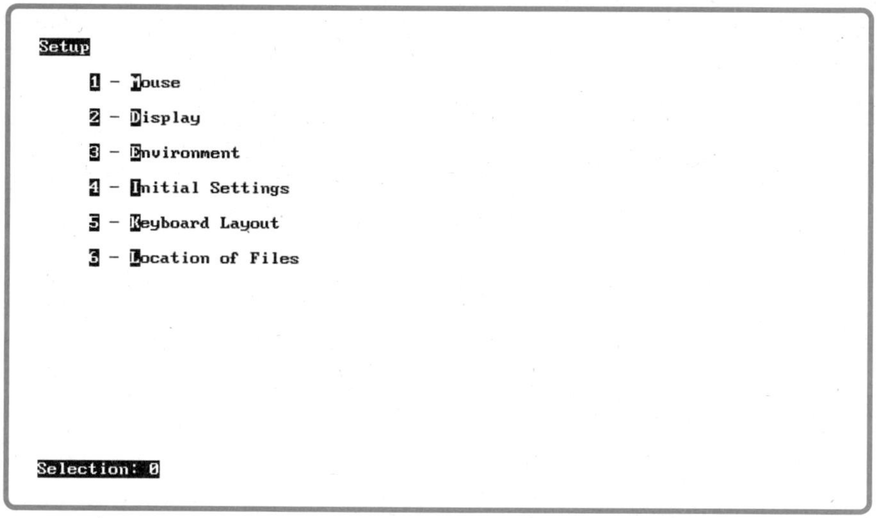

Figure 4.2

The Setup menu.

```
Setup
    1 - Mouse
    2 - Display
    3 - Environment
    4 - Initial Settings
    5 - Keyboard Layout
    6 - Location of Files




Selection: 0
```

Recovering After an Accident

If you set timed backup and sometime afterward experience a computer power failure, you will want to recover the timed backup copy of your document. Before trying the recovery, make sure the problem with the power supply is over. Then turn on your computer and start WordPerfect. A message like this appears:

```
Old Backup File Exists. 1 Rename; 2 Delete:
```

Press ⬜1 to rename the WP{WP}BK file. A message to rename the file is displayed:

```
New Name:
```

Type in the file name and press ⮐Enter. The backup file is renamed and WordPerfect is available for use.

```
Setup: Backup
      Timed backup files are deleted when you exit WP normally.  If you
      have a power or machine failure, you will find the backup file in the
      backup directory indicated in Setup: Location of Files.

         Backup Directory

   1 - Timed Document Backup              Yes
       Minutes Between Backups            30

   Original backup will save the original document with a .BK! extension
   whenever you replace it during a Save or Exit.

   2 - Original Document Backup           No

Selection: 0
```

Figure 4.3

Automatic Backup Options screen.

> **CAUTION:** Don't give the recovered backup file the same name as the "old" file you were working with, in case the "old" file is a more complete copy. You may want to look at it later.

You would then look at the contents of the timed backup file you renamed as well as the contents of the last version of the document you saved. Just like any other WordPerfect document, each document can be retrieved by using ⇧Shift‑F10 (Retrieve Text) or Retrieve from the **File** menu. (You'll find Quick Steps for retrieving a document in Chapter 5.)

In a Jam? A Possible Use of Backup Files

A possible (but not customary) use of backup files is to "lose" edits you may have made since the last automatic backup. Just use F7 (Exit) or select Exit from the **File** menu to leave your document without saving it, but don't leave WordPerfect. Retrieve the backup file from the location WordPerfect files are stored (on a hard disk, this is usually the WP51 directory). The text will reflect the file at the point of last backup. Because you have to be very aware of the timing of the latest edits, only use this approach in a pinch.

What's Next?

In this chapter, you learned how to save your work and exit WordPerfect. In addition you learned about how you can protect access to your documents with passwords and how WordPerfect can be used to protect your documents via automatic backup features. Further information about automatic backups follows.

Redirecting Backups

WordPerfect maintains backup files in the same directory as the WordPerfect system files. On most hard disks, this is the WP51 directory. If you are short on space in that area and want to redirect WordPerfect to save the files in another directory, follow these steps:

1. Press Shift-F1 (Setup) or select Setup from the **File** menu.

2. Select 6 - Location of Files.

3. Select 1 - Backup Files.

4. Enter the drive and path where you want Backup Files stored.

Refer to *The WordPerfect Bible* by Susan Baake Kelly for more information on changing the location of other WordPerfect files.

Ways to Retrieve a Document

▲ If you know the document name, press ⇧Shift-F10 (Retrieve) or select Retrieve from the **File** menu.

▲ If you don't know the document name, press F5 (List Files) or select List Files from the **File** menu, highlight the document, and select 1 Retrieve.

To Retrieve a Document into Another Document

1. Place the cursor where the document will be retrieved.

2. Use any retrieve method described above in "Ways to Retrieve a Document."

To View a Document (Not Edit)

1. Press F5 (List Files) or select List Files from the **File** menu.

2. Press ↵Enter.

3. Highlight the document.

4. Select 6 Look.

To Change the Drive and Directory Designation

1. Press F5 (List Files) or select List Files from the **File** menu.

2. Press = (equals sign).

3. In response to the New directory prompt, type in the desired drive and directory.

Ways to Retrieve a Document

Now that you have learned how to save a document, retrieving it becomes important. This chapter covers the options for retrieving documents including a basic retrieve, viewing a document before it is retrieved, retrieving a document stored on another drive or directory, and retrieving a document into an existing document.

Retrieving a Document

The term "retrieving a document" refers to moving the document from disk storage into RAM (and onto the screen). It is also referred to as "loading" or "opening" a document. You'll most often use the procedure when you wish to edit the document.

> **TIP:** If you have assigned a password to a document, you will be asked to enter the password when the document is retrieved. (Chapter 4 covers how to add a password to protect a document.)

Retrieving When You Know the Name

If speed is your goal, knowing its name when you want to retrieve a document is the fastest approach. Start from a "blank" WordPerfect screen, and use the following Quick Steps.

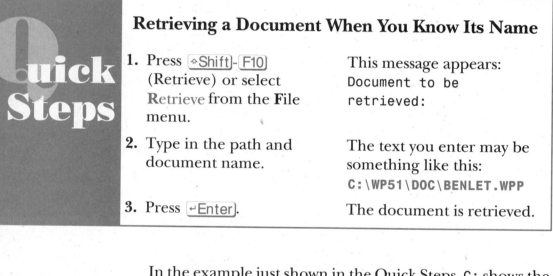

Quick Steps

Retrieving a Document When You Know Its Name

1. Press ⇧Shift-F10 (Retrieve) or select **R**etrieve from the **F**ile menu.

   This message appears: Document to be retrieved:

2. Type in the path and document name.

   The text you enter may be something like this: C:\WP51\DOC\BENLET.WPP

3. Press ↵Enter.

   The document is retrieved.

In the example just shown in the Quick Steps, C: shows the drive, WP51 and DOC are directories, and BENLET.WPP is the document name. The directory and document name are always set off by backslashes.

After typing in the document name and pressing ↵Enter, you may see a message like this:

ERROR: File not found - filename

This means that one of the following has occurred:

▲ You have made a typographical error in the document drive, directory, or name.

▲ The information is incorrect.

▲ The file does not exist on the disk.

Whatever the reason, WordPerfect cannot match the information you provided with a document on the disk. If, after carefully checking your typing accuracy, you cannot determine the problem, it may be that you've forgotten the document name. In this event, use the approach described in the next section.

Retrieving When You Don't Know the Name

Sometimes you'll want to retrieve a document but not remember its name. Or, you'll attempt to retrieve a document by name and get a message like this:

```
ERROR: File not found BENLET.WPP
```

In either case, you can consult WordPerfect for a list of document names and select a document from the list. Read on to learn how.

Figure 5.1 shows an alphabetical list with the document BENLET.WPP highlighted. The highlighted (or selected) document appears in a different color or in reverse video characters (usually light characters in a dark box). To select from the list, you use the arrow keys or a mouse to highlight the desired document name. The drive and directory for these files appears at the top of the screen. Selections you can make are shown at the bottom of the screen and numbered.

Figure 5.1

*List of documents
with BENLET.WPP
highlighted.*

```
04-26-92  10:13a              Directory C:\WP51\DOC\*.WPP
Document size:        0    Free: 34,648,064 Used:      22,891      Files:        5

.     Current    <Dir>                  ..    Parent    <Dir>
ADDRESS  .WPP   12,546  02-10-92 12:48p   BENLET   .WPP      934  02-21-92 01:31p
LET1     .WPP      793  04-23-92 03:29p   NOTE     .WPP    2,471  04-07-91 07:48a
PHONE    .WPP    6,147  01-26-92 07:24p

1 Retrieve; 2 Delete; 3 Move/Rename; 4 Print; 5 Short/Long Display;
6 Look; 7 Other Directory; 8 Copy; 9 Find; N Name Search: 6
```

To retrieve a document when you don't know its name, follow the next Quick Steps.

Retrieving a Document When You Don't Know Its Name

1. Press F5 (List Files) or select List Files from the File menu.

   The current directory, path, and *.* for file names appears—for example, C:\WP51\DOC*.*.

2. Enter a new drive and directory, if necessary (keep the *.* notation in place of a document name), and press ↵Enter.

   The List Files screen appears, showing the contents of the drive and directory you entered. Figure 5.2 shows an example.

3. Highlight the document to be retrieved, and then select 1 Retrieve.

   The document is retrieved.

> **TIP:** If you are sure about the document's first letter, or extension, or some other portion, you can narrow the search by specifying some parameter other than *.* for the document name. For example, if you remembered that the document started with D, you could use D*.*; if you knew the extension was WPP, you could use *.WPP.

From the List Files screen, you can move to another directory. For example, on the screen shown in Figure 5.2, the Parent directory is highlighted. *Parent directory* is another name for the superior or higher directory. Figure 5.3 shows the result after you press ⏎Enter twice with the Parent directory highlighted. The files of that directory appear. You can then select files from this screen.

```
04-26-92  10:13a              Directory C:\WP51\DOC\*.WPP
Document size:        0   Free: 34,648,064 Used:       22,891      Files:      5

      .   Current   <Dir>                     ..   Parent    <Dir>
  ADDRESS .WPP    12,546  02-10-92 12:48p   BENLET  .WPP       934  02-21-92 01:31p
  LET1    .WPP       793  04-23-92 03:29p   NOTE    .WPP     2,471  04-07-91 07:48a
  PHONE   .WPP     6,147  01-26-92 07:24p








  1 Retrieve; 2 Delete; 3 Move/Rename; 4 Print; 5 Short/Long Display;
  6 Look; 7 Other Directory; 8 Copy; 9 Find; N Name Search: 3
```

Figure 5.2

Parent directory highlighted.

Figure 5.3

Parent directory files.

```
04-30-92  01:14p              Directory C:\WP51\*.*
Document size:        0   Free: 34,461,696 Used:    4,079,639       Files:    94

.    Current    <Dir>                  ..    Parent     <Dir>
DOC      .       <Dir>  04-04-92 06:38p  8514A   .VRS     5,226  09-25-91 12:00p
ARROW-22.WPG        187  09-25-91 12:00p  ATI     .VRS    37,635  09-25-91 12:00p
BALLOONS.WPG      3,187  09-25-91 12:00p  BANNER-3.WPG       719  09-25-91 12:00p
BICYCLE .WPG        607  09-25-91 12:00p  BKGRND-1.WPG    11,391  09-25-91 12:00p
BORDER-8.WPG        215  09-25-91 12:00p  BULB    .WPG     2,101  09-25-91 12:00p
BURST-1 .WPG        819  09-25-91 12:00p  BUTTRFLY.WPG     5,349  09-25-91 12:00p
CALENDAR.WPG        371  09-25-91 12:00p  CERTIF  .WPG       679  09-25-91 12:00p
CHARACTR.DOC     47,008  09-25-91 12:00p  CHARMAP .TST    39,271  09-25-91 12:00p
CHKBOX-1.WPG        653  09-25-91 12:00p  CLOCK   .WPG     1,811  09-25-91 12:00p
CNTRCT-2.WPG      2,753  09-25-91 12:00p  CONVERT .EXE   109,591  09-25-91 12:00p
CURSOR  .COM      1,452  09-25-91 12:00p  DEVICE-2.WPG       657  09-25-91 12:00p
DIPLOMA .WPG      2,413  09-25-91 12:00p  EGA512  .FRS     3,584  09-25-91 12:00p
EGAITAL .FRS      3,584  09-25-91 12:00p  EGASMC  .FRS     3,584  09-25-91 12:00p
EGAUND  .FRS      3,584  09-25-91 12:00p  FIXBIOS .COM        50  09-25-91 12:00p
FLOPPY-2.WPG        475  09-25-91 12:00p  GAVEL   .WPG       887  09-25-91 12:00p
GENIUS  .VRS     12,885  09-25-91 12:00p  GLOBE2-M.WPG     7,785  09-25-91 12:00p
GRAB    .COM     16,450  09-25-91 12:00p  GRAPHCNV.EXE   122,368  09-25-91 12:00p
HANDS-3 .WPG      1,117  09-25-91 12:00p ▼ HPLASEII.PRS   24,311  04-30-92 12:48p

1 Retrieve; 2 Delete; 3 Move/Rename; 4 Print; 5 Short/Long Display;
6 Look; 7 Other Directory; 8 Copy; 9 Find; N Name Search: 6
```

CAUTION: Do not press ⏎Enter after highlighting the document. Pressing ⏎Enter has the same effect as selecting 6 Look from the selections at the bottom of the screen. The document will only be available for you to view; it will not be available for editing.

TIP: If you are on the List Files screen and decide not to select a document, press F7 (Exit) to return to what you were doing before pressing F5 (List Files).

Viewing a Document Without Retrieving It

If you have a lot of documents or a number of documents with similar names, viewing the List Files screen can be confusing. You may still have no clue as to which document to retrieve.

Retrieving the incorrect document and then repeating the process to find the correct one is time consuming and frustrating. WordPerfect gives you a way to avoid this situation by letting you look quickly at a document before retrieving it. You can easily look at several documents before retrieving the correct one.

The following Quick Steps detail how to view a document without retrieving it.

Looking at a Document

1. Press F5 (List Files) or select List Files from the File menu.

   The current directory, path, and *.* for file names appears.

2. Type in drive, path and file name information, if needed and press ↵Enter.

   A screen listing the documents appears.

3. Highlight the document name to be retrieved, and then select 6 Look.

   The document appears on-screen.

Quick Steps

Continues

Continued	4. View the document, using the arrow keys to *scroll* (move backward or forward) its text.	
	5. Press F7 (Exit) when done.	You're returned to the document list.
	6. Press F7 (Exit) to return to the document screen.	The document screen appears.

Changing the Designated Drive and Directory

The drive and path that WordPerfect automatically brings up is the *default directory*. That is, if no other drive and directory path is indicated, the default directory is used.

Each time you save a document, retrieve a document, or search for a document, the default directory name appears when you press F5 or select List Files from the **File** menu. If you consistently use a drive and path different from the one that automatically appears, you may enter that drive and path to come up each time.

To change the default drive and directory, follow the next Quick Steps.

Changing the Default Drive and Directory

1. Press [F5] (List Files) or select List Files from the **F**ile menu.

A message like the following appears: `Dir C:\WP51\*.*`. This message displays the current drive; the path, if any; and *.* to indicate "all file names with all extensions (or no extension)."

2. Press [↵Enter].

The List Files screen appears, showing the documents on the drive and directory.

3. Select 7 **O**ther Directory.

A message like this appears, showing the current drive and directory: `New directory = C:\WP51`.

4. Type in the new drive and path information, and press [↵Enter].

A message like this appears, indicating the new drive, path, and files to select: `Dir C:\WP51\DOC\*.*`.

5. Press [↵Enter].

The files for that drive and directory appear.

6. Press [F7] (Exit).

You are returned to your document.

Quick Steps

The next time you list files, retrieve text, or save a document, the new default is used if no other drive or directory is designated.

As an alternative, you can use the $\boxed{=}$ to quickly change directories. The following Quick Steps explain how to change the drive and directory with this shortcut method.

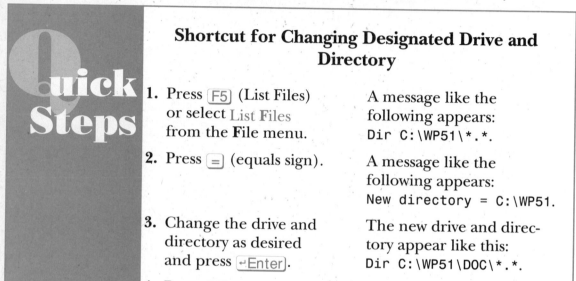

Quick Steps

Shortcut for Changing Designated Drive and Directory

1. Press $\boxed{\text{F5}}$ (List Files) or select List Files from the **File** menu.

   A message like the following appears:
   `Dir C:\WP51\*.*.`

2. Press $\boxed{=}$ (equals sign).

   A message like the following appears:
   `New directory = C:\WP51.`

3. Change the drive and directory as desired and press $\boxed{\text{↵Enter}}$.

   The new drive and directory appear like this:
   `Dir C:\WP51\DOC\*.*.`

4. Press $\boxed{\text{↵Enter}}$.

   The new drive and directory are set.

Retrieving One Document into Another

If you have a document on the screen, and then retrieve another document, the document you are retrieving is placed into the current document at your cursor position. This feature is useful for boilerplate text stored in a document that you want to retrieve into another document. Boilerplate is any text that you will use over and over such as an address or greeting. It is also one way to copy the complete contents of one file into another file. (Chapter 17 covers other ways to copy from one document to another.)

Figure 5.4 shows our document prior to retrieving the boilerplate text, Sincerely, Barbara J. Wiley. The closing is held in a document called CLOSE.WPP and can be retrieved into any letter. Figure 5.5 illustrates the document with boiler-plate text retrieved into it.

```
File Edit Search Layout Mark Tools Font Graphics Help      (Press F3 for Help)
Mr. David Randolph
Bennington Corporation
45 Superstition Highway
Phoenix, Arizona 85252

Dear Mr. Randolph;

     As I discussed,  I am very interested in pursuing a career
with the Bennington Corporation.  My complete resume is attached.
I look forward to speaking with you further on June 8th.  I'll meet
you at your corporate office location at 45 Superstition Highway.




C:\WP51\DOC\BENLET.WPP                    Doc 1 Pg 1 Ln 2.83" Pos 1"
```

Figure 5.4

Document before retrieving another document.

To retrieve one document into another, make sure the document you want to copy appears on your screen. Position your cursor in the location to be copied to. Use either of the following two retrieval methods:

▲ Press ⇧Shift-F10 (Retrieve) or select **R**etrieve from the File menu, type in the document name, and press ↵Enter. The document is retrieved.

▲ Press F5 (List Files) or select List Files from the **File** menu, enter the drive and path, then press ↵Enter. Highlight the document, select 1 **Retrieve**, and then press Y to this message:

```
Retrieve into current document? No (Yes)
```

The document is retrieved.

Figure 5.5

Document after retrieving another document.

```
File Edit Search Layout Mark Tools Font Graphics Help        (Press F3 for Help)
Mr. David Randolph
Bennington Corporation
45 Superstition Highway
Phoenix, Arizona 85252

Dear Mr. Randolph:

     As I discussed,  I am very interested in pursuing a career
with the Bennington Corporation.  My complete resume is attached.
I look forward to speaking with you further on June 8th.  I'll meet
you at your corporate office location at 45 Superstition Highway.

Sincerely,

Barbara J. Wiley



C:\WP51\DOC\BENLET.WPP                          Doc 1 Pg 1 Ln 3.5" Pos 2.6"
```

Retrieved text

Retrieve Can Save Typing Time

Consider how you may be able to use Retrieve to save typing time. Use Retrieve to combine two documents, then edit the new document, and save it under a new name.

For example, you may have a document with a standard memo heading and another document where you have written a report that you want to shorten into memo form. Let's also say that you need to retain both existing documents in their current form as well.

Just open the memo heading document file, then retrieve the entire paper into the file. Edit the new memo as needed (including any codes that existed in either document) and save it under a new name. Voilà... plenty of typing avoided.

What's Next?

In this chapter, you have learned how to retrieve a document whether or not you know the name of the document. You also learned how to look at a document before you retrieve it to make sure it is the document you want. Finally, you learned how to retrieve one document into another. A trick to retrieve text stored under certain conditions follows.

Retrieving Stored Text

Retrieving text is pretty straightforward, but here is one final advanced tip to pass on. When you block text, then copy, move, or delete text, it is stored. You can retrieve the last text stored by doing this:

1. Press `⇧Shift`-`F10` (Retrieve).
2. Press `↵Enter`. The stored text appears.

NOTE: The two-step technique just described only works if you used `Ctrl`-`F4` (Move) to copy, move, or delete. It doesn't work if you blocked text and pressed the `Del` key.

Selecting Paper Size and Type

1. Press ⇧Shift-F8 (Format) then select 2-Page or Page from the **L**ayout menu.
2. Select 7 - Paper Size/Type.
3. Select the paper size and type.

Change the Top and Bottom Margins

1. Press ⇧Shift-F8 (Format) then select 2-Page or Page from the **L**ayout menu.
2. Select 5 - Margins Top and Bottom.
3. Enter the new margin settings.

Set the Left and Right Margins

1. Press ⇧Shift-F8 (Format) then select 1-Line or Line from the **L**ayout menu.
2. Select 7 - Margins Left and Right.
3. Enter the new margin settings.

Changing Margins

Where the text appears on the page is easy to control with WordPerfect. You can set the size of margins, control the size and type of paper, use a variety of units of measure, and print "sideways" on a page.

Setting Margins

Margins are the amount of space from the edge of the paper to the text in your document. WordPerfect allows you to determine the size of your margins document by document. You can change margins within a document as often as you like.

Most WordPerfect users like to use inches to measure the margins. You may enter other units of measure, however, as described at the end of this chapter.

The procedure for controlling your margins is:

▲ Enter the paper size and type. This tells WordPerfect the dimensions of your paper.

▲ Identify the size of each margin: top, bottom, left, and right. WordPerfect will leave the margins as "white space."

WordPerfect fits your text in the space that remains. As a result, the line length of the text you enter is determined by the measurement from the left to the right of the page minus the left and right margins. The number of lines that WordPerfect fits on a page is determined by the length of the page minus the top and bottom margins.

Figure 6.1 shows the edge of the paper, the margins, and the area for WordPerfect to use for the letter.

Figure 6.1

Paper edge, margins, and document area.

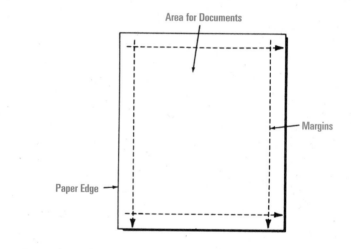

When you set the paper size/type and margins, you will use the Format menu. As you can see in Figure 6.2, a variety of formatting options are included on this menu.

```
Format
    1 - Line
            Hyphenation                 Line Spacing
            Justification               Margins Left/Right
            Line Height                 Tab Set
            Line Numbering              Widow/Orphan Protection

    2 - Page
            Center Page (top to bottom)  Page Numbering
            Force Odd/Even Page          Paper Size/Type/Labels
            Headers and Footers          Suppress
            Margins Top/Bottom

    3 - Document
            Display Pitch               Redline Method
            Initial Codes/Font          Summary

    4 - Other
            Advance                     Printer Functions
            Conditional End of Page     Underline Spaces/Tabs
            Decimal Characters          Border Options
            Language                    End Centering/Alignment
            Overstrike

Selection: 0
```

Figure 6.2

The Format menu.

Setting the Paper Size and Type

The first step in controlling margins is to set the paper size and type. WordPerfect's default (the setting which comes already established in WordPerfect) is 8.5" x 11" paper of standard weight. This default handles most common stationery and computer or typing paper. Depending on how your printer works, you may be able to use this setting for envelopes too, and just measure the address as if it were feeding onto an 8.5" x 11" sheet. For most work, you won't need to change the default settings. In fact, you will only need to change the paper size or type if you happen to use paper of a size other than 8.5" x 11", and a different type such as envelopes, letterhead, transparencies, labels, or cardstock.

If you want to add a setting, follow these steps:

1. Place the cursor in the location for entering the paper size/type code. Typically this is at the top of the page for the new paper size/type.

2. Press `⇧Shift`-`F8` (Format) to access the Format menu shown in Figure 6.2. Then, select 2-Page. The Format: Page menu appears. Or, simply select Page from the **L**ayout menu.

3. Select 7 - Paper Size/Type. The Format: Paper Size/Type menu appears.

4. If your paper size and type is not listed, select 2 - Add. If the paper size and type you want is already there, select it and skip to step 8.

5. If you choose to Add a paper size, you are taken to the Format: Paper Type menu. Select the type of paper you are using.

6. The Format: Edit Paper Definition options appears. Complete the information and press `⏎Enter`. Your addition appears on the Format: Paper Size/Type menu.

7. Select the paper size/type.

8. You are returned to the Format: Page menu. Complete another Format: Page option or press `F7` (Exit) to return to your document.

A code like the following one is placed in your document and may be viewed using Reveal Codes:

```
[Paper Sz/Typ:8.5" x 11",Standard]
```

Timesaving Idea

If you use different paper sizes/types often, consider setting up documents with the paper size, type, and correct margins to be used over and over. For example, if you use envelopes, you will need to not only identify the paper size/type, but position the address in the correct spot on the envelope.

A document just for envelope addresses can be a quick answer. This document would be set up with the correct paper size/type (envelope), and the correct top margin (from the top of the envelope). When you want to address a new envelope, you would need to open the envelope address document and copy or type in the new address, then print the page (in this case the envelope) for that address only.

If you like to put an envelope address page at the end of a letter, you could set up a document with the envelope paper size/type and margin information, retrieve it to a page at the end of the letter document, complete the address information, and then print.

Landscape Printing

All printers print in portrait orientation (such as a typical business letter where text is parallel to the short edge of the paper). Yours may allow for landscape orientation (or sideways, with print parallel to the long edge of the paper). Figures 6.3a and 6.3b illustrate these two print orientations. Figure 6.3a shows a typical letter (portrait). Figure 6.3b shows the envelope which accompanies the letter (landscape).

Figure 6.3a

Portrait printing.

```
Mr. David Randolph
Bennington Corporation
45 Superstition Highway
Phoenix, Arizona 85252

Dear Mr. Randolph:

     As I discussed, I am very interested in pursuing a career with
the Bennington Corporation.  My complete resume is attached.  I
look forward to speaking with you further on June 8th.  I'll meet
you at your corporate office location at 45 Superstition Highway.

Sincerely,

Barbara J. Wiley
```

Figure 6.3b

Landscape printing.

```
Barbara J. Wiley
3421 Pecos Way
San Diego, California 92123




                              Mr. David Randolph
                              Bennington Corporation
                              45 Superstition Highway
                              Phoenix, Arizona 85252
```

TIP: Landscape printing is useful for a document like a list or chart with a left margin that is too long to fit on an 8.5" wide sheet of paper. If you landscape print the document, you can have a left margin up to 11", thus allowing more text on a line.

Setting Top and Bottom Margins

The top margin setting is the measurement from the top edge of your paper to where the first line of your document will print. The bottom margin is the measurement from the bottom edge of the paper to where the last line of the document will print. The top and bottom margins are 1" unless you change them.

TIP: Top and Bottom margins are important to control if you print on letterhead. Just measure how far down from the top of the letterhead the text must fall. Set your top margin at this measure. Measure how far from the bottom of the letterhead text should stop for a pleasing effect. This is the length to enter for your bottom margin.

Let's walk through setting the top and bottom margins on a letter. The following Quick Steps detail the procedure.

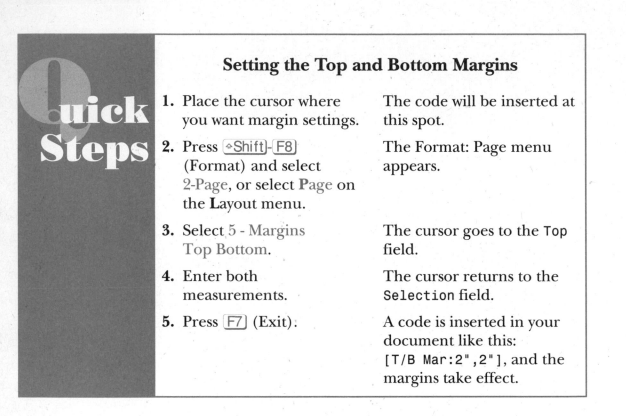

Quick Steps

Setting the Top and Bottom Margins

1. Place the cursor where you want margin settings.

   The code will be inserted at this spot.

2. Press ⇧Shift-F8 (Format) and select 2-Page, or select Page on the Layout menu.

   The Format: Page menu appears.

3. Select 5 - Margins Top Bottom.

   The cursor goes to the Top field.

4. Enter both measurements.

   The cursor returns to the Selection field.

5. Press F7 (Exit).

   A code is inserted in your document like this: [T/B Mar:2",2"], and the margins take effect.

Setting Right and Left Margins

The right margin is the space from the right edge of your paper to the rightmost characters of your document. The left margin is the space you want from the left edge of the paper to the leftmost characters in the document. The left and right default margins are set to be 1". You may change this setting.

The following Quick Steps detail how to set margins for the left and right of the page.

Setting the Left and Right Margins

1. Position the cursor and press ⇧Shift-F8 (Format) then 1 - Line or select Line on the **L**ayout menu.

   The Format: Line menu appears.

2. Select 7 - Margins Left Right.

   The cursor goes to the Left field.

3. Enter the left and right margin measurements.

   The cursor returns to the Selection field.

4. Press F7 (Exit) to return to your document.

   The code for the 2" left and right margins appears in the document: [L/R Mar:2",2"]. Text produced after this code has been established will be affected by the new setting.

Quick Steps

Figure 6.4 shows our letter with 1" margins. Since 1" margins are WordPerfect's default, there is no code for the margins in the document. Figure 6.5 shows the letter after the margins have been changed to 2". The lines in the letter are shortened and wrap around to accommodate the new, wider margins.

Figure 6.4

BENLET.WPP with 1" margins.

```
Mr. David Randolph
Bennington Corporation
45 Superstition Highway
Phoenix, Arizona 85252

Dear Mr. Randolph:

      As I discussed,  I am very interested in pursuing a career
with the Bennington Corporation.  My complete resume is attached.
I look forward to speaking with you further on June 8th.  I'll meet
you at your corporate office location at 45 Superstition Highway.

Sincerely,


Barbara J. Wiley
```

Controlling What is Visible on the Screen

If you set small (or no) margins or print in small characters, the text may extend right of what is visible on the screen. Some people like to view all the characters on the screen while they work on text then set the final margins and character size before printing. Do this by setting larger left and right margins for comfortable viewing as you work on the document. Then change the margins before you print to accommodate the printed result desired.

```
Mr. David Randolph
Bennington Corporation
45 Superstition Highway
Phoenix, Arizona 85252

Dear Mr. Randolph:

     As I discussed,  I am very interested in
pursuing a career with the Bennington Corpora-
tion. My complete resume is attached.  I look
forward to speaking with you further on June
8th.  I'll meet you at your corporate office
location at 45 Superstition Highway.

Sincerely,


Barbara J. Wiley
```

Figure 6.5
BENLET.WPP with 2" margins.

Setting the Unit of Measure

Most people who use WordPerfect keep inches as the default measure for margins and other measures. Additionally, the status line identifies the location of your cursor in inches. For example, these status line values:

```
Ln2" Pos 5"
```

indicate that the line where your cursor rests is 2" from the top edge of the paper and 5" from the left edge of the paper.

I use inches and recommend you use them, too. Besides their familiarity, the beauty of using inches is that if you want to place characters on the page, you can pick up a ruler and simply measure margins or other format options.

You may have a special need for another unit of measure, though. The units of measure available in WordPerfect are shown in Table 6.1.

Table 6.1
*WordPerfect's
Measurement Unit
Options.*

Measurement	Notation
inches	i or "
centimeters	c
points	p
1200ths of an inch	w
units for lines and columns	u

When you type in a type of measurement (such as a margin entry), you can enter the amount of the measurement followed by its notation. If inches is set as the default, the entry is converted to inches. For example, if you want a right margin to be 4 centimeters, enter `4c` in the `Right Margin` field. If the default is inches, WordPerfect converts 4 centimeters to 1.58" and displays that amount. Points is a special measurement used with particular type styles. If you are using a laser printer, you may want to use points occasionally.

WordPerfect allows you to control the measure used on menus along with the measure displayed in the status line. You can change the default for the unit of measurement.

To change the unit of measurement default, follow these steps:

1. Press ⇧Shift-F1 (Setup) or select Setup from the **File** menu.
2. Select 3 - Environment.

3. From the Setup: Environment screen, select 8 - Units of Measure. The Setup: Units of Measure screen appears (see Figure 6.6).

4. Select 1 - Display and Entry of Numbers for Margins, Tabs, etc.

5. Enter the type of measurement (i or ", c, p, w, or u).

6. Press F7 (Exit). The new defaults are set.

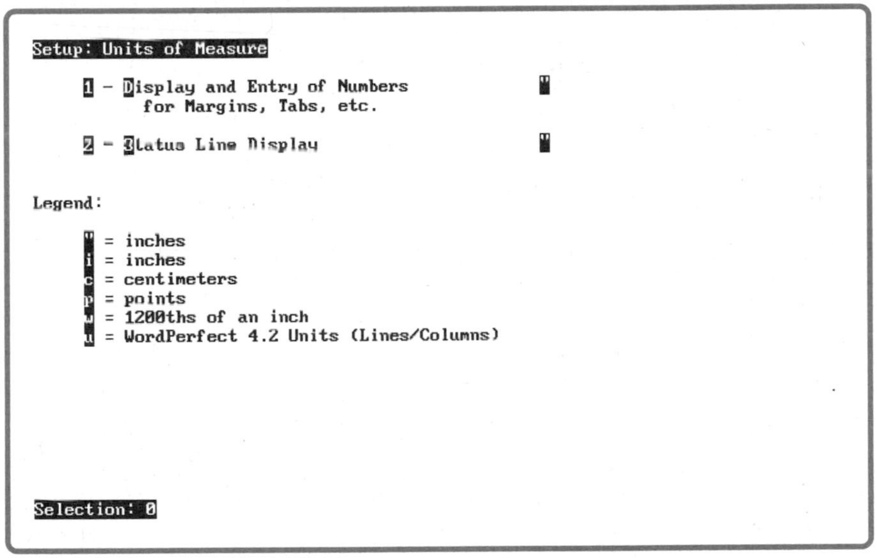

```
Setup: Units of Measure

     1 - Display and Entry of Numbers          "
            for Margins, Tabs, etc.

     2 - Status Line Display                   "


Legend:

     " = inches
     i = inches
     c = centimeters
     p = points
     w = 1200ths of an inch
     u = WordPerfect 4.2 Units (Lines/Columns)




Selection: 0
```

Figure 6.6

Setup: Units of Measure screen.

What's Next?

In addition to selecting or adding a paper type/size setting, you may copy, delete, or edit an existing paper type/size. Just do this:

1. Press ⇧Shift-F8 (Format) and select 2 - Page . Or, select Page from the Layout menu.

2. Select 7 - Paper Size/Type .

3. Follow the options on the screen.

Often, it is faster to copy a paper size/type than to add one because fewer settings may need to be entered. If you make a mistake, you can always edit the work or delete it and start again.

In This Chapter

Select the Printer File to Use

1. Press ⇧Shift-F7 (Print) or select **Print** from the **File** menu.
2. Select S - Select Printer.
3. Highlight a printer on the list and press ↵Enter, or select 2 - Additional Printers to choose one not listed.

Print a Document

1. Press ⇧Shift-F7 (Print) or select **Print** from the **File** menu.
2. Change any options desired, such as N - Number of Copies.
3. To print, select 1 - Full Document, 2 - Page, or 3 - Document on Disk. (For the latter, provide the document name.)

Printing Part of a Document

1. Block the text to print.
2. Press ⇧Shift-F7 (Print) or select **Print** from the **File** menu.
3. Press Y in response to the `Print Block? No (Yes)` message.

Print a Document from Disk

1. Press F5 (List Files) or select List Files from the **File** menu.
2. Change the directory name if desired, and then press ↵Enter to display the directory's contents.
3. Highlight the desired file and select 4 Print.

Control the Print

1. Press ⇧Shift-F7 (Print) or select **Print** from the **File** menu.
2. Select 4 - Control Printer and make the control selection.

How to Print Your Work

For most WordPerfect users, printing is the last step in getting desired results. This chapter covers what you need to know to identify your printer to WordPerfect, print all or part of a document, and control printing activity.

Setting Up Your Printer

When you installed WordPerfect, you identified the brand and type of printer you are using. You must also perform some setup operations from within WordPerfect before you can use your printer.

Press ⇧Shift-F7 (Print) or select **P**rint from the **F**ile menu. The Print menu shown in Figure 7.1 appears.

The currently selected printer is listed next to S - Select Printer. If you are using only one printer, and are not printing any fancy special effects, all you need to do is check that the name of the printer appears here.

Figure 7.1

The Print menu.

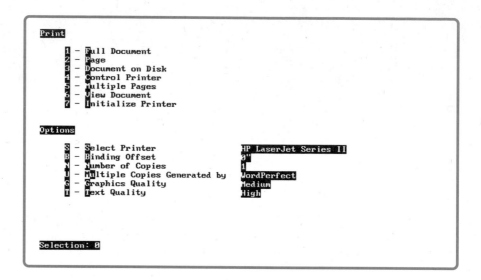

If you installed more than one printer and need to change the printer selected, or if you need to set up options for fancy printing jobs (like working with a laser printer), choose S - Select Printer. This displays the Print: Select Printer screen, which shows you the printers that you have installed. (Actually, each line represents a file that WordPerfect uses to communicate with a particular kind of printer.)

These are the options available from the Print: Select Printer screen:

1 - Select: To select a printer file other than the one highlighted.

2 - Additional Printers: To select other printer files that were installed. (See Appendix B for installation instructions.)

3 - Edit: To see the Select Printer: Edit menu shown in Figure 7.2. As you can see in the figure, you can edit:

The name of the printer file.

The port (the connection point of the computer to the printer cable).

Whether you are using a sheet feeder or another type of paper feeding device.

Cartridges, fonts, or print wheels (if your printer uses them; Chapter 8 covers more detail on this topic.)

The current initial font that will be used.

The paths to locate downloadable fonts (special character styles) or printer command files.

Printing to the hardware port to speed printing on computers not on a network.

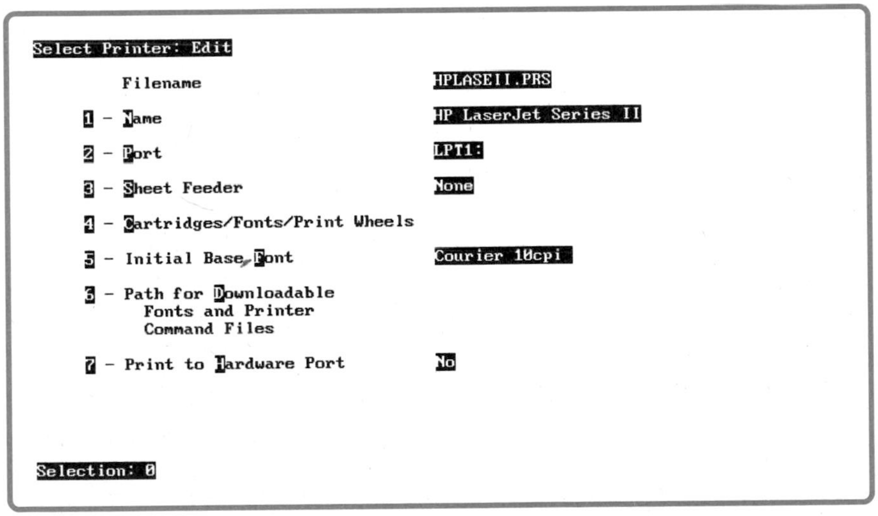

```
Select Printer: Edit

       Filename                         HPLASEII.PRS

  1 - Name                              HP LaserJet Series II

  2 - Port                              LPT1:

  3 - Sheet Feeder                      None

  4 - Cartridges/Fonts/Print Wheels

  5 - Initial Base Font                 Courier 10cpi

  6 - Path for Downloadable
        Fonts and Printer
        Command Files

  7 - Print to Hardware Port            No




Selection: 0
```

Figure 7.2

The Select Printer: Edit menu.

4 - **C**opy: To copy a printer file for editing through 3 - **E**dit.

5 - **D**elete: To delete a printer file you no longer need.

6 - **H**elp: To provide information important to setting print functions.

7 - **U**pdate: To update the printer file when you get a new printer file (such as one delivered with a later version of WordPerfect).

Press [F7] (Exit) select **E**xit from the **F**ile menu to return to the document screen when you have set up the printer.

Viewing a Document

Some WordPerfect formats don't show up on the editing screen. For example, headers, footers, footnotes, special fonts, and other formats may not appear. Figure 7.3 shows a page break in a draft chapter of a book. A header is set up to print at the top of each page and include the book title, chapter number, and page number, but you can't see it in Figure 7.3's draft mode. Through View Document, the header placement can be seen (see Figure 7.4).

Figure 7.3

Pages in a document.

Page break ————

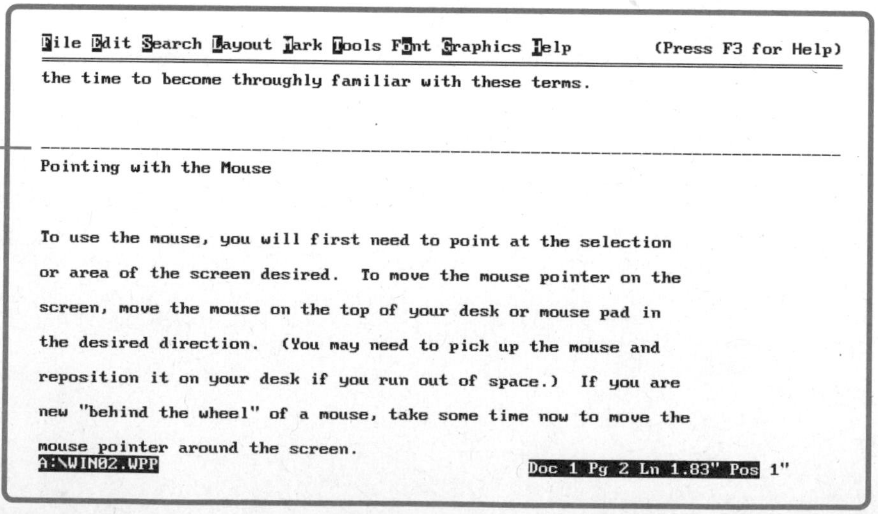

```
┌─────────────────────────────────────────────────────────────┐
│ File Edit Search Layout Mark Tools Font Graphics Help    (Press F3 for Help) │
│ the time to become throughly familiar with these terms.      │
│                                                               │
│ ───────────────────────────────────────────────────────────  │
│ Pointing with the Mouse                                       │
│                                                               │
│ To use the mouse, you will first need to point at the selection │
│ or area of the screen desired.  To move the mouse pointer on the │
│ screen, move the mouse on the top of your desk or mouse pad in │
│ the desired direction.  (You may need to pick up the mouse and │
│ reposition it on your desk if you run out of space.)  If you are │
│ new "behind the wheel" of a mouse, take some time now to move the │
│ mouse pointer around the screen.                              │
│ A:\WIN02.WPP                        Doc 1 Pg 2 Ln 1.83" Pos 1" │
└─────────────────────────────────────────────────────────────┘
```

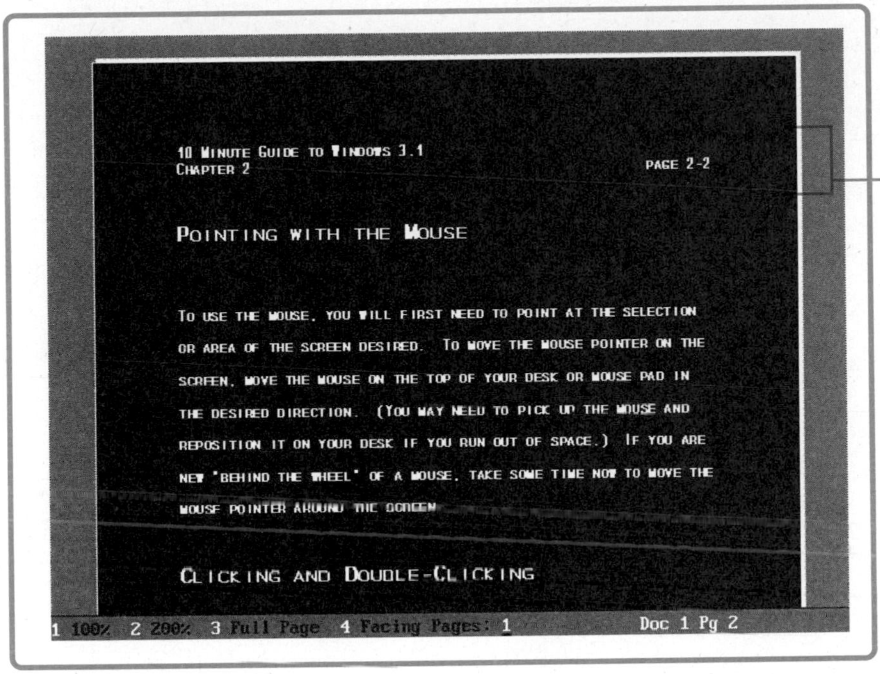

Figure 7.4

Viewing the pages through View Document.

The header appears in View Document mode.

```
10 MINUTE GUIDE TO WINDOWS 3.1
CHAPTER 2                                              PAGE 2-2


POINTING WITH THE MOUSE


TO USE THE MOUSE, YOU WILL FIRST NEED TO POINT AT THE SELECTION
OR AREA OF THE SCREEN DESIRED.  TO MOVE THE MOUSE POINTER ON THE
SCREEN, MOVE THE MOUSE ON THE TOP OF YOUR DESK OR MOUSE PAD IN
THE DESIRED DIRECTION.  (YOU MAY NEED TO PICK UP THE MOUSE AND
REPOSITION IT ON YOUR DESK IF YOU RUN OUT OF SPACE.)  IF YOU ARE
NEW "BEHIND THE WHEEL" OF A MOUSE, TAKE SOME TIME NOW TO MOVE THE
MOUSE POINTER AROUND THE SCREEN.


CLICKING AND DOUBLE-CLICKING

1 100%  2 200%  3 Full Page  4 Facing Pages: 1           Doc 1 Pg 2
```

To use View Document, press ⇧Shift-F7 (Print) to display the Print menu. Select 6 - View Document. The following options are available for viewing:

1 100%: To increase the display by 100%.

2 200%: To zoom in the maximum amount—200%.

3 Full Page: To display the entire page on the screen.

4 Facing Pages: To see even numbered pages displayed on the left and odd numbered on the right.

You may use PgUp/Dn, Home, arrow keys, and Go to (Ctrl-Home) to move through the document. When you are done viewing the document, press F7 (Exit) to leave the View Document screen.

Printing a Document

Once you have set up the printer, make sure your printer is ready to print:

▲ Is the cable between the printer and computer secure on both ends?

▲ Is the printer turned on? If not, make sure it is plugged in and then turn it on.

▲ Is the on-line light lit? If not, use the control panel to put the printer on-line (which means it is ready to receive your document from the computer).

▲ Is there paper in the printer and is it fed properly? If not, add paper and make sure it feeds smoothly into the printer.

When your printer is ready, and the document to print is showing on your screen, press ⇧Shift-F7 (Print) or select Print from the File menu. The Print screen shown in Figure 7.1 appears.

To print more than one paper copy, select N - Number of Copies, type in the number of copies you want, and press ↵Enter.

To print the entire document, select 1 - Full Document. To print only the page on which your cursor rests, select 2 - Page.

To "print" the document on a disk, select 3 - Document on Disk. (This option is discussed in detail later in this chapter.) When you print a document on a disk, you will be required to enter the name of the document before it is printed.

The following Quick Steps explain how to print a document.

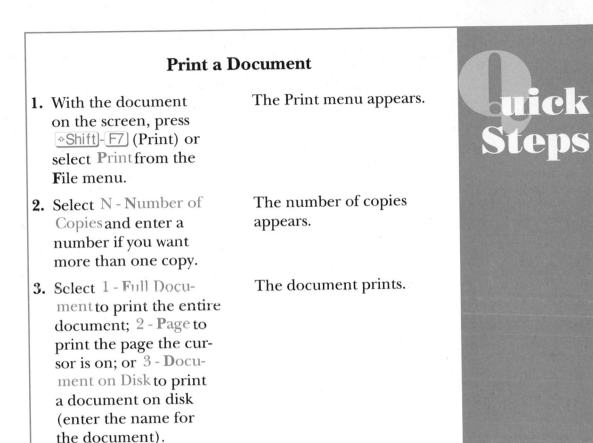

Print a Document

1. With the document on the screen, press ⇧Shift-F7 (Print) or select **P**rint from the **F**ile menu.

   The Print menu appears.

2. Select N - Number of Copies and enter a number if you want more than one copy.

   The number of copies appears.

3. Select 1 - Full Document to print the entire document; 2 - Page to print the page the cursor is on; or 3 - Document on Disk to print a document on disk (enter the name for the document).

   The document prints.

Quick Steps

Printing on Different Paper Sizes and Types

You may have more than one paper size/type in a document. For example, you may have a letter to be printed on 8.5" x 11" paper followed by text to be printed on an envelope. In such a case, put the different paper sizes/types on different pages, then print each page separately by using ⇧Shift-F7 (Print), then 2 - Page. This will give you time to hand-feed the paper to the printer or change the paper that is automatically fed through the printer.

FYI Idea

Printing a Selected Part of a Document

If you want to print only a part of a document, you may block the text to print and then press ⇪Shift-F7 (Print) or select **P**rint from the **F**ile menu. This message appears:

    Print block? No (Yes)

Press Y and the block prints.

Printing a Document on Disk

Sometimes you may be editing one document but wish to print a different one. You don't have to quit editing the first document to print the second—instead, you can print the second document directly from disk.

Earlier in this chapter, we covered how to use ⇪Shift-F7 (Print) or **P**rint from the **F**ile menu, then 3-**D**ocument on Disk to print a file on disk. What follows is a second method to perform the same activity.

To print a document on disk, press F5 (List Files) or select **L**ist Files from the **F**ile menu. Make sure the drive and path for the files you want are entered at the prompt. For instance:

    Dir C:\WP51*.*

To have only document files appear, change the file designation from *.* to *.WPP (or whatever file extension you regularly use). Press ↵Enter.

The List Files screen appears (shown in Figure 7.5). Use the arrow keys to highlight the file you want to print. (In Figure 7.5 the BENLET.WPP file is highlighted.)

```
02-21-92  01:58p           Directory C:\WP51\DOC\*.*
Document size:        0   Free: 12,881,920 Used:        5,749      Files:        8

      Current    <Dir>                  ..    Parent     <Dir>
ADDRESS .WPP      712  02-21-92 01:32p  BENLET  .WPP      706  02-21-92 01:32p
BENLET1 .WPP      934  02-21-92 01:31p  BENLET2 .WPP      753  02-21-92 01:44p
CHAPTER2.WPP      830  02-21-92 01:49p  CLOSE   .WPP      354  02-21-92 01:36p
LET1    .WPP      722  02-21-92 01:31p  LET2    .WPP      738  02-21-92 01:32p




1 Retrieve; 2 Delete; 3 Move/Rename; 4 Print; 5 Short/Long Display;
6 Look; 7 Other Directory; 8 Copy; 9 Find; N Name Search: 3
```

Figure 7.5
The List Files screen.

Select 4 Print and this prompt appears:

```
Page(s): All
```

Leave the number of pages "as is" to print the entire document or type in only those pages you want to print. Use a dash to indicate *through* or a comma to indicate *and*. Here are some examples:

3-8   prints pages 3 through 8

3,8   prints pages 3 and 8

Once the pages to print are identified, press ↵Enter. This message appears while the print order is sent to the printer:

```
*Please wait*
```

You are returned to the List Files screen. Press F7 (Exit) to return to your document. The pages you indicated will be printed.

The following Quick Steps summarize how to print a document on disk.

Quick Steps

Printing from Disk

1. Press F5 (List Files) or select List Files from the **File** menu.

    The List Files screen appears.

2. Highlight the document to print and select 4 Print.

    The prompt Page(s): All appears.

3. Type in the pages to print and press ↵Enter.

    The pages print.

4. Press F7 (Exit) to go back to your document.

    You are returned to your document.

Controlling the Print Operation

Sometimes after starting a print job, you change your mind. To stop the printing, press ⇧Shift-F7 (Print), or select Print from the **File** menu and then select 4 - Control Printer. The Print: Control Printer screen shown in Figure 7.6 appears. Notice that information about the Current Job (document being printed) appears. Then a Job List (the list of waiting documents) appears. Notice that each waiting job is assigned a number. Finally, the number of `Additional Jobs Not Shown` (if any) appears. The options from which you may select appear at the bottom of the screen.

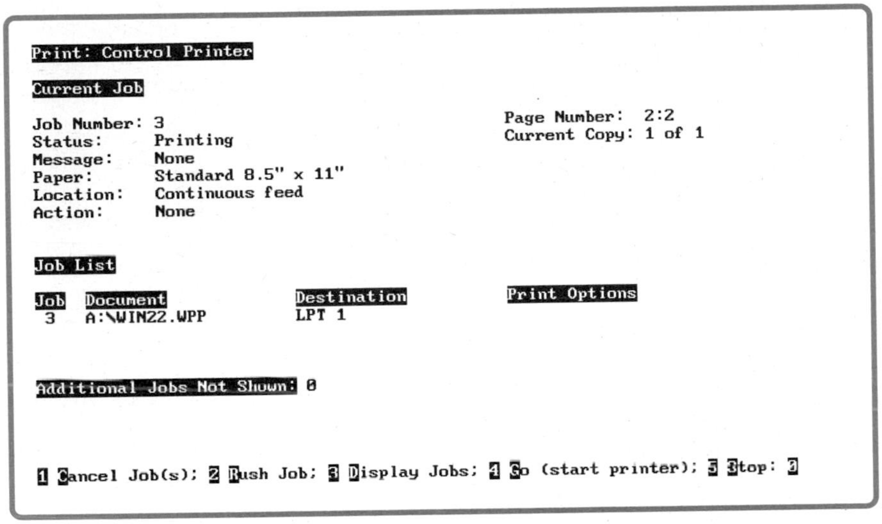

Figure 7.6

Print: Control Printer screen.

```
Print: Control Printer

Current Job

Job Number:  3                          Page Number:  2:2
Status:      Printing                    Current Copy: 1 of 1
Message:     None
Paper:       Standard 8.5" x 11"
Location:    Continuous feed
Action:      None


Job List

Job  Document              Destination         Print Options
 3   A:\WIN22.WPP          LPT 1



Additional Jobs Not Shown: 0



1 Cancel Job(s); 2 Rush Job; 3 Display Jobs; 4 Go (start printer); 5 Stop: 0
```

To control a print job, select one of these options:

1 **C**ancel Job(s): To cancel printing. Enter the number of the job (shown in the `Job List` on the screen).

2 **R**ush Job: To move a print job ahead of other documents waiting to be printed. Identify the number of the job to be printed next and press ↵Enter.

3 **D**isplay Jobs: To see which jobs are waiting to print if `Additional Jobs Not Shown` has a value. If all jobs are displayed on the screen when you make this selection, WordPerfect lets you know with a message.

4 **G**o (start printer): To start the printer after it has been stopped.

5 **S**top: To stop the printer to adjust paper or perform another activity. Use 4 **G**o (start printer) to start the printer again.

What's Next?

There are two advanced print features that are not needed by most users but that you might find useful. For example, when you press ⬆Shift-F7 (Print), or select **P**rint from the **F**ile menu you may have noticed the following:

U - **Mu**ltiple Copies Generated by: To identify whether WordPerfect or your printer will generate multiple copies (primarily for use when a network is involved).

G - **G**raphics Quality: To identify the quality level at which you want graphics printed (you may also specify "Do Not Print" graphics).

T - **T**ext Quality: To enter the quality level for text to be printed (Do Not Print the text, Draft, Medium, High).

If you omit printing graphics, the document will typically print faster. If you use Draft quality for graphics and/or text, you may be able to extend the life of your printer ribbon, and your document may print faster.

Experiment with these options, using your WordPerfect manual for reference. They can lead to a more professional touch and, in some cases, save time.

The following options are covered in Chapter 11:

5 - **M**ultiple Pages: To print a selection of pages in a document.

B - **B**inding Offset: To create a page for double-sided printing or copying. A wider "center" margin is created to allow space for binding or holes to be punched. You may specify how far the text should be shifted beyond the regular margin as it is printed.

In this chapter, you learned about printing on paper. It is possible you may want to print to a file. Read on to learn more about the "why" and "how."

Print to Disk

Let's say that you have WordPerfect installed on a computer that is not connected to a printer. If you wanted to print a file, you could copy it onto a floppy disk and take it to someone's computer who has a printer. If that person had WordPerfect, you could load the file into WordPerfect on that computer and print out your file. But what if that person did not have WordPerfect installed?

To solve this potential problem, WordPerfect offers the Print to Disk feature. It lets you send the print output to a file rather than to an actual printer; then later that file can be copied to a printer directly from DOS.

CAUTION: When you print a file to disk, the print file that is created is *not* a usable document file; it is written in a language understandable *only* to the printer.

Follow these steps to print a file to disk.

1. Press ⟨⇧Shift⟩-⟨F7⟩ (Print) or select Print from the **File** menu. The main Print menu appears.

2. Choose S - Select Printer. A list of installed printers appears.

3. Highlight the printer on which you will eventually print the document. (If it's not listed, you'll need to install it; see the instructions in Appendix B.)

4. Select 3 Edit. The Select Printer: Edit screen appears.

5. Select 2 - Port. A list of available ports appears.

6. Select 8 Other. A `Device or Filename:` prompt appears.

7. Type the full path and name of the print file you want to create, and press ⟨↵Enter⟩. You can use any name and extension, but a unique extension such as `.PRT` will help you distinguish the file from others on your disk.

8. Press ⟨F7⟩ (Exit) twice, or click the right mouse button twice.

9. Print the document as you normally would. Instead of sending the document to your printer, WordPerfect sends it to the specified disk file.

CAUTION: Don't forget to change the port selection back to a regular LPT or COM port when you're finished, or to specify a different file name to print to, or the next time you print a document it will overwrite the print file you just created.

Change the Size or Appearance of Characters

1. Press `Ctrl`-`F8` (Font) or select the **Font** menu.
2. Select the size or appearance attributes desired.

Change the Base Font While Working in a Document

1. Press `Ctrl`-`F8` (Font) and select 4 Base Font or select Base Font from the **Font** menu.
2. Highlight the desired font and choose 1 Select.

Change the Initial Base Font Set in the Printer File

1. Press `Shift`-`F7` (Print) or select Print from the **File** menu.
2. Select S - Select Printer, highlight the printer, then select 3 - Edit.
3. Choose 5 - Initial Base Font and select the font desired.

Change the Document Initial Font

1. Press `Shift`-`F8` (Format) then select 3 - Document or select Document from the **Layout** menu.
2. Select 3 - Initial Base Font and choose the font desired.

Convert Case

1. Block the text to convert.
2. Press `Shift`-`F3` (Switch) or select Convert Case from the **Edit** menu.
3. Choose Upper or Lower case.

Giving Characters a New Look

Changing the look of your characters can add emphasis, interest, and clarity to your documents. For example, Figure 8.1 shows a sample resumé before any appearance options are applied. Figure 8.2 shows the same resumé after some of the character formats available in WordPerfect have been used.

The available character enhancements possible depend not only on WordPerfect, but on your printer as well. Not all printers are capable of printing all of WordPerfect's character options. You can experiment with your printer to see which results are possible for you.

WordPerfect's Font Menu

WordPerfect's Font menu controls the look of your characters. With the Font options, you can control the typeface, type size, placement, and appearance of characters. Figure 8.3 shows some of the options available.

Figure 8.1

*The sample resumé
before appearance
options are applied.*

```
                        Barbara J. Wiley
                         3421 Pecos Way
                    San Diego, California 92123

Experience:

     1988-present      Programmer      Barney Corporation, 4566
                                       Oakway, Austin, Texas 78759
                                       (512) 253-9900.

                                       Cobol and PL1 in an IBM
                                       environment.

     1985-1988        Operator        Beverly World, PO Box 843,
                                       Austin, Texas 78777
                                       (512) 435-9000.

Education:

     Bachelor  of Science (Computer Science)
     University of Iowa, Iowa City, Iowa.
     Awarded 1984.

Affiliations:

     Data Processing Professional Group, 1985 to present.
```

Figure 8.2

*The sample resumé
after appearance
options are applied.*

**Barbara J. Wiley
3421 Pecos Way
San Diego, California 92123**

Experience:

1988-present	Programmer	Barney Corporation, 4566 Oakway, Austin, Texas 78759 (512) 253-9900.
		Cobol and PL1 in an IBM environment.
1985-1988	Operator	Beverly World, PO Box 843, Austin, Texas 78777 (512) 435-9000.

Education:

Bachelor of Science (Computer Science)
University of Iowa, Iowa City, Iowa.
Awarded 1984.

Affiliations:

Data Processing Professional Group, 1985 to present.

This chapter will explain the various options available on the Font menu, and will provide tips for using character appearance effectively.

Bold:	Bold text can **emphasize**.
Underline:	Underline can add <u>interest</u>.
Double Underline:	Double underlines can add even <u>more!</u>
Redline:	Redline text can set off text.
Strikeout:	~~Strikeout~~ does the same.
Shadow:	**Shadow** is another look.
Small Cap:	SMALL CAP gives this appearance.
Superscript:	Use superscript in footnotes.[2]
Subscript:	Subscript is good for text like H_2O.
Fine:	Fine text is one size.
Large:	**Large is another.**
Extra Large:	**EXTRA LARGE IS ANOTHER.**
Some type styles:	Helvetica
	Times Roman
	PRESENTATION
	Courier.

Figure 8.3

Some effects you can create with the Font menu.

Changing the Font

Your printer has specific typeface and type size capabilities (which can be augmented through various means, as you will learn in the "Font Cartridges and Soft Fonts" section later in this chapter). On many printers, it is possible to print in more than one typeface and/or more than one type size. For example, Figure 8.4 shows the sample resumé printed with the headings in a large Helvetica font and the body in a smaller Times Roman font.

NOTE: *Typeface* refers to the general "family" of the letters. Helvetica is an example of a typeface; Times Roman is another. (This book is printed in New Baskerville.) Text in a particular typeface can appear in a variety of *type sizes*, from about 6 points (6/72 of an inch) to as high as 70 points or more, depending on the printer's capabilities. For our purposes, the term *font* means the combination of typeface and type size.

Figure 8.4

The sample resumé with Helvetica and Times Roman fonts.

Barbara J. Wiley
3421 Pecos Way
San Diego, California 92123

Experience:

1988-present   Programmer   Barney Corporation, 4566 Oakway, Austin, Texas
                                  78759 (512) 253-9900.

                                  Cobol and PL1 in an IBM environment.

1985-1988   Operator   Beverly World, PO Box 843, Austin, Texas 78777
                                  (512) 435-9000.

Education:

Bachelor of Science (Computer Science)
University of Iowa, Iowa City, Iowa.
Awarded 1984.

Affiliations:

Data Processing Professional Group, 1985 to present.

WordPerfect offers several ways to control fonts. Each method allows you to choose from the same list of fonts, which is determined by the fonts available to your particular printer.

Setting the Initial Base Font

The *initial base font* is set up through the Select Printer: Initial Font screen. This font is used for all documents unless another font is specified using one of the other two methods (discussed later in this chapter).

To change the initial base font (in the printer file), follow the next Quick Steps.

Setting the Initial Base Font

1. Press ⬆Shift-F7 (Print) or Print from the File menu.

   The Print menu appears.

2. Choose S - Select Printer.

   The Print: Select Printer menu appears.

3. Highlight the desired printer file, and select 3 Edit.

   The Select Printer: Edit menu appears.

4. Choose 5 - Initial Base Font.

   The Select Printer: Initial Font menu appears (see Figure 8.5).

5. Highlight the desired font and choose 1 - Select.

   The font appears as the Initial Base Font on the Select Printer: Edit screen.

6. Press F7 (Exit) as needed to return to your document.

Quick Steps

Figure 8.5

*The Select Printer:
Initial Font screen.*

```
Select Printer: Initial Font

* Courier 10cpi
  Courier 10cpi Bold
  Helv 14.4pt Bold (B)
  Letter Gothic 10cpi (R)
  Line Draw 10cpi (Full)
  Line Draw 10cpi 14pt (R)
  Line Draw 12cpi (Full-Cr)
  Line Draw 12cpi (Full-LG)
  Line Draw 12cpi (Full-PE)
  Line Printer 16.67cpi
  PC Line Draw 10cpi 14pt (R)
  Presentation  6.5cpi Bold (R)
  Presentation  8.1cpi Bold (R)
  Presentation 10cpi Bold (R)
  TmsRmn  8pt (B)
  TmsRmn 10pt (B)
  TmsRmn 10pt Bold (B)
  TmsRmn 10pt Italic (B)




1 Select; N Name search: 1
```

Setting the Document Initial Font

You can set the default font for an individual document through
the Document: Initial Font screen. This font setting is valid for
the active document only and overrides the font set in the Select
Printer: Initial Font screen.

To set the Document Initial Font, use the following Quick
Steps.

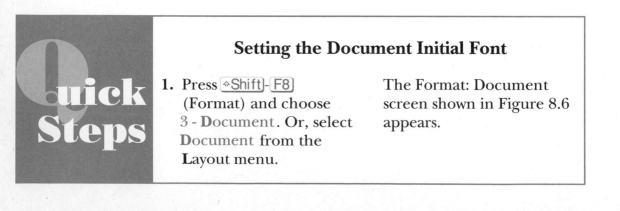

**Quick
Steps**

Setting the Document Initial Font

1. Press ⇧Shift-F8
   (Format) and choose
   3 - Document. Or, select
   Document from the
   Layout menu.

The Format: Document
screen shown in Figure 8.6
appears.

2. Select 3 - Initial Base Font.

The Document: Initial Font screen appears.

3. Choose the font desired, then choose 1 - Select.

The font appears as the Base Font on the Format: Document screen.

4. Press F7 (Exit) to return to your document.

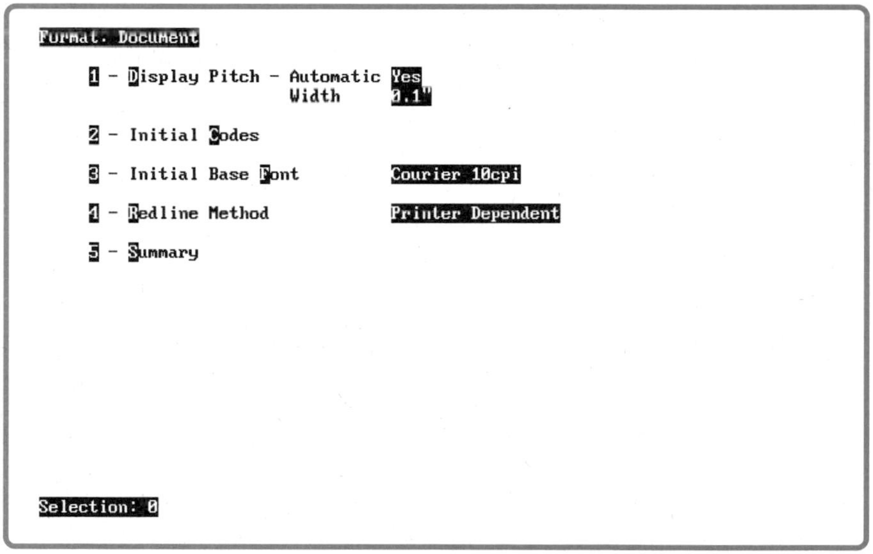

```
Format. Document

 1 - Display Pitch - Automatic Yes
                        Width     0.1"

 2 - Initial Codes

 3 - Initial Base Font        Courier 10cpi

 4 - Redline Method           Printer Dependent

 5 - Summary










Selection: 0
```

Figure 8.6

The Format: Document screen.

Changing the Base Font

The final font setup option is the one you will use most often if your printer has a variety of font capabilities—changing the Base Font. This option overrides any fonts set through the other methods. It inserts a font code at the beginning and end of the selected text, just as when you select a size or appearance attribute (as you will see later in the chapter). Text after the font code will appear in the font selected until you enter a new font code. (If you later want to delete the font selection, just delete the code.)

To change the base font, use the following Quick Steps.

Changing the Base Font

1. Place your cursor where the font is to change. (All text from the cursor forward will be affected.)

2. Press Ctrl-F8 (Font) and select 4 Base Font. Or, select Base Font from the Font menu.
   The Base Font menu appears, displaying the available typefaces and sizes for your printer.

3. Highlight the desired font and choose 1 Select.
   You are returned to your document. A code for the font is placed in the document.

When you choose a base font (using any of the methods we've discussed), you are defining a combination of typeface and type size to be the "normal" font for your document. Once you have defined what is "normal," you can concentrate on creating variations to make your document more interesting.

Controlling Character Size

No matter how carefully you choose your base font, there will be times when you want to make certain words larger or smaller. WordPerfect offers several options for changing the size of text for emphasis, aesthetic appeal, or simply to fit more text on a page.

> **CAUTION:** Whether you can use these options or not depends on your printer. If your printer has only one font, in one size, it will print in that font and size, regardless of the size options you choose through WordPerfect.

WordPerfect offers an easy way to change the size of selected text without messing up your base font—it lets you change the *size attribute* of text. This is different from changing the size of a font.

Font size is measured in *points* (there are 72 points in an inch). When you change font size, you change from one point size to another. That's what you did when you were setting the font in the previous section.

In contrast, when you change the size attribute of text, you don't specify a point size—you specify in words how you want the size to change. For example, you might specify "very large." When you do this, WordPerfect examines the size of the currently-selected font and multiplies its size by a fixed percentage to determine how big "very large" would be in comparison to it.

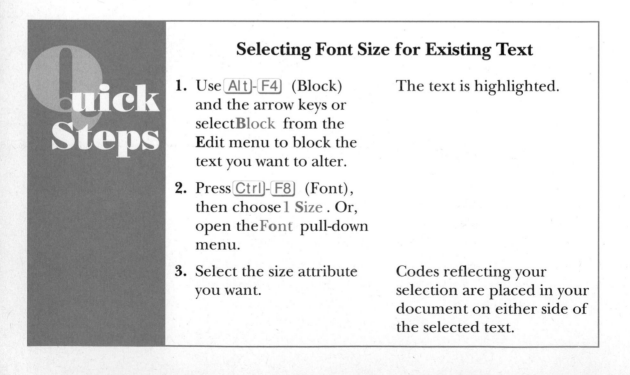

NOTE: The menu that displays the size choices also displays options for superscript and subscript. These are not really size attributes, but rather position attributes. They are discussed in the next section.

You can use the following words to change the size attribute:

Fine

Small

Large

Very Large

Extra Large

To assign a size attribute to already-typed text, use the following Quick Steps.

Selecting Font Size for Existing Text

1. Use [Alt]-[F4] (Block) and the arrow keys or select **B**lock from the **E**dit menu to block the text you want to alter.

   The text is highlighted.

2. Press [Ctrl]-[F8] (Font), then choose 1 **S**ize . Or, open the**F**ont pull-down menu.

3. Select the size attribute you want.

   Codes reflecting your selection are placed in your document on either side of the selected text.

Or, to change the size of text you are about to type, follow the next Quick Steps.

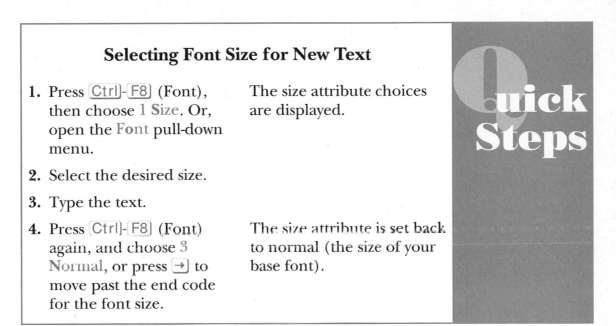

Selecting Font Size for New Text

1. Press `Ctrl`-`F8` (Font), then choose 1 Size. Or, open the Font pull-down menu.

   The size attribute choices are displayed.

2. Select the desired size.

3. Type the text.

4. Press `Ctrl`-`F8` (Font) again, and choose 3 Normal, or press `→` to move past the end code for the font size.

   The size attribute is set back to normal (the size of your base font).

Controlling Character Position

In some instances, you may want characters to appear slightly above or below the normal line of text. WordPerfect offers two common options for positioning text:

Superscript: Superscript characters are placed somewhat above the line of normal text. Text in superscript is often used for footnotes and formulas. Most printers are capable of printing superscript text.

Subscript: Subscripted characters are placed slightly lower than the line of text. Formulas often require subscripted text. Common printers can handle this option.

You set subscript or superscript exactly the same way that you set size attributes (see the previous section). You can either set it for existing text or for new text, just as you can with size attributes.

WordPerfect is not "what you see is what you get." That is, the actual sizes and positions of characters appear on the screen as different colors rather than as they will actually look when you print. Figure 8.7 illustrates the appearance of the size attribute and position options on-screen, both in the document and Reveal Codes screen.

> **TIP:** You can change both size and position for the same text. For example, you can set text to Fine, Superscript for footnote numbering.

Figure 8.7

Character size and position attributes in both the document and Reveal Codes screen.

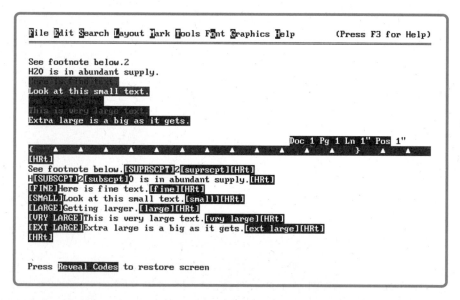

Altering the Appearance of Characters

> **NOTE:** *Appearance*, as WordPerfect uses it, means the presence or absence of attributes such as bold, italic, underline, redline, and strikeout.

WordPerfect's appearance options have something for everyone. Figure 8.8 shows some of the appearance options you can select. The options available are:

Normal: Normal text is text with no appearance codes. It is the default text for the document.

Bold: Bold text is heavier than normal text. Usually, bold text is displayed on-screen as brighter or in a different color than other text.

Italic: If your printer handles italic text, you can introduce a typeset quality to your documents. Use it sparingly to emphasize key words or phrases. Use it throughout invitations or announcements to give them an elegant appearance.

Underline: Text may be printed with a single underline. (You cannot type in text and then use the underline key to underline it unless you select the text first.)

Double underline: Text may be printed with two underlines. Some printers do not handle this option. If your printer does, it can give your documents an unusual touch.

Redline: This option is often used to display edits that should be reviewed. Text to be added can be shown in redline.

Strikeout: When showing edits made to a document, you can use strikeout to illustrate text to be removed.

Outline: This special style is useful as an attention-getter, although many printers do not handle the style.

Shadow: This creates a shadow effect by offsetting a character from itself. Shadow is effective for use in flyers and advertisements.

Small Caps: Regardless of whether you enter the text in upper- or lowercase letters, the text is printed in small uppercase (capital) letters.

Figure 8.8

Examples of character appearance options.

```
Normal

Bold

Underline

Double Underline

Italic

Shadow

SMALL CAPS

Redline

Strikeout
```

The process for changing an appearance is similar to that for changing a size attribute. The following Quick Steps detail how to control character appearance for existing text.

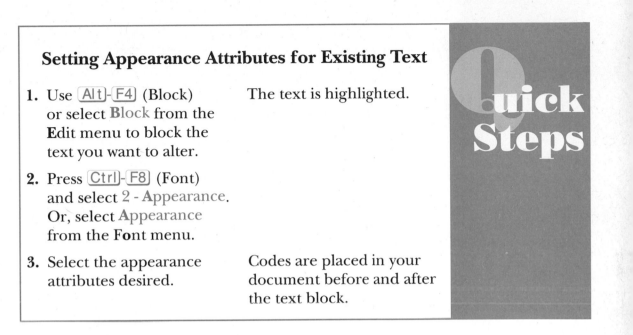

Setting Appearance Attributes for Existing Text

1. Use `Alt`-`F4` (Block) or select **B**lock from the **E**dit menu to block the text you want to alter.

   The text is highlighted.

2. Press `Ctrl`-`F8` (Font) and select 2 - **A**ppearance. Or, select **A**ppearance from the **Fo**nt menu.

3. Select the appearance attributes desired.

   Codes are placed in your document before and after the text block.

After the appearance is set, codes are placed around the text in your document. Figure 8.9 illustrates the document and Reveal Codes screen for the appearances. If you have a color monitor, redline appears in red.

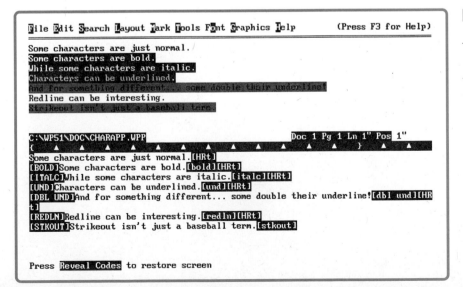

Figure 8.9

Appearances in the document and Reveal Codes screen.

To change the appearance for text you are about to enter, press Ctrl-F8 (**Font**) and 2-**Appearance** or select **Appearance** from the **Font** menu. Type the text. Then select a different appearance or Normal (to return to the default appearance). Or, press → to move beyond the ending appearance code.

As with size choices, you can combine appearances, or you can combine size and appearances. For example, you can select Very Large Bold Italic text. Just make the necessary selections.

TIP: After blocking text, you can press a single key to make text bold or underlined. Block the text. Press F6 (Bold) or F8 (Underline).

CAUTION: If you have a daisywheel printer, where characters are printed by pressing an image of the letter against a ribbon, the character sizes on the wheel dictate the characters you may use. If you have a dot-matrix printer, the sizes available through the printer are the options available to you. (Many printers have self-tests which can be run to show the character sizes available. See your printer manual for how to run the self-test.) If you have a laser printer, you may have more options via fonts that are on cartridges or are downloadable. The bottom line is, even though WordPerfect has many character size and appearance options, your printer may not handle printing each option. Even if the appearance shows up on-screen, the printer may not be able to print the result.

Redline and Strikeout

Redline and strikeout have a nifty bonus. When you use them (usually to illustrate edits to a document), you can automatically strip the strikeout text from your document. The editing process is as follows:

1. Enter text to be inserted in redline and text to be deleted in strikeout.

2. Review the text as it will be edited. Delete any redlined text that you decide you don't want inserted. Type in (using normal text) any stricken text that you decide to retain. This way, when you apply the automatic removal of the marks, you get the intended effect.

3. Automatically remove the strikeout text (the text is deleted) and leave or remove the redline codes. (The redline text will always stay in place.) To do this, press Alt-F5 (Mark Text) and type 6 - Generate or select Generate from the Mark menu. Press 1 - Remove Redline Markings and Strikeout Text from Document. Type y at the "Delete" question in order to remove the redline appearance and delete the text marked with strikeout.

Using Font Cartridges and Soft Fonts

Many printers, particularly laser printers, will print additional fonts (combinations of typefaces and sizes) that you purchase separately as a cartridge (that plugs into the printer) or as software that you install on your computer (also called *download-able fonts* or *soft fonts*).

If you have a cartridge installed, you need to tell WordPerfect what cartridge you want to use. If you have soft fonts installed, you need to indicate where (in what directory) your soft fonts are stored and which fonts you want to use. Do this via the following steps:

1. Press ⟨⇧Shift⟩-⟨F7⟩ (Print) or select **P**rint from the **F**ile menu.

2. Choose S - **S**elect Printer to go to the Print: Select Printer screen.

3. Choose 3 **E**dit to go to the Select Printer: Edit screen.

4. Select 4 **C**artridges/Fonts/Print Wheels to go to the Select Printer: Cartridges/Fonts/Print Wheels screen shown in Figure 8.10. This screen shows you what fonts may be built into your printer (you cannot make changes in these). It also identifies the number of cartridges or print wheels your printer handles and the space available for soft fonts.

5. Select **C**artridges, **S**oft Fonts, or **P**rint Wheels, and then select the fonts to use. (Note: You can only select the number of cartridges which your printer will handle or number of soft fonts that consumes the available space.) If you have selected soft fonts, you may have to select a font group first.

6. If you are using soft fonts, press ⟨F7⟩ (Exit) as needed to return to the Select Printer: Edit screen. (A message may appear as fonts are updated.) If you are not using soft fonts, press ⟨F7⟩ (Exit) as needed to return to your document and continue working.

7. If the soft fonts are on a different directory from your printer files (typically the WP51 directory on a hard

disk), specify the path for downloadable fonts now. From the Select Printer: Edit screen, select 6 - Path for Down-loadable Fonts and Printer Command Files. Enter the drive and path to the soft fonts directory. Press F7 (Exit) as needed to return to your document.

8. There is one final step for soft font users. If the soft fonts on the Select Printer: Cartridges/Fonts/Print Wheels screen were marked with an asterisk (*), you must run the Initialize Printer option every time you turn on your printer. To do this, press ⇧Shift-F7 (Print) or select Print from the File menu. Select 7 - Initialize Printer.

```
Select Printer: Cartridges/Fonts/Print Wheels

Font Category                        Quantity        Available

Built-In
Cartridges                              2               0
Soft Fonts                            350 K           350 K




NOTE: Most fonts listed under the Font Category (with the exception of Built-In)
are optional and must be purchased separately from your dealer or manufacturer.
If you have fonts not listed, they may be supported on an additional printer
diskette.  For more information call WP at (801) 225-5000.

If soft fonts are marked '*', you must run the Initialize Printer option in WP
each time you turn on your printer.  Doing so deletes all soft fonts in printer
memory and downloads those marked with '*'.

If soft fonts are not located in the same directory as your printer files, you
must specify a Path for Downloadable Fonts in the Select Printer: Edit menu.

1 Select; 2 Change Quantity; N Name search: 1
```

Figure 8.10
Select Printer: Cartridges/Fonts/ Print Wheels screen.

The steps above are the basic steps for selecting a cartridge or soft font for use. Dealing with cartridges and soft fonts can become very complex. If you run into trouble, consult your *WordPerfect Reference* or a more advanced book.

Convert Case

With WordPerfect, you can block text and convert it to upper-
or lowercase. A few character-based options are not on the Font
menu—Convert Case is one of them, so the procedure for using
it is a little different from the other procedures in this chapter.
To convert text to upper- or lowercase, follow these steps:

1. Block the text to convert, including the punctuation.

2. Press ⇧Shift-F3 (Switch) or select Convert Case from
   the **E**dit menu.

3. Identify whether you want the result in upper- or lowercase.

The text in the selection is displayed according to your
choice. The only exceptions are that when uppercase text is
converted to lowercase, the "I" in "I'm" and the first letter of a
new sentence remain in uppercase.

TIP: Make sure to block text using Alt-F4 (Block) or
select **B**lock from the **E**dit menu before pressing ⇧Shift-F3
(Switch). If you do not, you will be switched to a new screen
(Document 2) which allows you to use two WordPerfect
documents at once. If you accidentally end up in Document
2 (Doc 2 appears in the lower right corner), simply press
⇧Shift-F3 (Switch) to return to your original document.

WordPerfect Characters

WordPerfect Characters are characters that are not available on your keyboard. You can print out these special characters if you have a graphics printer or if you have a font that contains the characters.

WordPerfect Characters include *diacritics* (for phonetic values such as accent e (é) and tilde n (ñ)). To use one of the over 1500 characters available:

1. Position your cursor where you want the character and press [Ctrl]-[V] (Compose) or select Characters from the Font menu. The prompt Key= appears on the lower left of the screen.

2. Type in the number of the character set containing the character you want.

3. Type in a comma (,) or press [↵Enter].

4. Enter the number of the character to create. Appendix C includes a list of WordPerfect Character sets.

For example, suppose you want an e with an accent over the e. You would press [Ctrl]-[V] (Compose). After the Key= prompt, type in 1,41 and press [↵Enter]. The é appears on your screen.

Special Characters include ANSI characters and IBM PC Extended Characters such as boxes, lines, and other symbols. To use either, simply hold down [Alt], press [0], then type the corresponding number on the *numeric* keypad (not the numbers across the top of your computer keyboard). Release the [Alt] key. To see a partial list of the possible symbols and their corresponding numbers, see Appendix C.

CAUTION: Not all graphic displays will show all characters possible through WordPerfect. Not all printers will print each character. Experiment with your display and printer to see what capabilities are available.

Create Unusual Effects

Combining keyboard characters or WordPerfect special characters with unusual fonts can create pleasing graphical effects. For example, you can use the IBM PC Extended Character Set circle (character 248 shown in Appendix C) with a large font size for an unusual bullet for a bulleted list. Or, you could use an extra small character size with multiple pipes (II) on your keyboard for an unusual line style.

What's Next?

This chapter covered the basics to meet 99 percent of most user's special character requirements. However, you may be among the 1 percent with exceptional needs.

The Printer Functions screen in WordPerfect allows for more detailed control of characters. Follow these steps to see it in action:

1. Press `⇧Shift`-`F8` (Format) and choose 4 - **O**ther, or select **O**ther from the **L**ayout menu.

2. Select 6 - **P**rinter Functions. The Format: Printer Func-
    tions menu appears. From this menu, you can control
    Printer commands.

The commands available on this menu are commands to
your printer which affect the printed result (but not the appearance of text on your screen). Check your printer manual to see
what commands may be available and useful to you in your work.
This screen also allows you certain typesetting capabilities:

Kerning

Word Spacing/Letter Spacing

Word Spacing Justification Limits

Baseline Placement for Typesetters

Leading Adjustment

WordPerfect also handles AutoFont technology and the
handling of custom fonts. This is handled through the
WordPerfect Printer Program (PTR.EXE).

If any of these capabilities sound beneficial in your work,
research them more through the *WordPerfect Reference* or a more
advanced WordPerfect book (such as *The WordPerfect Bible,*
published by Sams).

Types of Alignment

▲ Left Indent: Press F4 or select Align then Indent from the **L**ayout menu.

▲ Right and Left Indent: ⇧Shift-F4 or select Align then Indent from the **L**ayout menu.

▲ Hanging Indent: F4 (Left Indent) or select Align then Indent from the **L**ayout menu followed by ⇧Shift-Tab (Margin Release) or select Align then Margin Rel from the **L**ayout menu.

▲ Center Text: ⇧Shift-F6 or select Align then Center from the **L**ayout menu.

▲ Flush Right: Alt-F6 or select Align then Flush Right from the **L**ayout menu.

Justifying Text

1. Press ⇧Shift-F8 (Format) then select 1 - Line or select Line from the **L**ayout menu.

2. Select 3 - Justification then pick 1 Left, 2 Center, 3 Right, or 4 Full.

Line Spacing

1. Press ⇧Shift-F8 (Format) then 1 - Line or select Line from the **L**ayout menu.

2. Select 6 - Line Spacing.

Changing Default Initial Codes

1. Press ⇧Shift-F1 (Setup) or select Setup from the **F**ile menu then 4 - Initial Settings.

2. Select 5 - Initial Codes, enter the codes, and press F7 (Exit).

Aligning Text

Though you can align text the old fashioned way (using the spacebar to place characters), there are faster methods yielding more pleasing results. A few key presses allow you to indent, center, justify, and place text flush right. You may also control linespacing and set initial codes to create your own default settings to save more time when new documents are created.

Indenting Text

Using WordPerfect's indent feature is different from using the `Tab↹` key. When you use the `Tab↹` key, only the first line is indented. When you use WordPerfect's indent feature, you indent the entire paragraph. You can type as many lines as you wish, and then press the `↵Enter` key to end the paragraph (and the indention).

For example, text with indents has been added to the letter shown in Figure 9.1. Each paragraph in the body of the letter starts with a Tab, so only each paragraph's first line is indented. The list of attachments was created with WordPerfect's Left Indent feature. Each dash is followed by an indent, followed by text. Notice that the first line of attachments wraps around to line up with the indented text above.

Later in the letter, a quote is indented from both the right and left.

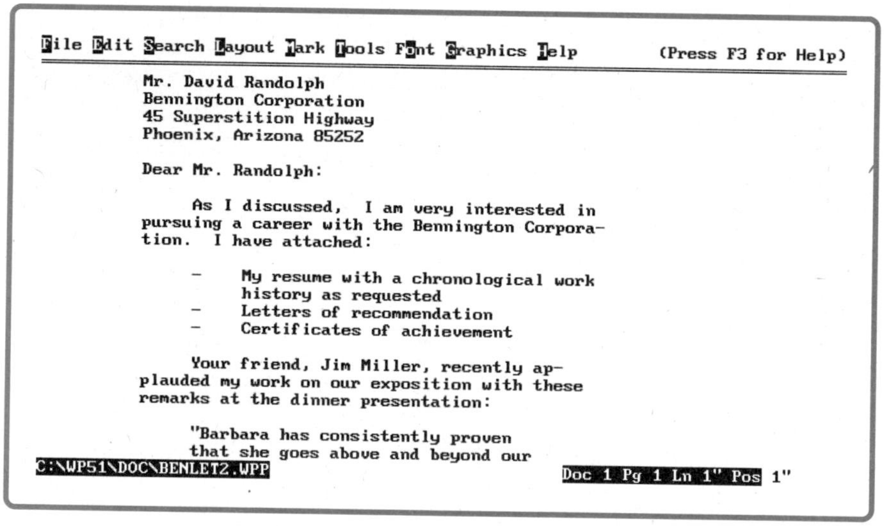

Figure 9.1

Text with indents.

```
File Edit Search Layout Mark Tools Font Graphics Help        (Press F3 for Help)

         Mr. David Randolph
         Bennington Corporation
         45 Superstition Highway
         Phoenix, Arizona 85252

         Dear Mr. Randolph:

             As I discussed,  I am very interested in
         pursuing a career with the Bennington Corpora-
         tion.  I have attached:

             -    My resume with a chronological work
                  history as requested
             -    Letters of recommendation
             -    Certificates of achievement

             Your friend, Jim Miller, recently ap-
         plauded my work on our exposition with these
         remarks at the dinner presentation:

             "Barbara has consistently proven
             that she goes above and beyond our
C:\WP51\DOC\BENLET2.WPP                              Doc 1 Pg 1 Ln 1" Pos 1"
```

You can indent either from the left or from both the right and the left with WordPerfect. A third type of indent is a *hanging indent,* which leaves the first line of the paragraph at the left margin and indents the following lines at the next tab setting. Hanging indents are useful for lists set off by bullets or numbers.

All indents align with the tab settings in WordPerfect. For now, you should work with the default tab settings. (Chapter 10 covers how to change tab settings.)

The following Quick Steps summarize each kind of indent.

Setting the Left Indent

1. Press [F4] (Left Indent) or select **Al**ign then **In**dent from the **L**ayout menu until the appropriate tab setting is reached.

   An Indent code is embedded in your text. The [± Indent] code appears.

2. Type in the text you want indented.

   The text automatically aligns with the last indent entered.

3. Press [↵Enter] to complete the indent.

   Any text in the paragraph immediately following the indent is indented.

Quick Steps

Setting Left and Right Indents

1. Press [⇧Shift]-[F4] or select **Al**ign then **In**dent from the **L**ayout menu for Left/Right indent.

   The code [± Indent] is placed in your text.

2. Type in the text.

   The text aligns along the left tab setting and an equal distance from the right side.

3. Press [↵Enter] to complete the indent.

   The text in the paragraph following the Left/Right indent is set in from the left and right margins.

Quick Steps

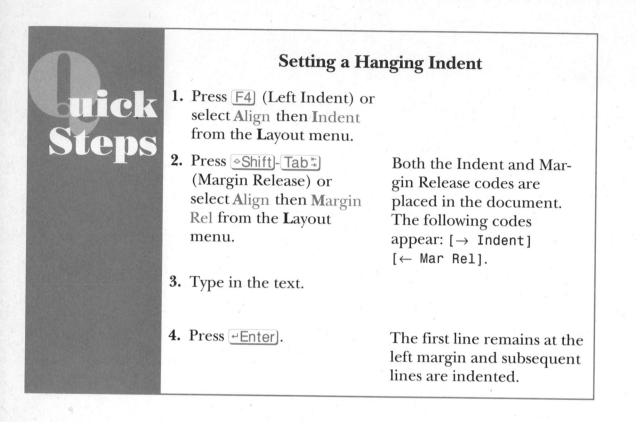

Quick Steps

Setting a Hanging Indent

1. Press `F4` (Left Indent) or select **Align** then **Indent** from the **Layout** menu.

2. Press `⇧Shift`-`Tab⇕` (Margin Release) or select **Align** then **Margin Rel** from the **Layout** menu.

   Both the Indent and Margin Release codes are placed in the document. The following codes appear: `[→ Indent]` `[← Mar Rel]`.

3. Type in the text.

4. Press `↵Enter`.

   The first line remains at the left margin and subsequent lines are indented.

Indenting Existing Text

You may apply all the indent options to existing text. Just insert the indent code(s) where you want the indents created.

Centering Text

The old-fashioned way of centering text was to count the number of characters in the text to be entered, subtract that number from the number of characters possible in the line, divide by two, space in that number of spaces, and begin typing. This tedious operation is replaced with the ⊲Shift⊳-F6 (Center) key combination or by selecting Align then Center from the Layout menu.

Just place your cursor in the line and press ⊲Shift⊳-F6 (Center) or select Align then Center from the Layout menu. A code is placed in your text and the cursor goes to the center of the line. Type in your text. As you type, the characters move to the left or right to even the centering. When you are done, press ⏎Enter. To remove centering delete the code.

Figure 9.2 shows centered text with Barbara J. Wiley's return address.

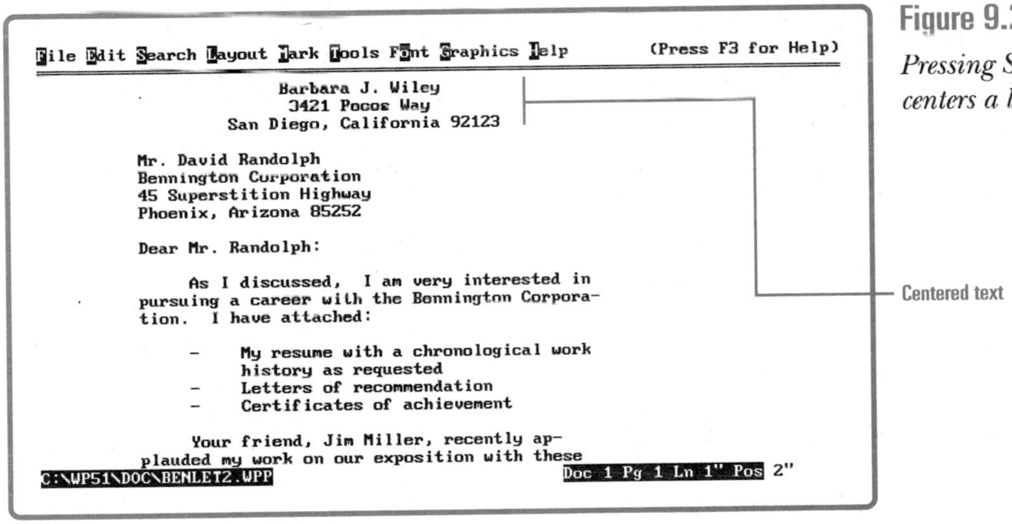

Figure 9.2

Pressing Shift – F6 centers a line.

You can also center existing text or multiple lines. Just block the text and press ⊲Shift⊳-F6 (Center) or select Align then Center from the Layout menu. This message appears:

```
[Just: Center?] No (Yes)
```

Select Yes to center the text. The text in the block is centered and the appropriate codes(s) inserted.

Placing Text Flush Right

Figure 9.3 demonstrates the Flush Right option on the date line. You don't have to count text or backspaces; just press `Alt`-`F6` (Flush Right) or select Align then Flush Right from the **L**ayout menu. The cursor goes to the right margin. As you type in the text, it moves left. Press `↵Enter` and the text aligns with the right margin. Press `↵Enter` to stop typing text that is flush right.

   To make existing text flush right, place the cursor before the text and press `Alt`-`F6` (Flush Right).

> **TIP:** To "flush left" text, just type it in at the left margin and press `↵Enter` to start a new line.

Figure 9.3
Flush right date line.

```
┌─────────────────────────────────────────────────────────────┐
│ File Edit Search Layout Mark Tools Font Graphics Help         │
│                                            (Press F3 for Help)│
│                    Barbara J. Wiley                           │
│                    3421 Pecos Way                             │
│               San Diego, California 92123                     │
│                                                               │
│          Mr. David Randolph                                   │
│          Bennington Corporation                               │
│          45 Superstition Highway                              │
│          Phoenix, Arizona 85252                               │
│                                          May 12, 1991         │
│                                                               │
│          Dear Mr. Randolph:                                   │
│                                                               │
│               As I discussed, I am very interested in         │
│          pursuing a career with the Bennington Corpora-       │
│          tion.  I have attached:                              │
│                                                               │
│               -    My resume with a chronological work        │
│                    history as requested                       │
│               -    Letters of recommendation                 │
│               -    Certificates of achievement                │
│ C:\WP51\DOC\BENLET2.WPP            Doc 1 Pg 1 Ln 2.5" Pos 6.5" │
└─────────────────────────────────────────────────────────────┘
```

The date ends at the right margin.

Creating a Pleasing Effect

You can create a pleasing effect by combining tab, indent, center, and flush right capabilities. For example, you may want a top of a report to have the name of the report indented on the left, the date in the center, and the page number flush right. Just indent, type in the name of the report, center and type in the date, then flush right and enter the page number. The effect might look like this:

```
Bennington Report      January 10, 1992
Page 6
```

Later chapters in this book cover how to make such a heading appear on each page of the document and how to have WordPerfect consecutively page number for you. For now, just consider how you can combine alignment capabilities for the result you want.

Justifying Text

Justification refers to the even vertical alignment of text between margins in a document. When you enter a justification code, all the text that follows that code will be justified until a new justification code is entered or the original one is deleted. WordPerfect's default is called *full justification*, which lines up text evenly between right and left margins. Figure 9.4 shows the Barbara Wiley letter with full justification.

Figure 9.4
Letter with full justification.

Barbara J. Wiley
3421 Pecos Way
San Diego, California 92123

Mr. David Randolph
Bennington Corporation
45 Superstition Highway
Phoenix, Arizona 85252

May 12, 1991

Dear Mr. Randolph:

As I discussed, I am very interested in pursuing a career with the Bennington Corporation. I have attached:

- My resume with a chronological work history as requested
- Letters of recommendation
- Certificates of achievement

Your friend, Jim Miller, recently applauded my work on our exposition with these remarks at the dinner presentation:

"Barbara has consistently proven that she goes above and beyond our expectations. And... always within budget no less!"

I look forward to speaking with you further on June 8th. I'll meet you at your corporate office location at 45 Superstition Highway.

Sincerely,

Barbara J. Wiley

WordPerfect makes four types of justification possible:

▲ *Left* justification for most documents.

▲ *Right* justification for special layouts.

▲ *Full* justification (text aligned evenly on left and right margins) for a formal appearance.

▲ *Center* justification (text centered on every line) for special layouts.

Figure 9.5 illustrates an advertising piece with each type of justification applied.

Figure 9.5

Four types of justification.

```
Start the day right with the newest in
breakfast juices.  It has a fresh taste for
your family.  You'll never place the fruit
taste...
                                                    Flush left

                                  It's not grape
                                 It's not orange
                              It's not grapefruit
                                                    Flush right

Never in the history of our company have we
made such a product.  It is unmatched in the
breakfast fruit juice category.  To thank you
for  your  support,  we  are  offering  a  free
sample.
                                                    Justified

            Just enter your name in the
               box below and mail to:

                    Oki Offer
                    PO Box 346
                Wilmington, Ill 45322
                                                    Centered
```

To justify text:

1. Place the cursor where you want to begin the justification.

2. Press ⇧Shift-F8 (Format) and then select 1 - Line, or choose Line from the Layout menu. The Format: Line menu appears.

3. Select 3 - Justification. A prompt line like this appears:

```
Justification: 1 Left; 2 Center; 3 Right;
4 Full: 0
```

4. Select the type of justification you want. A justification code is placed in your document at the cursor location.

To remove or change the justification, delete the first code or enter the code for another type of justification.

Controlling Line Spacing

Line spacing refers to the number of lines between each printed line. The default is single spacing. However, you can double or triple space or space by any number of lines you want to enter. The following Quick Steps detail how to set line spacing.

Quick Steps

Setting Line Spacing

1. Press ⇧Shift-F8 (Format) and type 1 - Line, or select Line from the Layout menu. | The Format: Line menu appears.

2. Select 6 - Line Spacing, enter the number of lines, and press ⏎Enter.

3. Press F7 (Exit) to return to your document.

A code like this is placed in the document: [Ln Spacing: 3]. The text following the inserted code follows the new line spacing setting.

Initial Codes

You may want to change some of WordPerfect's defaults. For example, you may want to change WordPerfect's default of single line spacing. If you typically use double spacing, you may get tired of having to set the line spacing for each document. You can change this initial code (and others) through the Initial Code option.

You can change the initial codes via one of two routes depending on the outcome you want.

To affect all documents you will create, change the default. To change a default:

1. Press ⇧Shift-F1 (Setup) and select 4 - Initial Settings. Or, select Setup from the **File** menu, and then Initial Settings.

2. From the Setup: Initial Settings menu, select 5 - Initial Codes. You are taken to the Initial Codes screen like that shown in Figure 9.6.

3. Enter the new line spacing or any other codes you want as the new default(s).

4. Save the entries by pressing F4 (Exit) until you return to your document.

These initial codes are applied to every document you create from then on until you change the codes again.

To change the codes for a document only:

1. Press ⇧Shift-F8 (Format) and select 3 - Document (or select Document from the Layout menu).

2. Select 2 - Initial Codes. The same screen shown in Figure 9.6 appears.

3. Enter the codes and press F7 (Exit) when done.

The benefit of using this option (versus just putting the codes in the document screen) is that if you give the document to someone else to use, the codes will not transfer with the document. This is especially useful if you create a document for printing in a fancy font or margin setting which you also need to transfer over a modem or pass on to someone else for a different use. Placing the codes in the Initial Codes screen using the second method will mean the codes will be omitted from the document when it is transmitted via modem.

TIP: Any codes you enter directly in the body of a document take precedence over the Initial Codes.

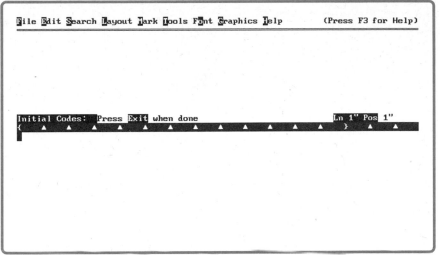

Figure 9.6
Initial Codes screen.

CAUTION: The initial codes become the new defaults. The codes for the settings don't appear in your document. Therefore, if you give your document on a disk to someone with different initial codes, your settings will not be in place.

What's Next?

Tabs come into play when you indent or flush right text. The next chapter will provide the necessary information for you to control where text appears on your screen when it is indented or flush right.

A function few users need to change is Line Height. This is the space allowed for a line. Typically, it is set to Automatic and WordPerfect selects the best line height according to your printer and font selections. However, if you use very small or very large characters and want to control the line height yourself, you may.

1. Press ⬆Shift-F8 (Format) and select 1 - Line or select Line from the Layout menu.

2. Select 4 - Line Height.

3. Select 2 Fixed.

4. Enter the desired line height.

Another advanced function is Display Pitch. Display Pitch allows you to change the space assigned to tabs, indents, or column gutters (the space between the columns). To access Display Pitch:

1. Press ⬆Shift-F8 (Format) and select 3 - Document or select Document from the Layout menu.

2. Select 1- Display Pitch.

3. Select No at the Automatic Yes (No) prompt.

4. Type the desired display pitch and press ⏎Enter.

Now you know how to access these features, but it takes a considerable knowledge of typesetting and publishing to use them effectively. Consult a more advanced text for the nuances of setting Line Height and Display Pitch, and if you get into trouble, just set the features back to Automatic.

In This Chapter

Default Tabs

•

Tab Types and Settings

•

Dot Leaders

•

Decimal/Align Characters

•

Columns

•

Tables

Entering Tabs

1. Press `⇧Shift`-`F8` (Format) then 1 - Line or select Line from the **L**ayout menu.
2. Select 8 - Tab Set.
3. From the tab line, enter an **L**, **D**, **C**, or **R** for new tabs, or use `Del` to clear old tabs. For dot leaders, type a period (**.**) over the tab setting letter.

Temporarily Decimal Aligning Text

1. Press `Ctrl`-`F6` (Tab Align), or select Align then Tab Align from the **L**ayout menu.

Setting the Decimal/Align Character

1. Press `⇧Shift`-`F8` (Format) and 4 - Other or select Other from the **L**ayout menu.
2. Select 3 - Decimal/Align Character and enter the character desired.

Using Columns

1. Press `Alt`-`F7` (Math/Columns) and select 1 Columns, or select Columns from the **L**ayout menu.
2. Select 3 Define, complete the definitions, and press `F7` (Exit).
3. Select 1 On at the Columns prompt.
4. Enter text in columns. Press `Ctrl`-`↵Enter` to start a new column.
5. Press `Alt`-`F7` (Math/Columns) and select 1 Columns, or select Columns from the **L**ayout menu. Select 2 Off.

Creating a Table

1. Press `Alt`-`F7` (Math/Columns) and then select 2 - Tables, or select Tables from the **L**ayout menu.
2. Select 1 - Create.
3. Enter the number of columns and rows for the table.
4. With the cursor in the table, press `F7` (Exit) to go to document-editing mode or `Alt`-`F7` (Math/Columns) to go to table-editing mode.

Using Tabs, Columns, and Tables

Arranging text on the screen can be streamlined with the use of tabs, columns, and tables. This chapter not only covers how to delete tabs but how to add a variety of tabs specific to your needs. You will also learn how to create columns and tables which can simplify working with text you want to have remain together in columns or columns and rows.

Default Tabs

A *tab* in WordPerfect is like a tab setting on a typewriter, only better. At the basic level, you press the Tab↹ key to indent the first line of a paragraph, or select F4 (Indent) to indent the entire paragraph. The cursor moves to the next column marked by a tab setting and a [Tab] or [Indent] code appears in your text. At a more sophisticated level, according to the type of tab setting you enter, you can align characters on the left, the right, by any character, or you can center the characters.

WordPerfect comes with defaults of tab settings every half inch. The sample resume shown in Figure 10.1 was created with WordPerfect default tab settings. (The tab settings are denoted by triangles on the dividing line between the editing screen and the Reveal Codes area.)

Notice that with tabs set every half inch, F4 (Indent) had to be pressed several times to complete the entries. As you'll learn later in this chapter, you can set new tab settings anywhere you like. By entering your own tab settings, you can reduce the number of times you have to press Tab⇄ or F4 (Indent).

Figure 10.1

Resumé with default tabs.

Tab defaults ——

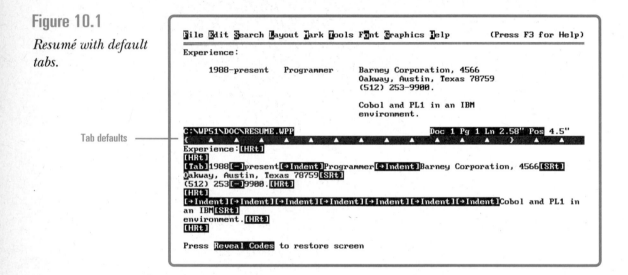

Tab Types and Settings

WordPerfect uses four types of tabs:

▲ Left

▲ Decimal

▲ Center

▲ Right

The fund-raising activities included on the resume, shown in Figure 10.2, illustrate each type of tab setting. A description of each type follows.

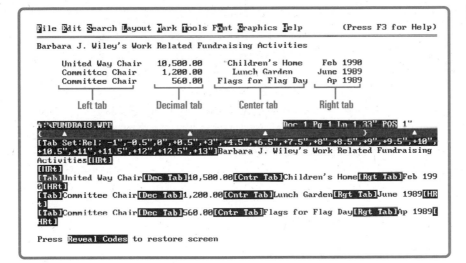

Figure 10.2

Types of tab settings.

Left Tab Setting

The left tab setting is the default used by WordPerfect. When you use a left tab setting and then begin typing, the text is entered one space to the right of the tab setting. The [Tab] code is placed in your text. In Figure 10.2, the titles (such as Committee Chair) are aligned under the standard left tab setting.

Decimal Tab Setting

You set a decimal tab to align text (usually dollar amounts) on a decimal point. Text you type in is entered to the left of the decimal tab until you press the decimal point (a period). The [Dec Tab] code is entered into the text. Then the text is entered to the right. This feature is especially helpful when you want to enter columns of financial figures, as in Figure 10.2, where the money raised is aligned under the decimal point.

Center Tab Setting

The center tab is used to center text under the tab setting. As you type, the text is centered automatically, just like when you use the ⇧Shift-F6 (Center), or select Justify then Center from the Layout menu. Setting a center tab setting enables you to enter text before and after the centered text on the line, as shown in Figure 10.2. You can also see that the [Cntr Tab] code is entered into the text.

Right Tab Setting

The right tab setting is used to align text on a rightmost character. As you enter text, it moves left until you finish typing. The code [Rgt Tab] appears in the text. In Figure 10.2, the year is entered using the right tab setting, which makes an even right margin. You can, however, place the right tab setting anywhere in a line.

To use each of these tab settings, you don't need to press special keys—just the standard Tab⇄ or F4 (Indent). You do, however, need to set tab settings to tell WordPerfect where to place the tabs and what type of tab setting to use.

Changing Tab Settings

You can set up WordPerfect to use any of the four types of tab options. First, however, you need to decide where you want tab settings placed. To determine an exact location, just measure your page and identify the location of the tab settings from the left edge of the page. Or, you can "eyeball" the tab locations and begin entering new tab settings. You will have to visualize the tab setting effect as you work. The following Quick Steps detail how to set tabs.

Quick Steps

Adding and Deleting Tabs

1. Place your cursor where you want the new tab settings.	Text after the location will be affected.
2. Press Shift-F8 (Format) and type 1 Line. Or, select Line from the Layout menu.	The Format: Line menu appears. The current tab setting appears next to `8 - Tab Set.`
3. Select 8 - Tab Set.	The Tab line appears, as shown in Figure 10.3. Current tabs are denoted by `L` (left), `R` (right), `C` (center), and `D` (decimal).
4. If you want to delete existing tabs, position your cursor on one of them and press Del or Backspace.	The letter marking the tab disappears from the Tab line.

Continues

Continued

5. If you want to add a tab setting, type in **L** (left), **R** (right), **C** (center), or **D** (decimal) at the spot where you want the tab to be.

A letter marking the tab appears on the Tab line.

6. Press F7 (Exit) until you return to your document and begin using the tab settings.

A tab setting code is entered in your document for each tab you entered (see Figure 10.4), and text you enter after the code is affected.

Figure 10.3

Tab line.

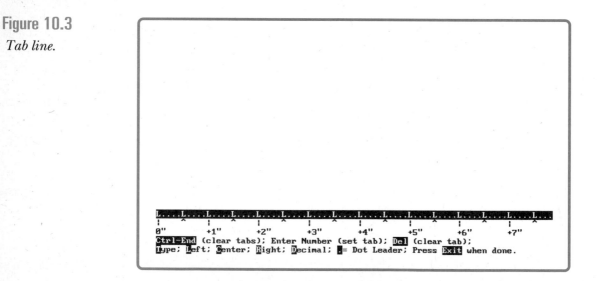

```
L....L....L...L....L....L....L....L....L....L....L....L....L....L....L....
 !    ^   !   ^   !    ^   !    ^   !    ^   !    ^   !   ^   !    ^
0"       +1"      +2"      +3"      +4"      +5"      +6"      +7"
Ctrl-End (clear tabs); Enter Number (set tab); Del (clear tab);
Type; Left; Center; Right; Decimal; = Dot Leader; Press Exit when done.
```

CAUTION: Once you view the Tab line after selecting 8 - Tab Set, a new tab-setting code will be entered into the document even if you don't make any changes, and even if you press F7 (Exit) or Esc to leave the line. To stop the operation and *not* enter the new tab setting, press F1 (Cancel).

NOTE: The current tab setting you will see will either include Abs or Rel. *Abs* means "Absolute," which is WordPerfect's way of saying that the tab settings are measured from the edge of the paper and not from your left margin. So, setting a tab setting at 3" means the tab setting will be 3" from the left edge of the paper, not 3" from the left margin setting. Conversely, *Rel* means "Relative" to the left margin setting.

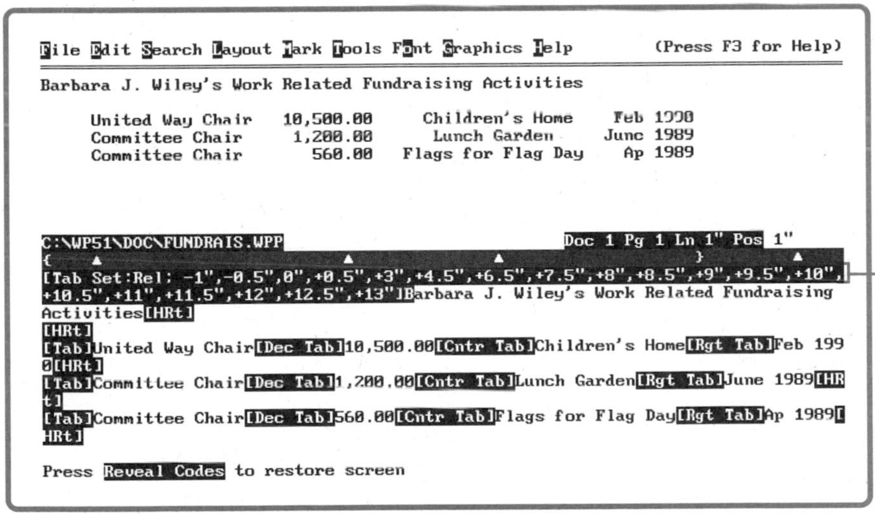

Figure 10.4
Codes signifying tabs set.

There are several benefits to becoming familiar with how to set tabs:

▲ You can use all four types of tabs instead of being stuck with left tabs only.

▲ By setting your own tabs, you can reduce the number of times you have to press the Tab⇥ or F4 (Indent) key.

▲ You can use tabs to easily change the layout of your text. Simply by entering new tab settings, the text after those tab settings is rearranged.

As long as you do not delete a tab setting code, it remains in the text. When you change the tab settings, the new tab codes are inserted after the old ones. If you change your mind and want to revert back to the old settings, you can just delete the new codes.

Figure 10.5 shows an example of changing tab settings and then reverting to the old ones. A new set of codes has been entered in the figure, moving the text. Notice that the original code is still in the text and that the new tab-setting code follows. To go back to the old tab settings, highlight the second tab-setting code and press Del, and the text is restored to its earlier appearance.

Figure 10.5

The old tab code remains in the document unless you delete it.

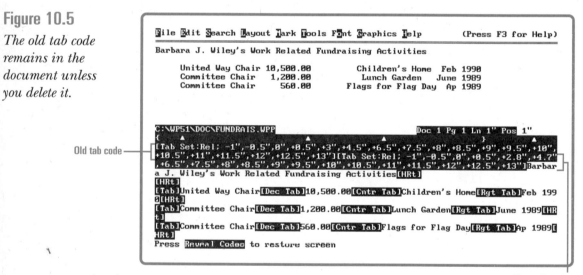

Old tab code

New tab code

Dot Leaders

Occasionally, you may want to enter a row of dots (called *dot leaders*) between the text at tab settings. In Figure 10.6, dot leaders have been added to some of the tab settings.

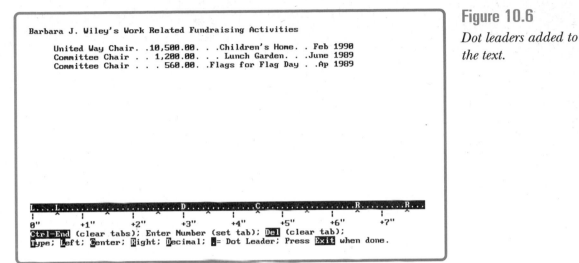

Figure 10.6
Dot leaders added to the text.

> **TIP:** You can mix dot leader tabs with other tabs set in the same tab setting.

To enter a tab setting to include dot leaders, view the Tab line as described in the previous "Adding and Deleting Tabs" Quick Steps. Place the cursor on a left (L), right (R), or decimal (D) tab in the Tab line and type a period (.). The tab setting is in reverse video (light letter on a dark box or vice versa). When you next use the tab setting, dot leaders appear. Adding dot leaders does not affect existing tabs.

Entering Headings

Often when you use tab settings, you are creating columns of text for which you want headings. You will want the headings to be aligned over the columns in most cases, rather than aligned the same way as the tabular data beneath them. If this is the case, you have several options:

▲ You can place your headings before the tab code (so that the earlier tab settings are used, if they are more appropriate than the newer ones).

▲ You can type in the headings using spaces instead of tabs.

▲ You can create a set of tab settings especially for the headings, and then create another set for the data after the headings are typed.

Of these three methods the latter is probably the most reliable, since by creating new tab settings especially for the headings, they will be exactly the way you want them.

> **CAUTION:** If you choose to use spaces rather than tabs, be aware that some printers do not measure the spaces between tab settings and the spaces entered with the spacebar in the same way. Thus, your headings can appear lined up on the screen but not when printed. You may need to experiment with your printer to get the outcome desired.

Changing the Decimal/Align Character

The default decimal/align character is a period (.). When you use decimal tab settings, you type in a period as the alignment character and the text lines up according to the period. You can use any character, however, not just a period to align by. For example, you might want to align text on an equals sign (=) as shown next:

```
6-9-4=19
  8-2=10

800-310=1110
```

To change the decimal/align character, follow these steps:

1. Press `⇧Shift`-`F8` (Format) and select 4 - **Other**, or select **Other** from the **Layout** menu. You are taken to the Format: Other menu.

2. Select 3 - **Decimal/Align Character**. Type in the keyboard character you want to use for the alignment and press `⏎Enter`.

3. Press `F7` (Exit) to go back to your document.

A code like this appears in your document identifying the decimal/align character:

```
[Decml/Algn Char:=,,]
```

The character after `Char:` is the new decimal/align character that will be used in text entered after the code. In this example, it is the equals sign. You can return to the period as the decimal/align character any time by deleting the code or by setting a period as the new decimal/align character.

Tab Align

Sometimes, you might want to align characters by the decimal/align character without changing to a decimal tab setting. For example, if you want to enter only a few lines of text aligned by a decimal/align character, it would be cumbersome to change the tab setting to a decimal tab, enter the text, then change the tab setting back to a left tab setting for the remainder of the document. Instead, you can use a key combination to use a tab setting temporarily as a decimal tab.

The `Ctrl`-`F6` (Tab Align) feature affects your work with a single tab setting in a single line. You can use the feature repeatedly to align multiple lines. Follow these steps:

1. Place your cursor before the tab setting under which you want to align the character.

2. Press `Ctrl`-`F6` (Tab Align). The [DEC TAB] code appears in your document and the cursor goes under the next tab setting. The message Align char== appears at the bottom left of your screen to remind you which character (in this case, the equals sign) has been chosen.

3. Type in the text. The text moves to the left.

4. Type the decimal/align character (in our example, the equals sign). The next text you type in will move to the right of the equals sign.

Columns

WordPerfect's Columns feature is useful to create any type of document with two to twenty-four columns on a page. Scripts, newsletters, and lists are popular applications.

The following are the types of columns shown in Figures 10.7a and 10.7b:

Newspaper: Text flows from the bottom of one column to the top of the next (good for newsletters).

Parallel (with or without block protect): Text is grouped across the page in rows. Related text across columns may be Block Protected to stay together on a page (good for lists where the text in each line relates).

```
----------------Roses, Roses, and More Roses----------------
A publication of the Rose Growers              Tempe, AZ/June 1991
```

```
     ROSE SHOW AUGUST 10TH          very   fatigued.    Since  our
                                    temperatures stay above 90 and
Don't miss the rose show on         are often in the 100s, the
August 10th.  All the beauties      plant can use up food faster
will be there and you should be     than it comes.
too!  Jan and Jerry Mulder will
be hosting the show for the         A common mistake of most rose
third year.  The show will be       growers is that they over prune
held  at  the  Civic  Gardens       their plants.    More foliage
Auditorium from 10 am until 8       allows  the  plant  to  store
pm.  The cost is $5.00.             energy  for  the  hot  summer
                                    months.

                                    A "to do" is cover your plants
     KEEPING PLANTS COOL            to protect them from the hot
                                    summer sun.  An easy way to do
As we in the desert know, very      that is to add a lath over the
hot weather can make a plant        roses  for  shade  during  the
                                    hottest part of the day.
```

Figure 10.7a
Newspaper columns.

```
            Rose Club Membership List and Status

Member's Name          Membership Status      Committee

Mulder, Jan            Active                 Rose Show

Mulder, Jerry          Active                 Rose Show

Nelson, Devon          Active                 Nominations

Zatto, Jessie          Inactive               -
```

Figure 10.7b
Parallel columns.

To get started, you must define and turn on columns. To do this, follow these next Quick Steps. Start with the cursor where you want the column to begin.

Quick Steps

Using Columns

1. Select Alt-F7 (Math/Columns) and then 1 **Columns**, or select **Columns** from the **Layout** menu.

   The Column options appear.

2. Select 3 **Define**.

   The Text Column Definition screen shown in Figure 10.8 appears.

3. Select 1 - **Type**, and choose the type of column you want (**Newspaper**, **Parallel**, or **Parallel with Block Protect**).

   The type you select appears next to the **Type** prompt.

4. Select 2 - **Number of Columns**, and type in the number of columns desired on the page.

   The number you enter appears next to the Number of Columns prompt.

5. Select 4 - **Margins** and type in the margins desired for each column. (See the note about margins that follows these steps.)

6. If you want to control the space between columns, select 3 - **D**istance Between Columns and enter the amount of spacing desired (the default is .5").

7. Press `F7` (Exit).

A Columns: prompt appears.

8. Select 1 **O**n.

The Column Definition and Column On codes appear in your document, such as: `[Col Def:Newspaper;2;1",` `4";4.5",7.5"][Col On]`.

9. Enter the text you want in the column. Press `Ctrl`-`⏎Enter` to start a new column.

The text appears in columns.

10. Press `Alt`-`F7` (Math/ Columns) then 1 - **C**olumns, or select **C**olumns from the **L**ayout menu. Select 2 **O**ff.

The Column Off code appears in the text and text you enter after the code will not be in columns. When you are returned to your document, you can see that codes are placed where the columns are defined.

NOTE: Margin entries are expressed in inches from the left edge of the paper. In the Figure 10.8 example, the left margin of the first column is 1" from the left edge of the paper and the right margin is 4" from the left edge of the paper. Column number 2 starts 4.5" from the left edge of the paper and ends at 7.5" from the left edge of the paper.

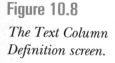

Figure 10.8

The Text Column Definition screen.

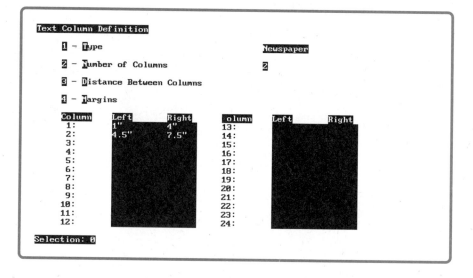

```
Text Column Definition
   1 - Type                              Newspaper
   2 - Number of Columns                 2
   3 - Distance Between Columns
   4 - Margins
 Column   Left      Right      Column   Left       Right
  1:      1"        4"          13:
  2:      4.5"      7.5"        14:
  3:                            15:
  4:                            16:
  5:                            17:
  6:                            18:
  7:                            19:
  8:                            20:
  9:                            21:
 10:                            22:
 11:                            23:
 12:                            24:
Selection: 0
```

CAUTION: When you enter the margin, spacing, and distance between columns, make sure your numbers match up. For example, there can't be 2 evenly spaced columns that are 4" wide each with a 1" space between columns on an 8.5" x 11" page. The request is for more width than is available on the page because 4" - 4" - 1" equals 9", not 8.5". When you enter the Number of Columns, the rest of the spacing will be automatically calculated for you.

Newspaper and Parallel Columns

Figure 10.9 illustrates codes for a newspaper format:

```
[Col Def:Newspaper;2;1",4";4.5",7.5"][Col On]
```

The definition code shows the type of column, Newspaper or Parallel, the Number of Columns, and the Margin Settings for each column. Then, the [Col On] code indicates that the following text will be in column format. Notice that the earlier text in the example is not in column format and provides the heading for our newsletter.

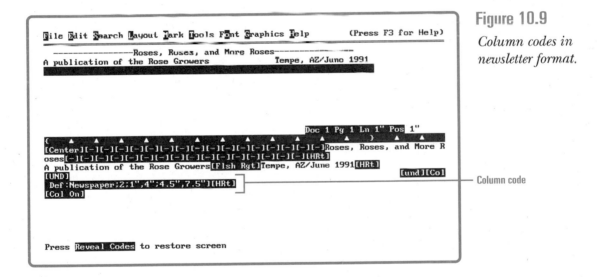

Figure 10.9

Column codes in newsletter format.

Column code

To enter text in a column, begin typing. You may use any typical editing features in columns along with fonts, graphics, and other effects.

> **TIP:** Some font sizes will give unusual on-screen results. For example, the font on-screen may make the columns longer than the line. However, print the document or use View Document to see the actual layout before you worry. The result is usually better than it seems on-screen.

When you want to begin a new column, press `Ctrl`-`⏎Enter` to create a hard page break. You go to the next column and a Hard Page Break code [HPg] is placed in your document. Figure 10.10 illustrates how the text wraps around in the newsletter column format.

Figure 10.10

Newspaper column format.

```
 File  Edit  Search  Layout  Mark  Tools  Font  Graphics  Help      (Press F3 for Help)
 ---------------------Roses, Roses, and More Roses-------------------
 A publication of the Rose Growers                    Tempe, AZ/June 1991

       ROSE SHOW AUGUST 10TH              very fatigued.  Since our
                                          temperatures stay above 90 and
 Don't miss the rose show on              are often in the 100s, the
 August 10th.  All the beauties           plant can use up food faster
 will be there and you should be          than it comes.
 C:\WP51\DOC\ROSES.WPP                            Col 2 Doc 1 Pg 1 Ln 1.67" Pos 4.5"
 {    ▲    ▲    ▲    ▲    }   {    ▲    ▲    ▲    ▲    }   ▲    ▲
 As we in the desert know, very[SRt]
 hot weather can make a plant[HPg]————————— End of column
 [HRt]
 Very fatigued.  Since our[SRt]
 temperatures stay above 90 and[SRt]
 are often in the 100s, the[SRt]
 plant can use up food faster[HRt]
 than it comes.[HRt]
 [HRt]
 A common mistake of most rose[SRt]

 Press Reveal Codes to restore screen
```

When you create a hard page break using parallel columns, a Hard Page Break code [HPg] is placed in the text. The cursor goes to the next column to the right in the line. When you are in the last column of the line, the column is turned off and a new column line is turned on. Codes appear in this order: Column Off [Col Off], a Hard Return [HRt] to skip a line, then Column On [Col On] to begin a new column line.

Figure 10.11 shows the placement of the codes for parallel columns. Notice the last [Col On], code which is set up to continue the entry of another set of parallel columns.

Parallel Columns with Block Protect

If you are creating parallel columns with block protect, you will also see block protection codes, as shown in Figure 10.12.

Here is a sample block protection code from the figure:

```
[Block Pro:On][Col On]Mulder[HPg]
American[SRt]
Pride[HPg]
TBD[HPg]
TBD[Block Pro:Off][Col Off]
[HRt]
```

First, block protection and the column are turned on ([Block Pro:On] and [Col On]). The text in the first column appears (Mulder) followed by a hard page break ([HPg]) for the next column. Then, the text in the second column (American) appears with a soft return [SRt] at the end of each line in the column. At the end of the text in the second column, a hard page break appears followed by the text in the third column, and another hard page break. Finally, the text for the fourth column appears (TBD). When the column line is complete, the block protect and column are turned off.

Figure 10.12

Parallel Columns with block protection codes.

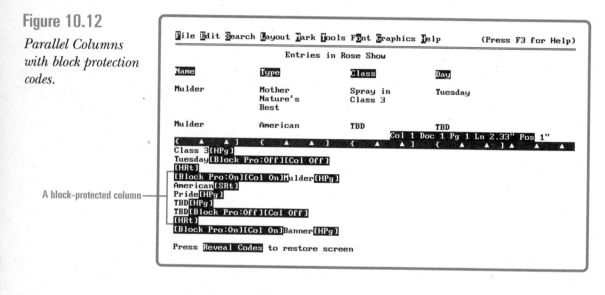

A block-protected column

 TIP: Always use block protection if you want to keep the lines that make up a single column on one page (rather than split between pages) when printed.

Working with Columns

There are some tricks to moving your cursor around in columns. The easiest way by far is to use the mouse. You can also use Ctrl-Home (Go To) and press an arrow key.

> **TIP:** Be careful when editing column text. Don't remove the important [Col On], [HPg], or [Col Off] codes by accident.

When you are ready to stop the column feature, place the cursor where you want columns to end and press Alt-F7 (Math/Columns) and then 1 Columns, or select Columns from the Layout menu. Select 2 Off. A [Col Off] code appears in your document.

Mailing Labels

Many people use sheet mailing labels for newsletters. These labels are typically on 8.5" x 11" paper with three or four labels across. With a little effort, you can use columns to set up addresses to be printed on the sheets. As you add or delete names from the list, the columns can be resized to fit on the label sheet.

To set up mailing labels, just type in the addresses. Make each address the same length in terms of the number of lines used. For example, you may have some addresses that are three lines long (name, street, city/state/ZIP) and others that are four lines long (name, company, street, city/state/ZIP). Add a blank line after the addresses that are three lines long. You will also want one or more blank lines between addresses depending on the length of the labels.

After the addresses are entered, set up a small (or no) left and right margin at the top of the document. Then, insert the columns definition. Measure the labels to determine the appropriate width of the columns. Turn the columns option on. Press Ctrl-↵Enter after the last address in each column.

Continues

Continued

You may want to test print the document before printing on the labels just to make sure the text lines up as you expected. When you add or delete addresses, you will need to change Ctrl - ↵Enter points at the end of each column. Be careful to keep the addresses aligned.

Tables

An attractive way to organize information is to use the Tables feature. Rather than using tabs or parallel columns to lay out information, a table grid is created for you. You may also enter formulas in tables for quick math calculations. Figure 10.13 shows a simple table. This table shows a small budget. The totals in the last line were calculated with formulas entered into the table.

Figure 10.13
A simple table.

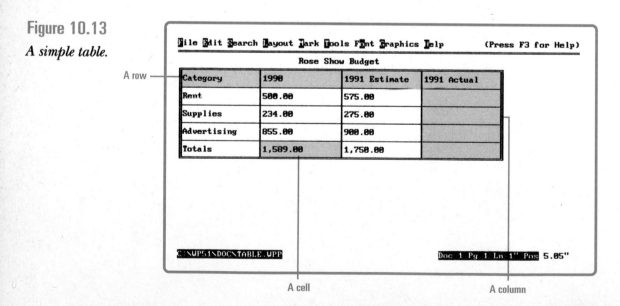

A row

A cell

A column

TIP: You may want to test a simple grid with your printer to see how the grid appears in final form.

As shown in Figure 10.13, tables are organized into rows, columns, and cells. A *row* is a single line of boxes across. For example, Figure 10.13 shows a row for Category. A *column* refers to the vertical boxes in the table. In the figure, the 1991 Actual cells are in a column. A *cell* points to a particular rectangular space in the table. In Figure 10.13, the total for the 1990 column (1,589.00) is contained in one cell.

Creative Uses for Tables

In addition to budgets, you can use tables to create inventory lists, expense accounts, financial reports, telephone lists, class enrollments, or employee lists.

Create a Table

Creating a table in WordPerfect is very straightforward; you just tell it how many rows and how many columns you want. To create a table, follow the next Quick Steps.

Creating a Table

1. Position your cursor where you want the top left corner of the table to begin.

2. Press `Alt`-`F7` (Math/ Columns) and select 2 **Tables**, or select **T**ables from the **L**ayout menu.

3. Select 1 - **C**reate.   This prompt appears:
   `Number of Columns:`

4. Enter the number of columns for the table and press `⏎Enter`.   This prompt appears:
   `Number of Rows:`

5. Type in the number of rows and press `⏎Enter`.   The table grid appears, as shown in Figure 10.14.

6. Press `F7` (Exit) to go into document-editing mode.   You are now ready to enter data into the table.

Notice that the Reveal Codes screen in Figure 10.15 shows the Table Definition code, a code for each row and cell, and a code identifying where the table feature is turned off. Once the grid is created, you can enter information in the table using regular WordPerfect features.

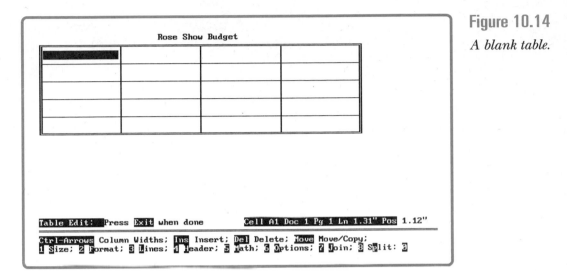

Figure 10.14

A blank table.

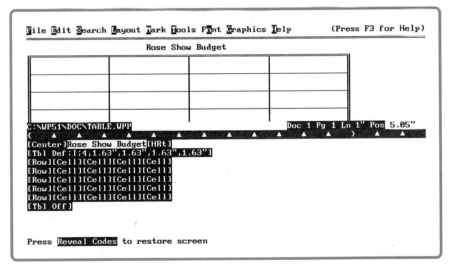

Figure 10.15

The Reveal Codes screen shows the table definition.

Enter a Formula

To add a formula, you will need to understand how each cell is identified. Starting in the upper left corner, columns are represented by letters starting with A and rows are represented by numbers starting with 1. The cell in the upper left corner of the screen is A1, the next cell to the right is B1. The cell below A1 is A2 and so on. See Figure 10.16.

Figure 10.16

Identifying cells.

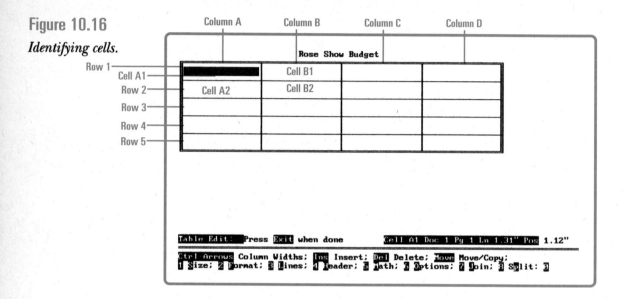

You can enter text (numbers and letters) into the table just as you type regular WordPerfect text. To enter formulas, you must leave document-editing mode by placing your cursor in the table and either pressing Alt - F7 (Math/Columns) or selecting Tables then Edit from the Layout menu. The editing features appear on the bottom of the screen. To enter a formula, select 5 Math and then 2 Formula. This prompt appears:

```
Enter formula:
```

To create a total in our example, the results of the following formula would be placed in cell C5:

```
C2-C3-C4
```

The formula tells you to add the values in cells C2, C3, and C4. (Of course, you must have numeric values in these cells, not text.)

You may use these symbols in formulas:

+   Add

–   Subtract (or negative number)

*   Multiply

/   Divide

Formulas are calculated left to right unless you put part of a formula in parentheses. In that case, the calculations in the parentheses are calculated first.

Once the formula is entered at the prompt, press ⏎Enter. If values are entered in the cells contained in the formula, the result is shown. Otherwise, enter values in the cells and use Table Edit mode to select 5 Math then 1 Calculate to calculate the result.

Edit a Table

Use the normal WordPerfect editing tools for entering and editing table text as well as formatting. You may control the formatting of a single cell or a number of cells you select (for example, an entire row or column). Formatting includes appearance, size, justification, column width, and so on. From the table editing options, select 2 Format then 1 Cell, 2 Column, or 3 Row Height as desired. Depending on which you select, you are presented with different menus of options, all of which are fairly self-explanatory.

For example, in Figure 10.17, the dollar amount cells were formatted for decimal align justification. This was accomplished using 2 Format, then 2 Column, then 3 Justify, and then 5 Decimal Align.

Figure 10.17

Decimal align justification.

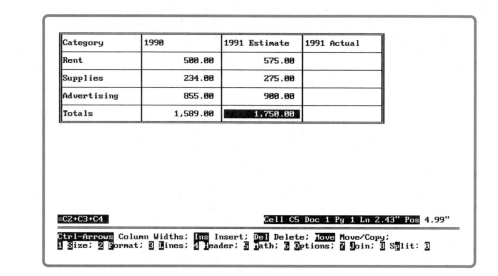

Sometimes you may want to add a row or column. To do this, place the cursor where you want the new row or column added. A new column will be added to the left of the cursor. A new row will be added above the cursor. From the table-editing options, select Insert by pressing the Ins key. This prompt appears:

    Insert: 1 Rows; 2 Columns: 0

Identify rows or columns. Then, this prompt appears:

    Number of Columns: 1

Enter the number of columns or rows. The table is updated. The column or row is added. If the entire line between margins is taken up by the table, the current cell will be split when a new column is added.

To delete a row or column, place the cursor in the row or column to delete. From the table editing options, select Delete by pressing the Del key. This prompt appears:

```
Delete: 1 Rows; 2 Columns: 0
```

Identify rows or columns. Then, a prompt like this appears:

```
Number of Columns: 1
```

Enter the number of columns or rows. The table is updated. To delete an entire table, you must select the whole table and press Del.

What's Next?

This chapter only touched on the power of using columns and tables. If you have a need for columns or tables for business or pleasure, you may want to master the basics described in this chapter then learn more.

For example, with a little research, you can speed up your work. There are additional quick cursor keys to move between columns, a way to quickly delete columns, and methods to speed the display of columns by turning off the Side-by-side Columns Display. There are quick movement keys for tables, methods to move and copy within tables, as well as other ways to handle math. Tables 10.1 and 10.2 list several of the quick movement keys.

Table 10.1

Quick Movement Keys for Columns.

Press	To move cursor
Ctrl-Home (Go To), → or ←	From column to column
Ctrl-Home (Go To), Home, → or ←	To first or last column on a page
Ctrl-Home (Go To), ↑ or ↓	To top or bottom of current column

Table 10.2

Quick Movement Keys for Tables.

Press	To move cursor
Ctrl-Home (Go To), Cell location (A3)	To a specific cell location
Home, ↑	To the first cell in a column
Home, ↓	To the last cell in a column
Home, ←	To the first cell in a row
Home, →	To the last cell in a row
Home, Home, ↑	To the first cell in the table
Home, Home, ↓	To the last cell in the table

Creating a Page Break

▲ Press Ctrl-⏎Enter.

Go To a Page

1. Press Ctrl-Home (Go To), or select Go To from the Search menu.
2. Type the desired page number.

Widow/Orphan Protection

1. Press ⇧Shift-F8 (Format) and select 1 - Line or select Line from the Layout menu.
2. Select 9 - Widow/Orphan Protection and choose Yes.

Conditional End of Page

1. Move the cursor directly above the text you want to keep together.
2. Press ⇧Shift-F8 (Format) and select 4 - Other or select Other from the Layout menu.
3. Select 2 - Conditional End of Page and enter the number of lines to keep together.

Block Protect

1. Use Alt-F4 (Block), or select Block from the Edit menu to block the text.
2. Press ⇧Shift-F8 (Format) and choose Yes or select Protect Block from the Edit menu.

Creating Multiple-Page Documents

As you become skilled with WordPerfect, you will use it for pages and pages of work. In this chapter, you will learn not only how to create multiple pages, you will learn how to control what amount of text appears on the pages, how to print multiple pages, and how to go to a specific page.

Creating Multiple Pages

So far, you've learned to create and print a document, complete with the tab settings of your choice. Now you're ready to create a document that is more than one page long.

WordPerfect allows you to create lengthy documents—the maximum length depends only upon your computer's storage and memory capacity. Usually, though, any document over fifty pages seems a bit cumbersome because it takes too long to move around the document and make the frequent saves necessary to protect the document.

In a long document, the pages appear on-screen one after another. Think of your document as a long scroll with lines marking the pages.

Using Different Page Formats in One Document

The pages in a document do not necessarily have to be printed on the same type of paper, nor do they need to have the same formatting. For example, one document may have a letter to be printed on letterhead on the first page. The margins would be set up to fit the letter on the letterhead. The second page of the document may contain the address for an envelope and have a paper size/type code for an envelope, different margins, and a copy of the address from the letter to be printed on the envelope. The last page of the document may be a multiple-page report for regular 8.5" x 11" paper. A new paper size/type code would be used along with margins and page numbering specific for the report. When you plan a document, keep in mind how easily you can load different paper in the printer. Also consider how to minimize disruption to others who may be sharing the printer.

There is more than one way to break a page. If you've been experimenting on your own, you may have already created an extra page by accidentally using WordPerfect's automatic page break feature.

Automatic Page Breaks

WordPerfect knows how many lines of text can fit on a page. It is a careful deduction of the paper size minus the margins (both set through the Format menu and covered in earlier chapters). The ln amount in the lower right corner of the screen shows how many inches of the page have been filled with text up to your cursor position. On a typical 11" piece of paper with 1" top and bottom margins, you will be able to type to about the 9" mark before WordPerfect inserts a page break automatically for you. The exact measure varies according to the line spacing you're using (such as single or double) and the line height. (Both are set through the Format menu.) If you edit the page and add or delete lines of text, the page break remains at the same line. The text, in effect, "moves" to fill the page.

On your screen, an automatic page break appears as a dashed line, as shown in Figure 11.1. Notice that on the Reveal Codes screen, the automatic page break is shown as [SPg] (soft page break). *Soft page break* is WordPerfect jargon for an automatically inserted page break. If you insert a page break manually, this is referred to as a *hard page break*.

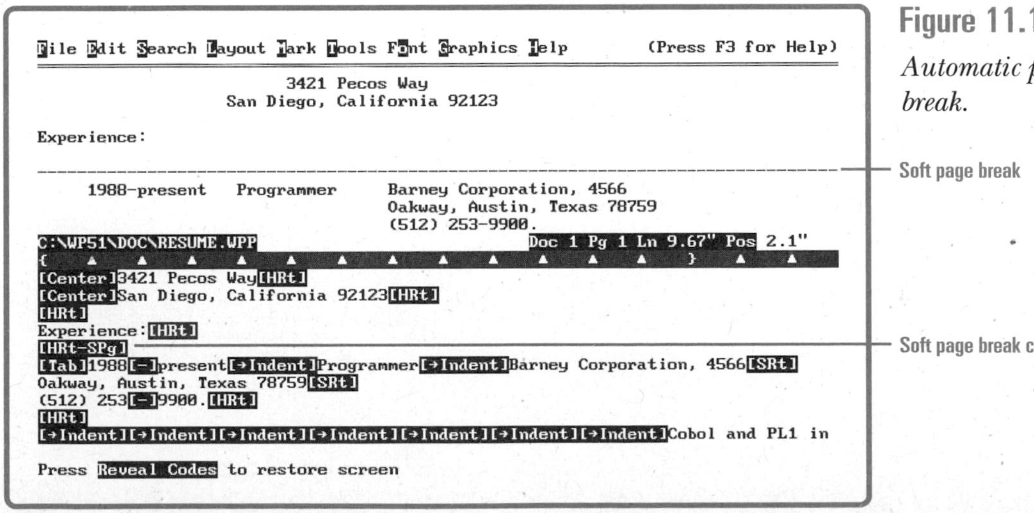

Figure 11.1

Automatic page break.

Soft page break

Soft page break code

Manual Page Breaks

You will often want a page break before WordPerfect enters one. For example, when you create a letter with several attachments, you may want to put the letter on the first page of the document and the attachments on subsequent pages, keeping all the related material in one WordPerfect document. When you print, you can insert letterhead for the first page and plain sheets after that.

Of course, you could press ⏎Enter enough times to take advantage of WordPerfect's automatic page break, but editing the text later could throw off the pages. Instead, use a manual (hard) page break.

To manually break a page, place the cursor on the line and column where you want the page to be broken. Press Ctrl-⏎Enter. A double dashed line like that shown in Figure 11.2 is inserted and the [HPg] (hard page break) code is inserted in your document. Text starting with the character your cursor is on appears after the manual page break. If you want to get rid of the manual page break, just delete the code.

> **TIP:** You may want a blank page in your document as a separator, or to later paste up an exhibit. To create a blank page, just enter two hard page breaks. For more blank pages, enter as many hard page breaks as you need.

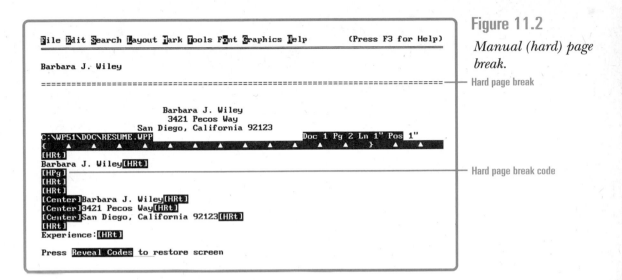

Figure 11.2

Manual (hard) page break.

— Hard page break

— Hard page break code

Moving Between Pages

Once you have multiple pages, you will want to be able to move from page to page quickly. The number of the page appears in the bottom right corner of your screen. In this sample line:

```
Doc 1 Pg 4 Ln 8" Pos 3"
```

your cursor is shown to be on page 4. To go directly to page 15, press Ctrl-Home (Go To Page), or select Go To from the **S**earch menu. This prompt appears:

```
Go to
```

Type **15** and press ↵Enter. Your cursor goes to the upper left corner of the first line of page 15.

```
Doc 1 Pg 15 Ln 1" Pos 1"
```

To move only one page, press PgUp (to go up or "back" in the document) or PgDn (to go down or "forward" in the document). When you use either of these keys, you are taken to the upper left of the first line of that page.

Preventing Widows and Orphans

To many beginning users, the terms "widows" and "orphans" have to do with women who have lost their mates and children who have lost their parents. In word processing, the terms also have to do with losses—specifically, when a single line of a paragraph has been lost from the rest of its paragraph by being split off by a page break. A *widow* is the first line of a paragraph alone at the end of a page. An *orphan* is the last line of a paragraph isolated at the top of a page. Figures 11.3a and 11.3b show a widow and an orphan.

If you don't like the appearance of widows and orphans, you can ask WordPerfect to prevent them. The following Quick Steps detail how to protect against widows and orphans.

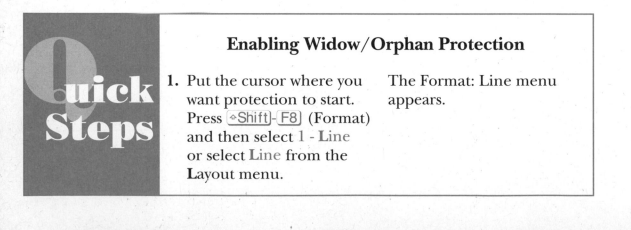

Quick Steps

Enabling Widow/Orphan Protection

1. Put the cursor where you want protection to start. Press Shift-F8 (Format) and then select 1 - Line or select Line from the Layout menu.

The Format: Line menu appears.

2. Select 9 - **W**idow/Orphan
Protection, choose **Y**es,
and press ⌐F7⌐ (Exit) to go
back to your document.

A code is inserted in your
text.

Figure 11.3a
A widow.

```
              Barbara J. Wiley
                3421 Pecos Way
          San Diego, California 92123

Mr. David Randolph
Bennington Corporation
45 Superstition Highway
Phoenix, Arizona 85252

                              May 12, 1991

Dear Mr. Randolph:

    As I discussed,  I am very interested in
pursuing a career with the Bennington Corpora-
tion.  I have attached:

        -    My resume with a chronological work
             history as requested
        -    Letters of recommendation
        -    Certificates of achievement

    Your  friend, Jim Miller, recently ap-
plauded my work on our exposition with these
remarks at the dinner presentation:

    "Barbara  has  consistently  proven
    that she goes above and beyond our
    expectations.  And... always within
    budget no less!"

    I look forward to speaking with you
```

—— Widow

Figure 11.3b

An orphan.

Orphan

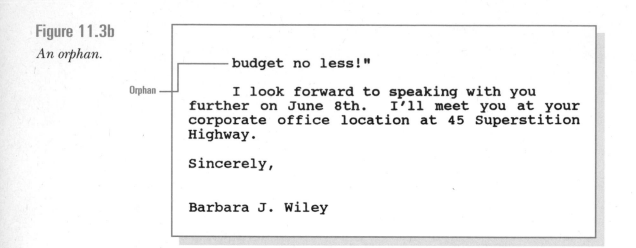

```
        budget no less!"

     I look forward to speaking with you
further on June 8th.  I'll meet you at your
corporate office location at 45 Superstition
Highway.

Sincerely,


Barbara J. Wiley
```

TIP: To protect an entire document, place the widow/orphan code at the beginning of the document.

Conditional End of Page

Sometimes you will want to keep several lines together in a document, even if it means letting a page run a little short. For example, in Figure 11.4, part of the sample resume is split by a soft page break automatically inserted by WordPerfect. The split is inappropriate. To keep the lines together, you could insert a manual page break above the lines. The problem with this is that if you edit text, the hard page break may end up cutting the page too short. A better solution is to enter a *conditional end of page*, which keeps together the number of lines you specify so that they can't be split between pages.

The following Quick Steps detail how to enter a conditional end of page. For our example, we'll keep the six lines at the bottom of Figure 11.4 together.

Entering a Conditional End of Page

1. Identify the number of lines to keep together and place the cursor before the first line.

   The lines after the cursor will be affected.

2. Press `⇧Shift`-`F8` (Format) and select 1 - **Other** or select **Other** on the **Layout** menu.

   The Format: Other menu appears.

3. Select 2 - Conditional End of Page, enter the number of lines to be kept together, and press `⏎Enter`.

   The lines are kept together on a page.

4. Press `F7` (Exit).

   You are returned to your document.

Quick Steps

The code [Cndl EOP:6] appears, indicating that six lines are to be kept together. The text that was split is automatically moved past the page break. Figure 11.5 shows the resumé after the conditional end of page code has been inserted. Notice the code placement.

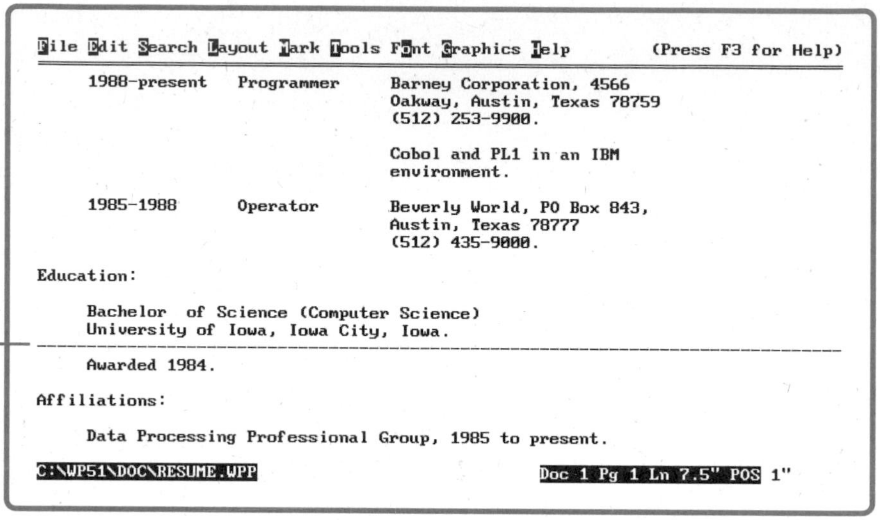

Figure 11.4

Resumé lines split by soft page break.

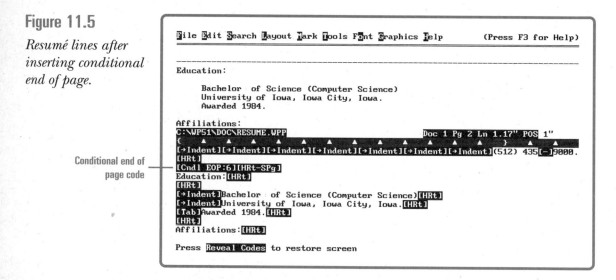

Figure 11.5

Resumé lines after inserting conditional end of page.

Block Protection

You may want to keep a given block of text together (versus specifying a particular number of lines). If so, use the *block protect* feature instead of the conditional end of page. With block protect, you can change the number of lines in the block through editing and the block will remain together on a single page.

This feature is especially useful for tables or any block that may be edited to a different number of lines. For example, Figure 11.6 shows text in a block protect. The entire block was moved to the start of a page. Notice the `[BlockPro:On]` and `[BlockPro:Off]` codes that mark the beginning and end of the block.

```
 File  Edit  Search  Layout  Mark  Tools  Font  Graphics  Help        (Press F3 for Help)
 ─────────────────────────────────────────────────────────────────────────────

 Education:

        Bachelor  of Science (Computer Science)
        University of Iowa, Iowa City, Iowa.
        Awarded 1984.

 Affiliations:
 C:\WP51\DOC\RESUME.WPP                            Doc 1 Pg 2 Ln 1.17" POS 1"
 {       ▲      ▲      ▲      ▲       ▲      ▲     ▲      }    ▲        ▲
 [→Indent][→Indent][→Indent][→Indent][→Indent][→Indent][→Indent](512) 435[-]9000.
 [HRt]
 [HRt-SPg]
 [Block Pro:On]Education:[HRt] ──────────┐
 [HRt]                                    │
 [→Indent]Bachelor  of Science (Computer Science)[HRt]  │
 [→Indent]University of Iowa, Iowa City, Iowa.[HRt]     │
 [Tab]Awarded 1984.[HRt]                  │
 [Block Pro:Off][HRt] ───────────────────┘
 Affiliations:[HRt]

 Press Reveal Codes to restore screen
```

Figure 11.6
Block protected text.

— Block protection codes

TIP: Since the text you are block protecting is to be placed on one page, you cannot block protect more than a pageful of text.

The following Quick Steps detail how to block protect text.

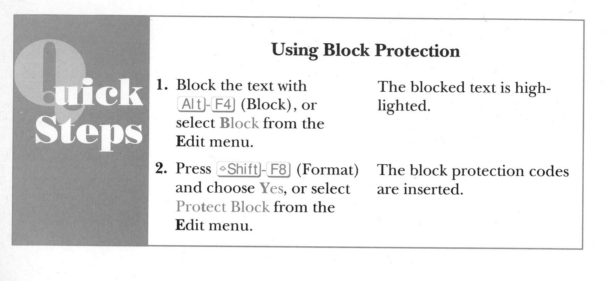

Using Block Protection

1. Block the text with
   Alt-F4 (Block), or
   select Block from the
   Edit menu.

   The blocked text is highlighted.

2. Press ⇧Shift-F8 (Format)
   and choose Yes, or select
   Protect Block from the
   Edit menu.

   The block protection codes
   are inserted.

Time the Addition of Page Controls

When should you add widow/orphan protection, hard
page breaks, conditional end of page codes, or block
protection? Many users find it most efficient to follow this
approach: If you want widow/orphan protection, enter it at
the beginning of the document. Enter other page controls
after you have created the text in your document and
completed editing the text. (If you enter special page break
codes and then do significant editing, you typically have to
redo the page breaks.) Once the document is complete,
take the time to pay attention to where the text is falling on
the page. Use block protection for tables or text that may be
later edited to a different length. Use conditional end of
page for text that is likely to remain the same in terms of
number of lines.

Printing Multiple Pages

Printing multiple pages is simple. When you press ⟨⇧Shift⟩-⟨F7⟩ (Print) or select Print from the File menu, the Print screen appears. Choose 5 - Multiple Pages. The Page(s): prompt appears. If you want a range of pages, enter them with a dash between the first and last page in the range. Enter individual pages with commas separating each page number. For example, the following entry will cause page 1 to print followed by pages 4 through 8, then page 12.

        1,4-8,12

This entry will print page 2 then print from page 6 through the end of the document.

        2,6-

This entry will print from the start of the document through page 6 then pages 22, 23, and 24.

        -6,22-24

TIP: Do not enter page numbers randomly (such as 5, 2, 7). Put them in the sequence in which they appear in the document (that is, 2, 5, 7).

Printing with a Binding Offset

Often, when people use multiple pages, they want to bind two-sided pages. The binding offset automatically shifts text away from the bound edge. (Pages are shifted right on the odd numbered pages and left on the even numbered pages.) This shifting makes plenty of room for holes to be punched or pages to be stitched.

To set the binding offset, press `⇧Shift`-`F7` (Print) or select **Print** from the **File** menu. The Print screen appears. Select B - Binding Offset. Enter the space to be left for the offset. When the document is printed, regular margin settings will remain the same and the binding offset is added to the margin.

What's Next?

Using a manual page break is desirable for dividing chapters or sections of smaller documents. If a document becomes much larger than 50 pages, it becomes cumbersome and time consuming to move between pages and work with the document. For that reason, you may want to create separate documents for each chapter or section then combine them into a master document for common operations such as creating tables of contents and indexes and printing.

A master document is a single document that links subordinate documents. To create a master document, just place the cursor in the document where you want to link a subdocument. Press `Alt`-`F5` (Mark Text) then select 2 Subdoc or select **Subdocument** from the **Mark** menu. The prompt Subdoc File-name: appears. Type in the path and name of the subdocument and press `↵Enter`. A box with the subdocument name appears in the master document. This represents the master document reference to the subdocument in condensed form.

You may expand the master document (for example, to print or to read the text in the subdocuments). Do this by pressing `Alt`-`F5` (Mark Text), 6 Generate, and 3 - Expand Master Document (or by selecting Master Document then Expand from the Mark menu). When a master document is expanded, the text as well as the subdocument reference appears in the master document. You may condense a master document by following the same process as expanding a master document and simply choosing the Condense option when it is presented.

For more information about master documents, consult an advanced WordPerfect reference.

Page Numbering Considerations

▲ Numbers may be entered anywhere in a document.

▲ Numbers may be roman or arabic style.

▲ Text may be entered with the page number.

▲ You may select from page positions to determine
the placement of page numbers.

Adding or Stopping Page Numbering (Not in Header)

1. Press ⇧Shift-8 (Format) then select 2 - Page, or
   select Page from the Layout menu.

2. Select 6 - Page Numbering and complete the
   options.

Suppressing a Page Number on a Single Page

1. Press ⇧Shift-F8 (Format) then select 2 - Page, or
   select Page from the Layout menu.

2. Select 8 - Suppress then 4 - Suppress Page
   Numbering.

Page Numbers

Once you develop documents with multiple pages, you will want to be able to number the pages. With just a little setup, WordPerfect does this for you automatically. You'll be able to select from a variety of page number appearances or develop your own unique look. In addition, you may insert a page number automatically in the body of a page to reference the page.

Page Number Choices

Numbering pages is handy for short documents and essential for most long documents. But don't tediously number each page in the document by hand. Instead, have WordPerfect automatically number your pages. WordPerfect allows you to select the:

▲ New page number (including the number with which to start consecutive numbering) and the type—roman or arabic.

▲ Style (number alone, or accompanied by text).

▲ Position of the number on the page.

You may change these options on any page you like and as often as you like in a document. A new code is inserted each time you enter page numbering options. The code affects the page on which it is entered and all following text until a new code is encountered.

CAUTION: Place the codes controlling page numbering at the top of a page. If you put text before the page codes, the page numbers may not print as you anticipated. If you accidentally put conflicting page numbering codes on a page, the page numbers won't number as you anticipated.

Numbering Type and New Page Number

New Page Number is WordPerfect's option to allow you to select the page number you want to start with at a given point in the document along with the type of number. The type may be roman (type I or i) or arabic (type 1).

For example, you might have several WordPerfect documents making up one long, printed document. The first three pages of the first document's introduction are numbered i, ii, and iii, and the next 15 pages in the document may be numbered 1 through 15. You then would want the first WordPerfect page of the second document to be numbered as page 16 with consecutive numbering continuing from there.

As you can see from this example, you can start new page numbering (number and type) at the start of a document or on any page. The page number you've assigned is displayed in the bottom right of the screen.

You have three type choices. You can choose lowercase roman numerals:

```
i, ii, iii, iv
```

You can pick uppercase roman numerals:

```
I, II, III, IV
```

Last, (and most often) you may use arabic numbers (WordPerfect's default):

```
1, 2, 3, 4
```

When you enter a new page number, a code like this appears in your document:

```
[Pg Num:4]
```

with the number identifying the new starting number. This number is displayed in the type (roman or arabic) you've chosen.

Style of Text/Page Number

Page Number Style is WordPerfect's option to allow you to enter the page number alone or to enter text along with the page number. As an example, you may want the first three pages of a document to have this text along with the page number:

```
Appendix A--Page 1

Appendix A--Page 2

Appendix A--Page 3
```

On the fourth page, you may want to change to the following style and continue it through the rest of the document:

```
Appendix B--Page 1
```

`Appendix A--Page` is the common style in this example, followed by WordPerfect's insertion of the "New Page Number" (the actual number and type of number) you've identified.

The text (`Appendix`) is just one way to use the page number style feature with text and symbols. (You can enter any text up to thirty characters in length.) For instance, you may want to insert a date:

```
June 10, 1992          (1)
```

a copyright notice:

```
1992 Sams   / Pg 1
```

the author's name:

```
By Kate Barnes   p. #1
```

a confidential notification:

```
CONFIDENTIAL: 1
```

identify the document as a draft:

```
!!!! D R A F T !!!! p. 1
```

or just add a decoration to the page number:

```
******** 1 ********
```

The text and page number appear when the document is printed.

> **TIP:** You may need to enter more than thirty characters along with a page number. If so, check out the discussion of headers and footers in Chapter 13.

When you set the style in WordPerfect, you enter the text along with a symbol (^B—entered by pressing Ctrl-B) for the page number. If the page number is to appear at the end of the text instead of within text, you can just enter the text (include a space if appropriate) and WordPerfect will automatically enter the ^B for you.

> **CAUTION:** Press Ctrl-B simultaneously. *Do not* press a caret (^) and a B. If you do, the caret and B will print in place of the desired page number.

When you enter a new page number style, this type of code is placed in the document:

```
[Pg Num Style: Confidential Draft/Page ^B]
```

The complete text of the style appears, along with ^B, which symbolizes the position of the page number.

"Inserting" New Pages After Pages Are Numbered

What if you create a lengthy document with consecutive page numbering, and want to "insert" pages later? If renumbering the document would take too long or multiple copies of the existing document have been distributed, add pages in between. For example, pages 17.1 through 17.5 could be added between page 17 and page 18.

You could just type in page numbers for these pages, however, that would leave some pages governed by automatic page number and others with page numbers typed in. If you wanted to print the document later, considerable editing would have to be done first to standardize how page numbers are assigned.

Instead, use WordPerfect's page numbering options to add a New Page Number with the appropriate Page Number Style. Continuing the example of adding pages 17.1 through 17.5, enter a code on what is to be page 17.1. Select a New Page Number of 1 (this will become the .1, .2, and so on). Enter a Page Number Style of 17.^B. After what is now page 17.5, enter a code with New Page Number set to 18 to return to the correct consecutive page numbering. When you print the pages they will be numbered correctly.

The specially numbered page codes can be easily removed. In Chapter 15 you will learn how to search for codes. If you end up with a document with multiple page changes and want to remove "inserted" page numbering, just search out the page codes and edit as desired.

Position on the Page

When it comes to positioning the page number, you are offered a variety of selections. Figure 12.1 illustrates the options. As shown in the figure, you can place the page number in the top left, top center, top right, bottom left, bottom center, or bottom right. The numbers in the Every Page diagram are simply identifiers for the position you can select. If you are printing pages that will be copied double sided, you can enter the page number on the upper outside (alternating top) of the page or the lower outside (alternating bottom).

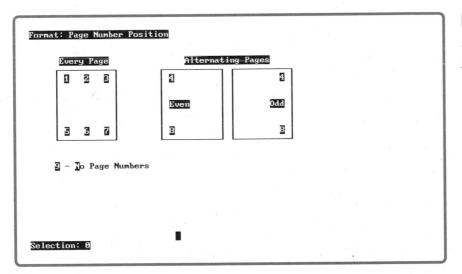

Figure 12.1
Possible page number positions.

Also notice in Figure 12.1 that you may select 9 - No Page Numbers. You can skip page numbers for one or more pages.

Once you add a position for a page number, a code like this appears in your document:

```
[Pg Numbering:Bottom Center]
```

The location of the page number is clearly shown.

Adding a Page Number

Now that you know *what* you can do, *how* do you do it? Here
are the steps.

1. Place the cursor before any existing text at the top of the
   page where you want page numbering to begin.

2. Press ⧖Shift-F8 (Format) then select 2 - Page, or select
   Page from the Layout menu.

3. Select 6 - Page Numbering. The Format: Page Numbering menu appears (see Figure 12.2).

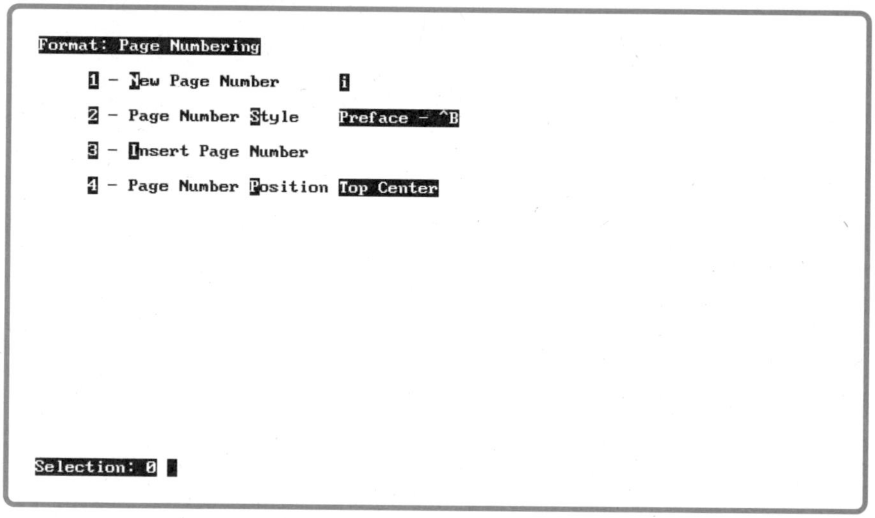

Figure 12.2

*The Format: Page
Numbering menu.*

```
Format: Page Numbering

    1 - New Page Number        i

    2 - Page Number Style      Preface - ^B

    3 - Insert Page Number

    4 - Page Number Position   Top Center




Selection: 0 
```

4. To enter the number of the page to use and the type of
   number (arabic or roman), select 1 - New Page Number.

5. Enter the page number in arabic or roman style and
   press ↵Enter.

6. To enter text before, after, or around the page number, select 2 - Page Number Style. Type in the text and press `Ctrl`-`B` to position the page number. If you don't press `Ctrl`-`B`, WordPerfect inserts the page number at the end of the text.

7. Press `⏎Enter` when you are done entering the text.

8. Select the positioning of the page number (or no page number) by choosing 4 - Page Number Position. The diagram shown in Figure 12.1 appears.

9. Select a page position by entering a number 1 through 8 and press `⏎Enter`.

10. Once you have entered all the desired selections, press `F7` (Exit) until you are returned to your document.

You may want to check the Reveal Codes screen to ensure that all the selections are as you desired. In the example shown in Figure 12.3, you can see codes placed in the document to yield a top, centered page number beginning with roman numerals after the text (`Preface  -  i`). The codes govern the page numbering until you enter new codes.

```
[Pg Num:i] [Pg Num Style: Preface - ^B] [Pg
Numbering: Top Center]
```

The page numbers will not appear on your page; they only appear when the document is printed.

The following Quick Steps summarize what you have learned about page numbering.

Using Page Numbering

1. Place your cursor at the top of a page.

2. Press ⇧Shift-F8 (Format) and select 2 - **P**age, or select **P**age from the **L**ayout menu.

   The Format: Page menu appears.

3. Select 6 - Page Numbering.

   The Format: Page Number-ing menu appears.

4. Select an option according to the page numbering you want.

5. Press F7 (Exit).

Figure 12.3

Page numbering codes in the Reveal Codes screen.

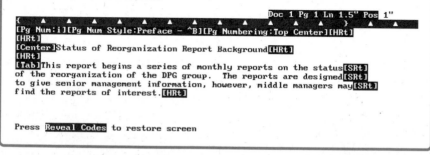

```
 File  Edit  Search  Layout  Mark  Tools  Font  Graphics  Help        (Press F3 for Help)


              Status of Reorganization Report Background
          This report begins a series of monthly reports on the status
      of the reorganization of the DPG group.  The reports are designed
      to give senior management information, however, middle managers may
      find the reports of interest.

                                                         Doc 1 Pg 1 Ln 1.5" Pos 1"
 {      ▲      ▲      ▲      ▲      ▲      ▲      ▲      ▲      ▲      ▲      }      ▲      ▲
 [Pg Num:i][Pg Num Style:Preface - ^B][Pg Numbering:Top Center][HRt]
 [HRt]
 [Center]Status of Reorganization Report Background[HRt]
 [HRt]
 [Tab]This report begins a series of monthly reports on the status[SRt]
 of the reorganization of the DPG group.  The reports are designed[SRt]
 to give senior management information, however, middle managers may[SRt]
 find the reports of interest.[HRt]


 Press  Reveal Codes  to restore screen
```

If you have graphics capabilities, you can view the page numbers on your screen by using ⇧Shift-F7 (Print) and then selecting 6 - View Document. Try your computer to see if it has this capability. If it does not, a message will appear. If it does, a screen like that shown in Figure 12.4 appears. (This figure displays the text enlarged to 200%.)

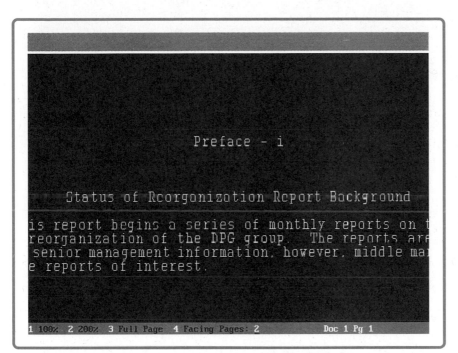

Figure 12.4

Page numbers appear with View Document.

Suppressing Page Numbers

You may want to suppress a page number on one page. This is sometimes required if you want to place a large graphic on a page or give a different look to the page. When you suppress the page number on a page, that page number remains in the consecutive count. For example, if you suppress the page number on page 3, the pages will be numbered 1, 2, (page 3 will have no page number), 4, 5, and so on.

To suppress a page number, use the following Quick Steps.

Suppressing a Page Number

Quick Steps

1. Press ⇧Shift-F8 (Format) and select 2 - **Page** or select **P**age from the **Layout** menu.

   The Format: Page menu appears.

2. Select 8 - **S**uppress (this page only).

   The Format: Suppress (this page only) menu appears (see Figure 12.5).

3. Select 4 - Suppress **P**age Numbering and choose **Y**es.

4. Press F7 (Exit) until you return to your document.

   The [Suppress:PgNum] code is placed in your document.

Figure 12.5

Format: Suppress (this page only) menu.

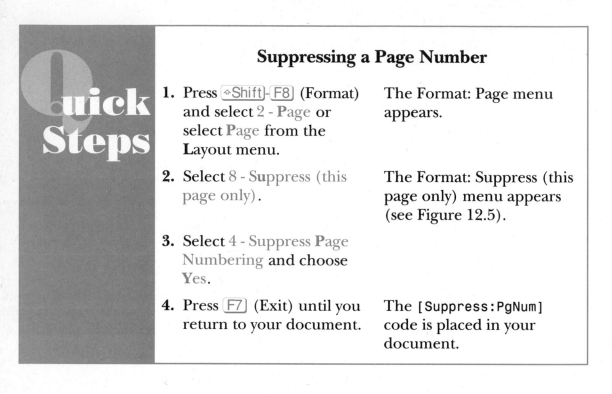

```
Format: Suppress (this page only)

     1 - Suppress All Page Numbering, Headers and Footers

     2 - Suppress Headers and Footers

     3 - Print Page Number at Bottom Center    No

     4 - Suppress Page Numbering               No

     5 - Suppress Header A                      No

     6 - Suppress Header B                      No

     7 - Suppress Footer A                      No

     8 - Suppress Footer B                      No




Selection: 0
```

Inserting the Page Number in the Body of the Page

For reference purposes, you may want to insert the page number in the body of the text. These phrases illustrate two examples:

```
Return to this page (page 3) when you have completed
the test.
```

```
The instructions follow (pg 4).
```

Use WordPerfect's feature for inserting page numbers (instead of typing in the page numbers yourself). That way, if the number of pages changes due to editing, the number that prints will always be correct.

To enter the page number, follow the next Quick Steps.

Entering the Page Number

1. Place the cursor in the body of the text where the page number is to appear.

2. Press ⇧Shift - F8 (Format) then select 2 - **P**age, or select **P**age from the **L**ayout menu.

3. Select 6 - Page Numbering.   The Format: Page Numbering menu appears.

4. Select 3 - Insert Page Number.   You are returned to your document and the ^B symbol appears in the document.

Quick Steps

This symbol will be replaced with the page number when the document prints. You can see the full code `[Insert Pg Num:^B]` with the Reveal Codes screen.

What's Next?

WordPerfect's header and footer features (covered in the next chapter) can affect page number placement. The use of headers and footers causes the text you enter to appear on each page. It is your option whether a header or footer includes a page number. Typically, when you use a header or footer, you will want the PageNumber Position on the Format: Page Numbering screen set to No page numbering. That way, you can add the page number in the header or footer at the location desired and experience no conflict with the page number entered automatically as described in this chapter.

In some cases, you may want to use both the automatic page numbering and use a header and/or a footer (with or without a page number). For example, you may want to put titles in the header without a page number symbol but have the pages numbered. Or, you may want to have a section number in the header or footer and a page number added with the approaches described earlier in this chapter. If that is the case, you will need to leave a blank line at the top of the header or the end of the footer to reserve space for the page number. Alternatively, you may leave space in the header or footer where the page number will fall. Read on to learn more about headers and footers.

Headers and Footers Are...

▲ A header is text that appears at the top of the document page (after the top margin).

▲ A footer appears at the bottom of the page (before the bottom margin).

Add a Header or Footer

1. Press ⬆Shift-F8 (Format) and select 2 - Page, or select Page from the Layout menu.

2. Select either 3 - Headers or 4 - Footers, and then either A or B.

3. Select 2 Every Page, 3 Odd Pages, or 4 Even Pages.

4. Enter the desired text and press F7 (Exit) or select Exit from the File Menu when you are done.

Edit or Discontinue a Header or Footer

1. Press ⬆Shift-F8 (Format) and select 2 - Page, or select Page from the Layout menu.

2. Select either 3 - Headers or 4 - Footers, and then either A or B.

3. Select 1 Discontinue or 5 Edit.

The Professional Touch: Headers and Footers

If you create multiple page documents such as reports or manuals, you will want to learn about the use of headers and footers. They add professionalism to any document. Better yet, they aren't hard to master. Basically, you will pass through several menus to set up a header or footer then use WordPerfect's regular editing features to enter the text.

What Are Headers and Footers?

A *header* or *footer* is common text that appears at the top (head) or the bottom (foot) of a page. Headers and footers can add a professional touch to a document to give it a first-rate appearance. Let's consider some examples.

A header or footer may include the name of a document, version number, notification of status (DRAFT or Confidential, for instance), author's name, page number, chapter or section numbers, graphics, or any other appropriate text you care to include. These are possible sample header or footer lines:

```
Chapter 3                              page 3-16

CONFIDENTIAL from President's office  page 6 of 9

Year End Report        - DRAFT -      by Jim Lindy

1992 Webber Corporation
```

Don't let these examples fool you. A header or footer can be more than a single line; in fact, it can include up to one pageful of text. This allows you great flexibility in the amount of information you can place in a header or footer. When you create headers and footers, you can use all of WordPerfect's editing features.

To place a page number in the header or footer, press Ctrl-B to get this symbol: ^B. Every time this symbol is encountered in a header or footer, WordPerfect will increment the page number by one. To start page numbering with a number other than 1, set the New Page Number to the desired first number (see Chapter 12 to review this procedure).

CAUTION: Do not use the Page Number Position feature (through Format, Page, Page Numbering) when you are using headers with page numbers, unless you want two page numbers. One page number will be positioned through that feature and the other page number will be the one contained in the header.

When you place the header or footer in the document, a code appears in your document to mark the start of the header or footer. The header or footer is then automatically repeated on each page or on alternating pages, depending on your selection. Every time you enter a new header or footer code, that header or footer is used until you enter another code. As a result, you can enter a header for front matter, such as:

```
Design Forward
```

Then, after those pages, enter the chapters:

```
Chapter 1 of Design                    page 1-1
```

Finally, enter a header for an appendix:

```
Design Appendix A                      App A-1
```

Because you can change headers and footers as often as you like, all parts of this document can be placed in one document file.

> **TIP:** When printed, headers and footers are placed under or above the top and bottom margins, respectively. They are not considered part of the margin setting.

Creating Headers and Footers

1. To create a header or footer, place the cursor at the top of the first page for the header or footer (before all codes except Paper Size/Type or Top/Bottom Margin codes).

2. Press ⬆Shift-F8 (Format) and select 2 - Page. Or select Page from the Layout menu. The Format: Page menu appears.

3. Select 3 - Headers or 4 - Footers. A line like this appears:

```
1 Header A; 2 Header B:
```

You can place two headers or footers on a page, which is useful if you have entered one header as Header A and then want to add more text to the header. Instead of editing it, you can add Header B. Get in the practice of always choosing Header A or Footer A first. Then, if a Header B or Footer B is necessary, you will know you are adding to the first header or footer on the page.

After selecting Header A or Footer A, you see a prompt line like this:

```
1 Discontinue; 2 Every Page; 3 Odd Pages; 4 Even
Pages; 5 Edit:
```

enabling you to place headers or footers on every page, just on odd numbered pages, or just on even numbered pages. (Editing and Discontinuing are covered later in this chapter.) For example, the text pages of this book have different headers for even and odd numbered pages. You will probably want the header on every page for most documents. Make the appropriate selection and you are taken to the header or footer screen. A sample of this screen is shown in Figure 13.1.

> **CAUTION:** Once you designate that a header or footer appears on every page, odd pages or even pages, that designation cannot be changed. You have to create a new header or footer with the proper designation, copy the contents from the old header or footer to the new, and then delete the old header or footer.

```
File Edit Search Layout Mark Tools Font Graphics Help    (Press F3 for Help)




















Header A: Press Exit when done                          Ln 1" Pos 1"
```

Figure 13.1
Header screen.

The header or footer screen is just like a regular WordPerfect screen. You can use any editing capability when you are entering the header or footer text. Once you've entered the text, press F7 (Exit) or select Exit from the **File** menu. Continue exiting until you return to your document screen. A code like this is placed in your document:

```
[Header A:Every page;Chapter 16[Flsh Rgt]Page
16[-]^B[HRt] By: Jim Wilson... ]
```

Let's take a closer look at the code example just shown. It first identifies whether the text is a header or a footer. In this example, it is a header. Then, the code identifies whether it is Header or Footer A or B. Next, the frequency of the header or footer appears. This header will appear on every page.

The beginning of the text and codes contained in the header are next shown. In the example, Chapter 16 is followed by a flush right code in order to place Page 16-^B at the right margin. The ^B is created by pressing Ctrl-B and it will be replaced with consecutive page numbering when the document is printed. A hard return follows and then the author's name.

The ellipses (...) indicate there is more text in the header than appears in the code. To see the complete header text, you would need to edit the header (which is described later in this chapter).

Adding Graphic Effects with Headers and Footers

Although headers and footers are typically used to provide information, don't forget that they can also be used for a pleasing graphic effect. You can use symbols created through WordPerfect's keyboard options (such as underlines or double underlines). Symbols from among the special characters supported by WordPerfect can be used (see Appendix C). Or, sophisticated graphics (like those covered in Chapter 21) can be placed in headers and footers.

Though creating and inserting graphic effects can take some time, a well designed header or footer can pay off in terms of the professional look of the document and ease of use.

Let's look at an example of a header and footer using the resumé for Barbara J. Wiley. In Figure 13.2, our RESUME.WPP document appears with headers and footers added. Notice in the Reveal Codes screen at the bottom that the code for Header A appears after the margin setting code. The code for Footer A follows the code for Header A, and both are set up to appear on every page.

Figure 13.3 shows the header that was entered. Notice that the header consists of two horizontal lines. Figure 13.4 shows the footer—a single line. The font code for Times Roman is entered (be sure your printer handles the font you choose). The text

Resume of Barbara J. Wiley follows. The flush right code places the current date in the right corner. The printed appearance of the first page of this resumé is shown in Figure 13.5. This header and footer will be printed on each page.

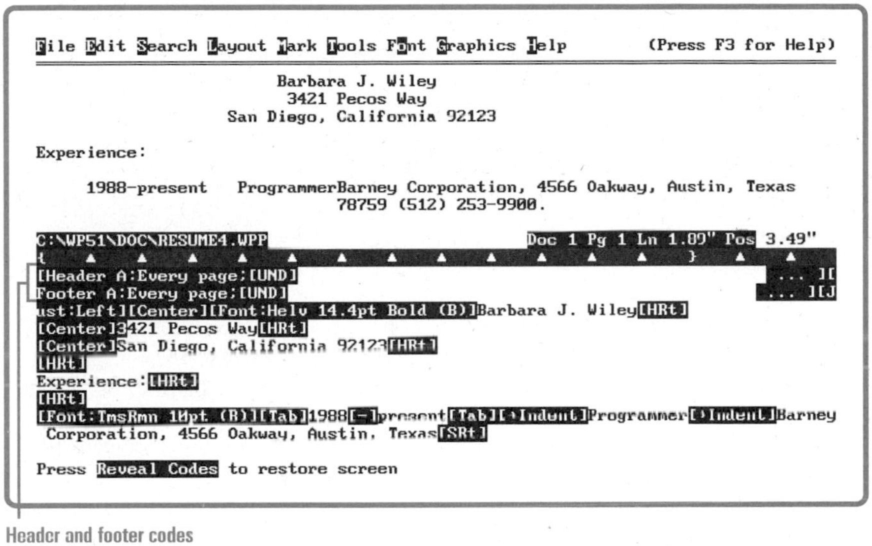

Figure 13.2

RESUME.WPP with header and footer codes.

Header and footer codes

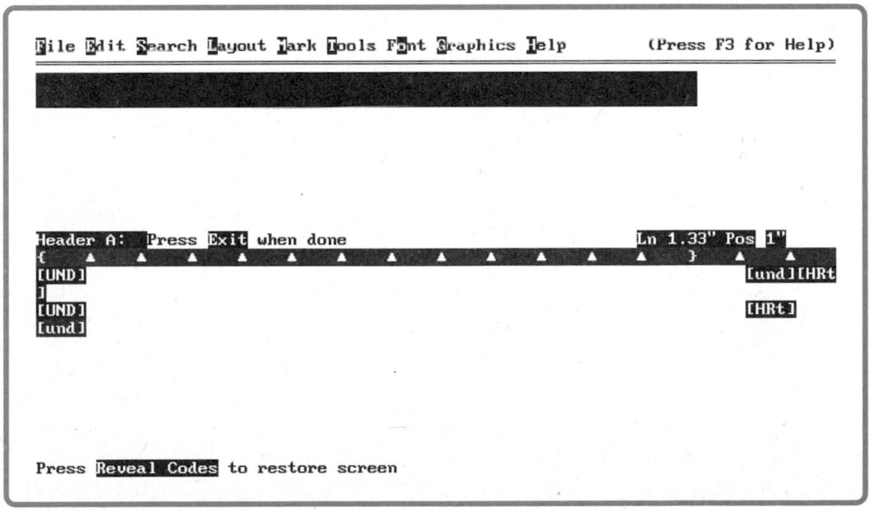

Figure 13.3

The header for the resumé.

Figure 13.4

The footer for the resumé.

```
File Edit Search Layout Mark Tools Font Graphics Help        (Press F3 for Help)

Resume of Barbara J. Wiley                        12/12/91




Footer A:  Press Exit when done                         Ln 1.5" Pos 1"
{       ▲      ▲      ▲      ▲      ▲      ▲      ▲      ▲      ▲   }      ▲
[UND]                                                       [und][HRt
]
[Font:TmsRmn 10pt (B)]Resume of Barbara J. Wiley[Flsh Rgt]12/12/91[HRt]
[HRt]


Press Reveal Codes to restore screen
```

Safety Checks for Headers and Footers

As you get accustomed to using headers and footers, you may find some surprising results when you print a document. For example, it is easy for a beginner to forget to enter enough blank lines in a header for appropriate spacing between the header text and the body of the document. It is also easy to forget that codes (such as margins or special fonts) entered in the document after the header or footer code will not take effect in the header or footer.

Follow these "safety checks" before you print. Check the Reveal Codes screen to make sure there are no unusual formatting codes accidentally placed around the header or footer. Make certain the header or footer code appears at the top of the page. Consider formatting codes. Are the appropriate codes contained in the header or footer? Finally, check the appearance of the header or footer through ⇧Shift-F7 (Print), 6 - View Document. Taking a few moments to double check the setup of your header or footer can save paper and time.

Barbara J. Wiley
3421 Pecos Way
San Diego, California 92123

Experience:

1988-present	Programmer	Barney Corporation, 4566 Oakway, Austin, Texas 78759 (512) 253-9900.
		Cobol and PL1 in an IBM environment.
1985-1988	Operator	Beverly World, PO Box 843, Austin, Texas 78777 (512) 435-9000.

Education:

Bachelor of Science (Computer Science)
University of Iowa, Iowa City, Iowa.
Awarded 1984.

Affiliations:

Data Processing Professional Group, 1985 to present.

Resume of Barbara J. Wiley 12/12/91

Figure 13.5

The printed result of RESUME.WPP with header and footer.

The following Quick Steps summarize how to add a header or footer.

Quick Steps

Adding a Header or Footer

1. Place the cursor in the location you want on the page for the header or footer.

2. Press ⇧Shift-F8 (Format) and select 2 - **P**age, or select **P**age from the **L**ayout menu.

   The Format: Page menu appears.

3. Select 3 - **H**eaders or 4 - **F**ooters.

   A prompt like this appears:
   1 Header **A**; 2 Header **B**:

4. Choose A (unless this is a second header or footer on the page).

   A prompt with new options appears.

5. Select the placement of the header or footer: 2 Every **P**age; 3 **O**dd Pages; or 4 **E**ven Pages.

   You are taken to the header or footer screen.

6. Enter the header or footer text just like any WordPerfect text.

7. When you are done, press F7 (Exit) or select **E**xit from the **F**ile menu until you return to the document screen.

   A code for the header or footer is placed in your document.

Editing Headers and Footers

Editing a header or footer is a lot like adding one. Follow these steps:

1. Place your cursor on or after the code representing the header or footer you want to edit.

2. Press ⇧Shift-F8 (Format) and select 2 - **P**age, or select **P**age from the **L**ayout menu.

3. On the Format: Page menu, select 3 - **H**eaders or 4 - **F**ooters.

4. Select Header or Footer A or B. This line appears:

   ```
   1 Discontinue; 2 Every Page; 3 Odd Pages; 4 Even
   Pages; 5 Edit:
   ```

5. Select 5 Edit. You are taken to the existing header or footer screen.

6. Edit it as you would any WordPerfect document screen.

7. When you are done, press F7 (Exit) or select Exit from the **F**ile menu until you reach the document screen. The new, edited header or footer takes effect.

Discontinuing Headers or Footers

Likewise, discontinuing a header or footer is only slightly different from adding and editing one. To discontinue the use of a header or footer:

1. Put your cursor on or after the header or footer code.

2. Press ⊕Shift-F8 (Format) and select 2 - Page, or select Page from the Layout menu.

3. Select 3 - Headers or 4 - Footers.

4. Select Header or Footer A or B. This line appears:

```
1 Discontinue; 2 Every Page; 3 Odd Pages; 4 Even
Pages; 5 Edit:
```

5. Select 1 Discontinue to discontinue the header or footer. Then press F7 (Exit) or select Exit from the File menu until you reach the document screen.

   A code like this is placed in your text:

```
[Header B:Discontinue]
```

You may also suppress a header or footer for a single page at a time. To do so:

1. Place the cursor at the top of the page where you want to suppress the header or footer.

2. Press ⊕Shift-F8 (Format) and select 2 - Page or select Page from the Layout menu.

3. Select 8 - Suppress (this page only). The Format: Suppress (this page only) menu shown in Figure 13.6 appears.

You may suppress all page numbering (including that in headers and footers) for the page. You can suppress all headers and footers on the page with a single setting. Or, you can choose which headers and footers on the page to suppress.

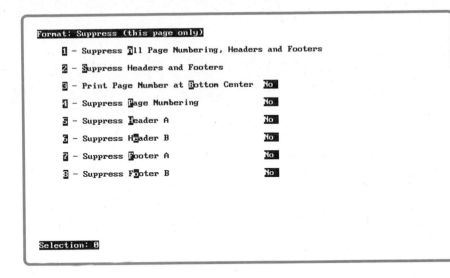

Format: Suppress (this page only)

```
Format: Suppress (this page only)

      1 - Suppress All Page Numbering, Headers and Footers

      2 - Suppress Headers and Footers

      3 - Print Page Number at Bottom Center    No

      4 - Suppress Page Numbering               No

      5 - Suppress Header A                      No

      6 - Suppress Header B                      No

      7 - Suppress Footer A                      No

      8 - Suppress Footer B                      No




Selection: 0
```

Figure 13.6

*The Format:
Suppress (this page
only) screen.*

What's Next?

There are two big challenges with headers and footers. The first is to consider (and troubleshoot, if necessary) how the header or footer will fit in with other formatting in the document to give you the look you want. The second is to use creativity to develop pleasing and useful headers and footers. Both challenges are met with thought and experimentation. When you experiment, do it incrementally. Start with a simple header, make sure it prints as expected, then add fancy formatting or graphics. That way, if you do run into trouble, you will be able to easily pinpoint exactly what to edit.

Checking Spelling

1. Press `Ctrl`-`F2` (Spell) or select Spell from the **T**ools menu.
2. Select the amount of text to check: 1 - **W**ord, 2 - **P**age, or 3 - **D**ocument.

Checking the Spelling in a Block of Text

1. Block the text with `Alt`-`F4` (Block), or select **B**lock from the **E**dit menu.
2. Press `Ctrl`-`F2` (Spell) or select Spell from the **T**ools menu.

Identifying the Supplemental Dictionary

1. Press `Ctrl`-`F2` (Spell) or select Spell from the **T**ools menu.
2. Select 4 - **N**ew Sup. Dictionary.
3. Enter the name of the dictionary.

Counting Words in a Document

1. Press `Ctrl`-`F2` (Spell) or select Spell from the **T**ools menu.
2. Select 6 - **C**ount.

Looking Up a Word

1. Press `Ctrl`-`F2` (Spell) or select Sp**e**ll from the **T**ools menu.
2. Select 5 - **L**ook Up and enter the word pattern.

Using the Thesaurus

1. Place the cursor on the word to look up.
2. Press `Alt`-`F1` (Thesaurus) or select **T**hesaurus from the **T**ools menu.
3. Select an option from the bottom of the screen.

Using the Speller and Thesaurus

Don't reach for that dictionary! Instead, use WordPerfect's Spell Checker. With it, you can check the spelling of a single word, a page, or an entire document. WordPerfect locates its built-in dictionary, looks up any unrecognized word, and suggests alternative spellings—more than any paper dictionary does.

WordPerfect's Spell Checker

Not every word that WordPerfect identifies is misspelled. WordPerfect matches the words in your document with those in its dictionary. If a match is not found, the word is identified. Some words may be properly spelled but not in WordPerfect's dictionary; some professional jargon and proper names, for example, are not included. You can add words to the dictionary, however, to accommodate unusual words you commonly use.

CAUTION: Just because a document spell checks okay does not mean your document is free from typographical or editorial errors. For example, this sentence would pass WordPerfect's spell checker with flying colors: "I never seen him be long to a group before." Though you wouldn't want to be identified as the author of that sentence, the words it comprises are correctly spelled. Remember, even when using spell check, you still need to carefully proofread documents to check sentence structure and appropriate use of words.

In addition to checking the spelling of words, WordPerfect finds double occurrences of a word, which is a common typographical error. In this next sentence the word "the" was entered twice: "Politics is a risky business for the the faint of heart." If you were to spell check a document containing this sentence, WordPerfect would point out the redundant word and enable you to fix the sentence.

WordPerfect also identifies double capital letters at the beginning of a word (JUst) as well as a small letter preceded by a capital letter (jUst).

TIP: Spell check the document when it is complete. Don't spell check a document early in development. You will just have to spell check it again after you edit it.

Correcting a Word, a Page, a Block, or a Document

To begin the spell check, place your cursor on the word, the page, or anywhere in the document you want to check in entirety. If you want to spell check a block of text, use Alt-F4, or select Block from the Edit menu, to block the appropriate text. Blocking text is useful when you've already spell checked a document, then edited a section, and now want to spell check only that edited section.

Press Ctrl-F2 (Spell) or select Spell from the Tools menu. If you are checking a word, page, or document, this menu appears at the bottom of the screen. (If you are checking a block, the spell check begins as soon as you designate the block.)

```
Check: 1 Word; 2 Page; 3 Document; 4 New Sup.
Dictionary; 5 Look Up; 6 Count:
```

To spell check a word, select 1 Word. To check the page your cursor is on, select 2 Page. To check the entire document, select 3 Document.

The spell check begins. WordPerfect skips those words that match words in the dictionary. When WordPerfect hits a word that is not in its dictionary, a screen like that shown in Figure 14.1 appears. The word identified as "misspelled" (persuing) is highlighted. This screen suggests spelling alternatives and prompts you for the possible actions to take.

Figure 14.1

Spelling alternatives.

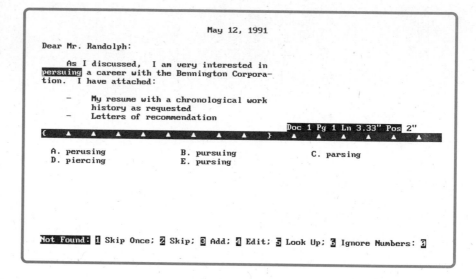

Select from these actions:

Letter (A-X): Enter the letter of the word you want from the suggested word list to substitute for the misspelled word (listed as A through E on Figure 14.1).

1 Skip Once: Skip this first occurrence of this word not identified in the dictionary.

2 Skip: Skip all occurrences of this word not identified in the dictionary.

3 Add: Add the word to the dictionary. Future occurrences of this word will be skipped in this and any other document you spell check.

TIP: Adding your own name to the dictionary is a good use of the Add feature.

4 Edit: If you don't like the alternatives WordPerfect presents, you may edit the word (or any part of the document, for that matter). When you select 4 Edit, your cursor goes to the document. Make your changes and then press F7 (Exit) in order to go back to spell checking.

5 Look Up: Look up a different word. This message appears: Word or Word pattern:. Type in the word (or a close likeness) and press ↵Enter. The word you enter is checked.

6 Ignore Numbers: This option skips numbers. Normally, WordPerfect stops on unusual number combinations.

Figure 14.2 shows an example of a double-word problem. If WordPerfect encounters double words, these options are available:

2 Skip: Skip the double occurrence.

3 Delete 2nd: Delete the second occurrence of the word.

4 Edit: Edit the text.

5 Disable Double Word Checking: Stop finding double words in this spell check session.

Figure 14.3 shows an irregular case (capitalization) problem. When WordPerfect comes across a word with the first two letters or just the second letter capitalized (JUst or jUst), these options come up:

2 Skip: Skip the word.

3 Replace: Change to the same word having only the first letter capitalized.

4 Edit: Edit the text.

5 Disable Case Checking: Stop locating case problems.

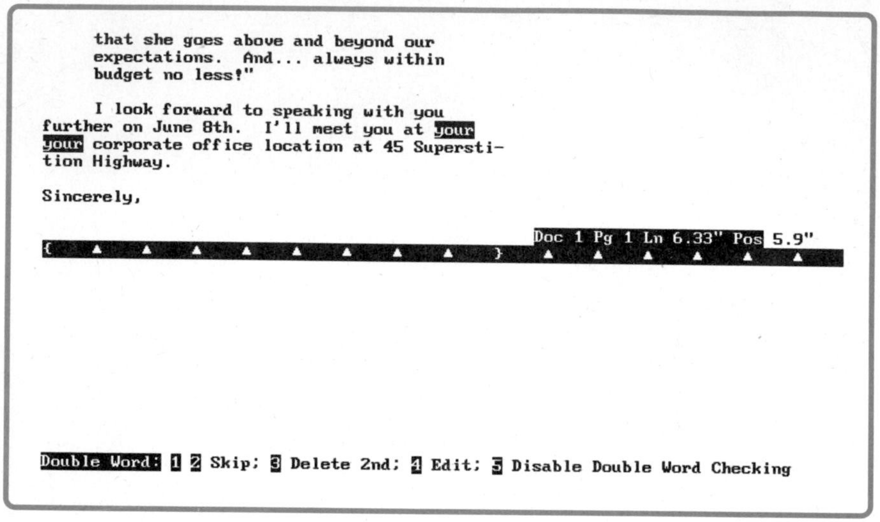

Figure 14.2
Double word.

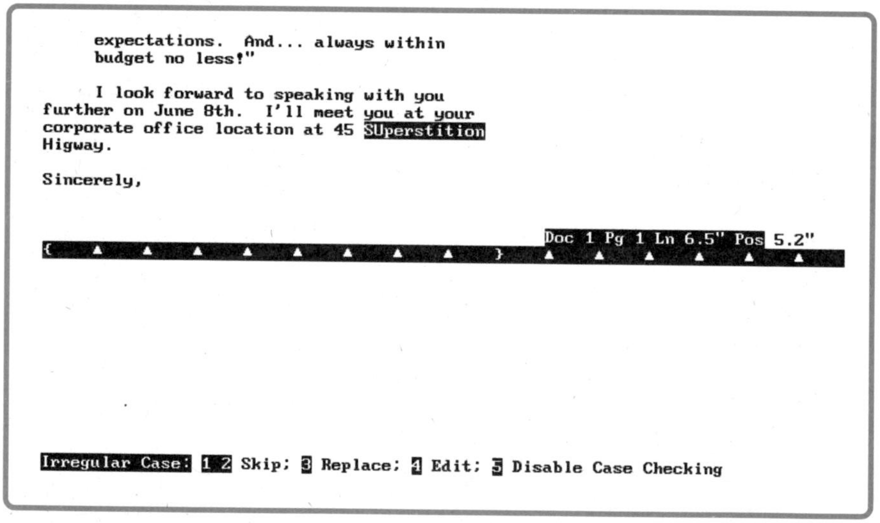

```
     that she goes above and beyond our
     expectations.  And... always within
     budget no less!"

     I look forward to speaking with you
further on June 8th.  I'll meet you at your
your corporate office location at 45 Supersti-
tion Highway.

Sincerely,

                                    Doc 1 Pg 1 Ln 6.33" Pos 5.9"
{    ▲    ▲    ▲    ▲    ▲    ▲    ▲    }    ▲    ▲    ▲    ▲    ▲

Double Word: 1 2 Skip; 3 Delete 2nd; 4 Edit; 5 Disable Double Word Checking
```

Figure 14.3
Capitalization.

```
     expectations.  And... always within
     budget no less!"

     I look forward to speaking with you
further on June 8th.  I'll meet you at your
corporate office location at 45 SUperstition
Higway.

Sincerely,

                                    Doc 1 Pg 1 Ln 6.5" Pos 5.2"
{    ▲    ▲    ▲    ▲    ▲    ▲    ▲    }    ▲    ▲    ▲    ▲    ▲

Irregular Case: 1 2 Skip; 3 Replace; 4 Edit; 5 Disable Case Checking
```

When you have finished spell checking, a message identifies the number of words checked. As the message says, press any key to go back to your document.

```
Word count: 234 Press any key to continue
```

When you check spelling, case is ignored by WordPerfect. When a word is substituted, the case of the original word is followed. Figure 14.4 shows the case of a word identified as misspelled, and Figure 14.5 illustrates the case after the substitution is made. Notice that the case remains the same.

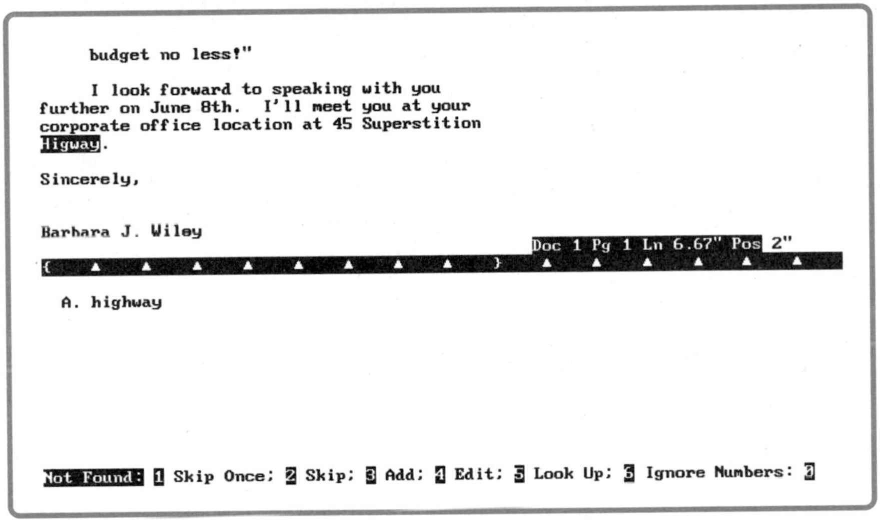

Figure 14.4

Case before substitution.

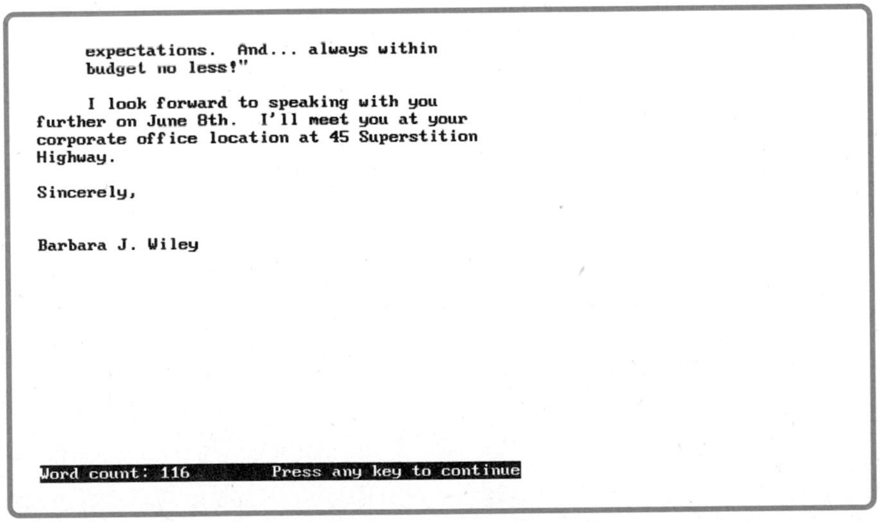

Figure 14.5

Case after substitution.

> **TIP:** If you are using the spell checker and want to quit, just press F1 (Cancel).

The Quick Steps which follow summarize the steps to spell check, to identify words not in the WordPerfect dictionary, and to respond to the words identified.

Spell Checking

1. If you wish, block the text with Alt-F4 or select **Block** from the **E**dit menu. Or place the cursor on the word, page, or document you wish to check.

   The text is highlighted. You have identified the text to spell check.

2. Press Ctrl-F2 (Spell) or select Spell from the **T**ools menu.

   If you are checking a word, page, or document (as opposed to a text block), a menu line appears at the bottom of the screen.

3. Select the amount of text to check: 1 **W**ord; 2 **P**age; or 3 **D**ocument.

   The first unrecognized word is found.

4. Replace the word or make another selection.

   Your selection is carried out. Spell checking continues until the final word is checked. Then, the word count appears and you are instructed to press any key to return to document editing mode.

Creating Supplemental Dictionaries

When you add a word to the dictionary, it is saved in a file named WP{WP}US.SUP. As you add words, you are creating a personal *supplemental dictionary*. To change the name of the supplemental dictionary, press Ctrl-F2 (Spell), or select Spell from the **Tools** menu, and select 4 - New Sup. Dictionary. Then enter a path and name to identify the dictionary you are using with this document. This feature enables you to create more than one supplemental dictionary. You could, for example, have a supplemental dictionary for legal terms, one for medical terms, and so on.

A Quick Way to Make a Supplemental Dictionary

Most people use the Add option during spell checking to add words to the supplemental dictionary. However, there is a quick route to assembling a supplemental dictionary of proper names and professional jargon that you use often.

First, make sure you are using the correct supplemental dictionary. If you want to change to a particular supplemental dictionary, press Ctrl-F2 (Spell), or select Spell from the **Tools** menu, and select 4 - New Sup. Dictionary then enter the name. Next, create a document with names and words you use often that are likely to be omitted from the WordPerfect dictionary. These would be proper names, professional jargon, and so on. Finally, spell check the document and add each word to the supplemental dictionary.

Looking Up a Word

You can look up a word as you work. Press Ctrl-F2 (Spell) or select Spell from the Tools menu. Pick 5 - Look Up, type in the word to look up, and continue as you would with any spell check procedure.

Counting Words

You can count the words in a document with the spell checker as well, regardless of whether you want to spell check the document. This is useful for writers who have a given length in mind. Just press Ctrl-F2 (Spell) or select Spell from the Tools menu. Select 6 Count and the spell checker counts the words in the document and displays the total.

Thesaurus

WordPerfect's Thesaurus feature is simple to use and often overlooked. When you say "that's not quite the word I want," call up WordPerfect's Thesaurus for other suggestions.

As shown in Figure 14.6, the following is a list of the available menu options from within Thesaurus:

1 Replace Word: The message Press letter for word appears. Press the letter before the suggested word and that word replaces the word marked by the cursor in your document.

2 View Doc: Scroll your document. This is especially helpful if you want to see the full context for the word you are replacing. The message `View: Press Exit` when done appears. Just press F7 (Exit) to go back to the Thesaurus screen.

3 Look Up Word: The prompt `Word:` appears. Type in a different word and press ↵Enter. Suggested substitutions for that word appear.

4 Clear Column: As you work in the Thesaurus, you may look up several words and not only fill all the columns but replace earlier columns of words with later columns of words. This option moves back to earlier columns.

Another option, which is not prompted on the screen, is available: press F7 (Exit) to leave. When you do this from the Thesaurus, you are returned to your document without substituting a word.

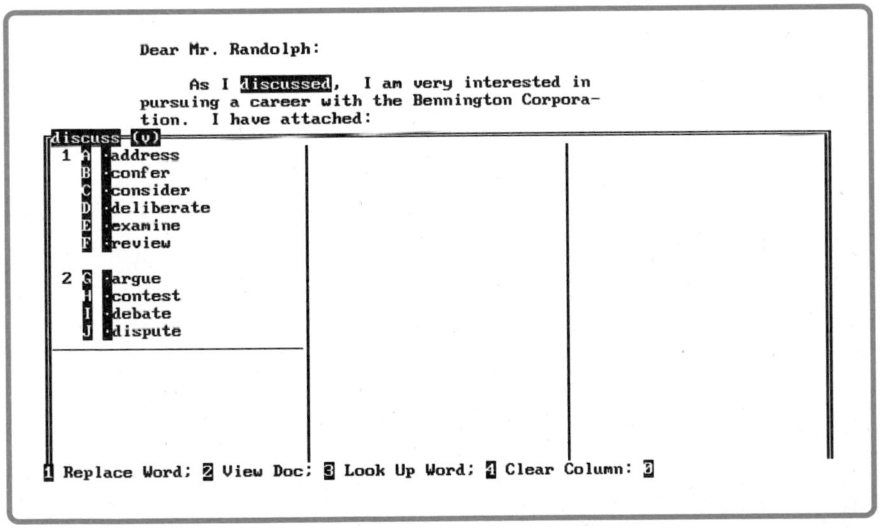

Figure 14.6

Thesaurus in action.

> **TIP:** If you fool the Thesaurus with a word it does not recognize, WordPerfect tells you Word not found and allows you to enter a word.

The following Quick Steps detail how to use the Thesaurus.

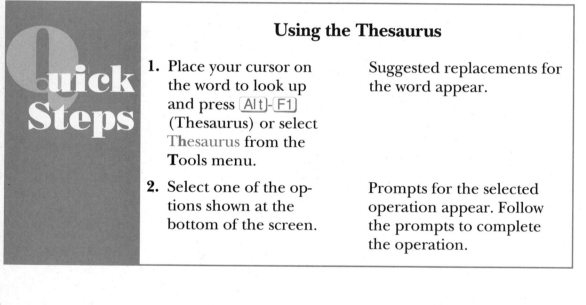

Using the Thesaurus

1. Place your cursor on the word to look up and press Alt - F1 (Thesaurus) or select Thesaurus from the **Tools** menu.

   Suggested replacements for the word appear.

2. Select one of the options shown at the bottom of the screen.

   Prompts for the selected operation appear. Follow the prompts to complete the operation.

What's Next?

If you work extensively with supplemental dictionaries, you will want to go do more reading on the topic. For example, you may password protect a supplemental dictionary, control where the supplemental dictionary is located, and edit the supplemental dictionary file.

For example, the default supplemental dictionary file is named WP{WP}US.SUP and may be edited like any WordPerfect document. Just retrieve the file in WordPerfect, enter one word per line, end each line with a hard return code `[HRt]`, and save the file.

You may also use the Speller Utility that comes with WordPerfect to compress the supplemental dictionary to take up less space. Once a dictionary is compressed, it cannot be edited through WordPerfect. It can only be edited through the Speller Utility. To see all the options on the Speller Utility menu, change to the directory containing the SPELL.EXE file by entering `cd\`*directory name* (the directory name is typically WP51). Then, type `spell`. Learn more about these topics by researching the supplemental dictionary and the Speller Utility.

If you commonly work in a different language, you will be pleased to know that WordPerfect has developed dictionaries in several languages. Contact the WordPerfect Corporation for more information.

Search and Replace Rules

▲ Search and replace occurs from the cursor location forward or backward.

▲ The character to search for must follow conventions such as case.

▲ To extend a search to headers, footers, graphics, etc., press `Home` before beginning the search or replace.

Searching

▲ To search forward, press `F2` (Search), or select Forward from the **S**earch menu, and follow the prompts.

▲ To search backward, press `⇧Shift`-`F2` (Search Backward), or select Backward from the **S**earch menu, and follow the prompts.

Replacing

1. Press `Alt`-`F2` (Replace) or select Replace from the **S**earch menu.

2. Choose Yes to confirm each replacement before it is made.

3. Enter the text to search for, including all codes, and then press `F2` (Search).

4. Enter the replacement text, including all codes, and then press `F2` (Search).

Search for and Replace (Almost) Anything

Searching and replacing characters is a feature that, at first, you may not think you'll use often. Read on. In this chapter, you will learn not only how to use Search and Replace, but you will also gain ideas about how to use Search and Replace creatively to solve problems.

Uses of Search and Replace

You use WordPerfect's Search feature to find text and codes in a document. You type in the text or codes to search for and WordPerfect finds the first occurrence. If you wish, you can then continue searching from that location.

There are more uses for Search than may meet the eye. You can search for text that you believe may be incorrectly entered. Or you can search for a key word in order to find a particular spot in a document. Search is also useful for checking headings, figure numbering, or bulleted text against tables of contents or indexes.

Using Search to Find "Bookmarks"

You may need to go from one part of a lengthy document to another to check information, and then return to your original spot. If so, just place a *bookmark* in your original spot so you can easily find your way back. In fact, bookmarks can be used to identify a part of a document for any purpose (such as adding information or a graphic later).

Here's how to proceed. Place special characters in the text where you want to return. Make sure the characters are unique and won't be used elsewhere in the document. Some users like to use a double asterisk and their name or instructions as a bookmark (such as ***Bill:check this out*). Go wherever you want in your document. Then, when you want to go back to the bookmark, simply search out the unique characters. Remember, you are just searching for a series of characters so you don't have to enter all the text in the bookmark.

Figure 15.1 illustrates one use of Search. Here, the document will be checked for "Bennington" being misspelled as "Benningtin." Notice that the last line of the screen shows the text that is sought. Figure 15.2 shows that the spelling is not found (notice the * Not found * message at the bottom of the screen). You know that in this document, at least, "Bennington" is not "Benningtin."

Figure 15.1
Checking for Benningtin.

```
File Edit Search Layout Mark Tools Font Graphics Help     (Press F3 for Help)
                      Barbara J. Wiley
                      3421 Pecos Way
                   San Diego, California 92123

Mr. David Randolph
Bennington Corporation
45 Superstition Highway
Phoenix, Arizona 85252

                              May 12, 1991

Dear Mr. Randolph:

     As I discussed,  I am very interested in
pursuing a career with the Bennington Corpora-
tion.  I have attached:

     -    My resume with a chronological work
          history as requested
     -    Letters of recommendation
     -    Certificates of achievement

-> Srch: Benningtin
```

Search prompt

Figure 15.2
Benningtin not found.

```
File Edit Search Layout Mark Tools Font Graphics Help     (Press F3 for Help)
                      Barbara J. Wiley
                      3421 Pecos Way
                   San Diego, California 92123

Mr. David Randolph
Bennington Corporation
45 Superstition Highway
Phoenix, Arizona 85252

                              May 12, 1991

Dear Mr. Randolph:

     As I discussed,  I am very interested in
pursuing a career with the Bennington Corpora-
tion.  I have attached:

     -    My resume with a chronological work
          history as requested
     -    Letters of recommendation
     -    Certificates of achievement

* Not found *
```

Prompt

The Replace feature goes a step beyond searching. With it, you identify both the text to find *and* the text to replace the found text. Replace is useful if you realize a proper name is misspelled consistently, a code is incorrectly used, or you wish to change formatting. For example, for a bulleted list, you might have entered text with a small "o" (to signify a bullet) followed by a tab. In order to change that to a dash followed by an indent, you could use Replace.

Let's take a look at an example. In our letter, bullets are created by a dash followed by an indent. We'll replace those with an indent, a small o, and an indent. Figure 15.3 shows at the bottom of the screen the text that will be searched. We include the indent after the dash because we only want to find occurrences where the dash is followed by an indent (not dashes that might be hyphens, for example). Figure 15.4 shows the text we want to use in replacement. Finally, Figure 15.5 illustrates the text after the replacement is made. Notice that the indents and small o's are now included.

Figure 15.3

The dash and indent entered for the search.

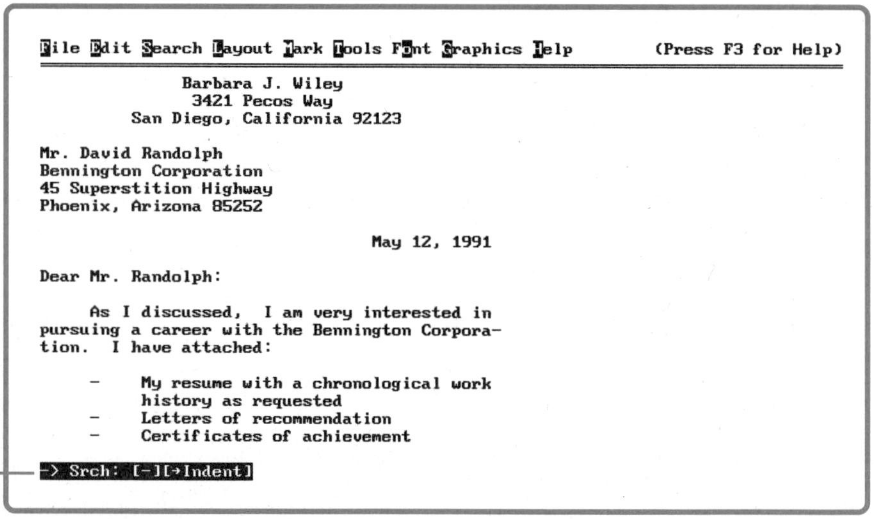

Text to search for

```
 File  Edit  Search  Layout  Mark  Tools  Font  Graphics  Help        (Press F3 for Help)
                          Barbara J. Wiley
                            3421 Pecos Way
                       San Diego, California 92123

              Mr. David Randolph
              Bennington Corporation
              45 Superstition Highway
              Phoenix, Arizona 85252

                                          May 12, 1991

              Dear Mr. Randolph:

                  As I discussed, I am very interested in
              pursuing a career with the Bennington Corpora-
              tion.  I have attached:

                  -      My resume with a chronological work
                         history as requested
                  -      Letters of recommendation
                  -      Certificates of achievement

              -> Srch: [-][→Indent]
```

You can check your replacements as you work or let WordPerfect do it alone. If you check replacements, WordPerfect stops at each occurrence. You then identify whether to replace that occurrence or not.

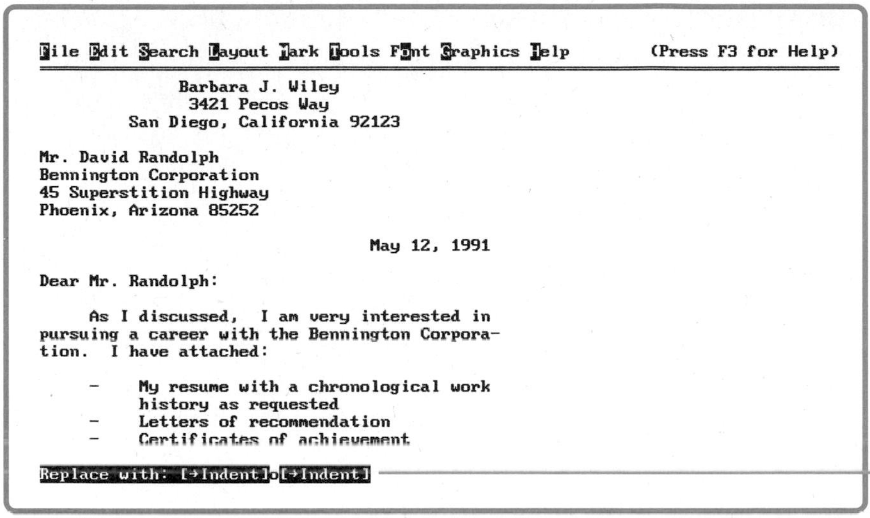

File Edit Search Layout Mark Tools Font Graphics Help   (Press F3 for Help)

```
                    Barbara J. Wiley
                    3421 Pecos Way
               San Diego, California 92123

Mr. David Randolph
Bennington Corporation
45 Superstition Highway
Phoenix, Arizona 85252


                         May 12, 1991

Dear Mr. Randolph:

     As I discussed,  I am very interested in
pursuing a career with the Bennington Corpora-
tion.  I have attached:

     -    My resume with a chronological work
          history as requested
     -    Letters of recommendation
     -    Certificates of achievement
```
Replace with: [→Indent]o[→Indent]

Figure 15.4

The indent, small o, and indent to replace.

— Replacement text

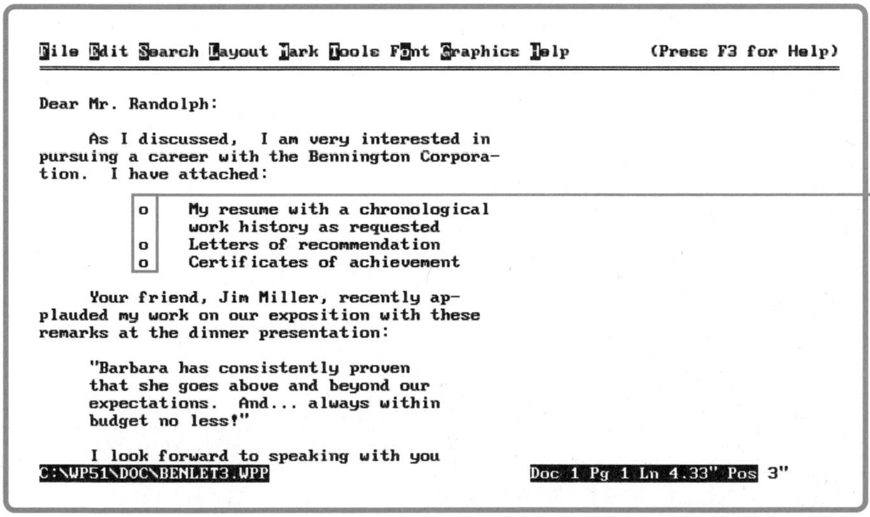

File Edit Search Layout Mark Tools Font Graphics Help   (Press F3 for Help)

```
Dear Mr. Randolph:

     As I discussed,  I am very interested in
pursuing a career with the Bennington Corpora-
tion.  I have attached:

          o │ My resume with a chronological
            │ work history as requested
          o │ Letters of recommendation
          o │ Certificates of achievement

     Your friend, Jim Miller, recently ap-
plauded my work on our exposition with these
remarks at the dinner presentation:

     "Barbara has consistently proven
     that she goes above and beyond our
     expectations.  And... always within
     budget no less!"

     I look forward to speaking with you
```
C:\WP51\DOC\BENLET3.WPP   Doc 1 Pg 1 Ln 4.33" Pos 3"

Figure 15.5

After replacements.

— The dashes have changed to o's.

When you use Search and Replace, the text you enter is important to identifying what will be found and, potentially, replaced. Here are the rules to keep in mind:

▲ When you enter the text to search out in lowercase letters, both lower- and uppercase letters will be found. (For example, entering `merger` will find `merger`, `Merger`, and `MERGER`.) If you enter uppercase letters, however, only matches with the same capital letters will be found. (If you enter `Merger`, `Merger` will be identified but not `merger` or `MERGER`.)

▲ When text is replaced, the case used in the replacement will match the replaced text. (For example, if `Merger` is encountered and you are replacing with the word `consolidation`, the replacement is entered with the first letter capitalized just like the text being replaced.)

▲ Pay attention to your use of spaces and hard returns when you search. If you enter spaces or press `⏎Enter`, the spaces or hard return will be included in the search. If you leave out spaces or hard returns, words that include the searched-out text will be found.

Searching Forward

Searching forward in a document means searching from your cursor location to the end of the document. If you want to search the entire document, press `Home`, `Home`, `Home`, `↑` to move to the top of the document (before any codes).

The following Quick Steps summarize how to search for text forward through a document.

Using Search Forward

1. Position your cursor where the search should begin. Press F2 (Search), or select Forward from the Search menu.

    This prompt appears: ->Srch:.

2. Enter the text and/or codes to search for and press F2 (Search).

    The text is found.

TIP: *Do not* press ↵Enter after entering the search text unless you want to search for hard returns.

Searching Backward

To search from your cursor location back to the beginning of the document is referred to as *searching backward.* To search from the end of the document to the beginning, press Home , Home , Home , ↓ to go to the end of the document (after all codes).

The following Quick Steps detail how to search for text backward through a document.

Using Search Backward

1. Position your cursor where the search should begin. Press ⬆Shift-F2 (Search Backward), or select Backward from the Search menu.

   This prompt appears:
   `<-Srch:.`

2. Enter the text and/or codes to search for and press F2 (Search).

   The text is found.

TIP: When you search, only the document text is searched. To search headers, footers, footnotes, endnotes, or graphic boxes you've created, press Home before using the ⬆Shift-F2 (Search Backward) option. Or select Extended from the Search screen and then Backward.

Replacing Text

Replacing text is like searching except that it goes an extra step. The following Quick Steps detail how to replace text.

Replacing Text

1. Position your cursor where the replace procedure should begin. Press [Alt]-[F2] (Replace), or select Replace from the **S**earch menu.

This prompt appears:
`w/Confirm? No (Yes).`

2. Choose Yes or No depending on whether you want to confirm each replacement.

This prompt appears:
`-> Srch:.`

3. Enter the text and/or codes to search for and press [F2] (Search).

This prompt appears:
`Replace with:.`

4. Enter the text and/or codes to replace and press [F2] (Search).

If you are confirming replacements, you are taken to the first one to respond Yes or No. Otherwise, all replacements are automatically made.

Quick **Steps**

TIP: Only the text in the document is searched and replaced. To search and replace in headers, footers, footnotes, endnotes, or graphic boxes you've created, press [Home] before using the [Alt]-[F2] (Replace) option. Or select Extended from the **S**earch screen and then select Replace.

What's Next?

The information contained in this chapter provides most of what you need to know about searching and replacing. However, there are some special entries you may make when searching or replacing.

These special codes may be used:

Key Press	Appearance	Outcome
Ctrl-V, Ctrl-X	^X	To represent a single character (cannot be the first character in the Search or Replace)
Ctrl-M	[SRt]	To search for a Soft Return Code
Ctrl-V, Ctrl-K	[SPg]	To search for a Soft Page Break

You may also enter WordPerfect codes. To search or replace a code, begin the Search or Replace as usual. Instead of typing in text, you may enter a code or a code and text. Just press the keys you would press for the function. (You must use the key presses rather than the menu choices.) For example, to search for the [BOLD] code, press F6 (Bold). *Do not* type in the actual brackets and capital letters for [BOLD] and don't select Appearance then Bold from the Font menu.

If you are typing in a code for replacement, you can only use the following codes:

Align	End Def
Center	Flush Right
Center Page	Font (Appearance and Size)

Columns On/Off

Hard Hyphen

Hard Page

Hard Space

Hyphen

Hyphenation Cancel

Indent (left; left and right)

Invisible Soft Return

Margin Release

Math On/Off

Graphics Box Number

Math Operators

Merge Codes

Note Number

Outline Off

Soft Hyphen

Tab Align

Tab Types

Widow/Orphan On/Off

Using the List Files Screen

1. Press [F5] (List Files), or select List Files from the
   File menu, select the desired directory, and press
   [⏎Enter].
2. Mark each document desired with an asterisk (for
   multiple documents) or highlight the document
   (for a single document).
3. Select 2 Delete, 3 Move/Rename, or 8 Copy.

Creating a New Directory

1. Press [F5] (List Files), or select List Files from the
   File menu, and make sure the path to the parent
   directory appears.
2. Press [=], enter the name of the new directory, and
   press [⏎Enter].
3. At the Create prompt, choose Yes.

Deleting a Directory

1. Delete or move all files from the subdirectory to be
   deleted.
2. Press [F5] (List Files), or select List Files from the
   File menu, and go to the parent directory.
3. Highlight the subdirectory to delete and select
   2 Delete.
4. Choose Yes at the Delete prompt.

Finding a File

▲ Press [F5] (List Files), or select List Files from the
   File menu, press [⏎Enter], then select N - Name
   Search, and type in the exact characters of the file
   name.
▲ Press [F5] (List Files), or select List Files from
   the **F**ile menu, press [⏎Enter], then 9 - Find to
   search files by name or contents with or without
   conditions.

Controlling Your Documents

When you start using WordPerfect, you'll have only a few documents stored on a disk, so managing them is easy. But as you create more documents, you may forget the names or the contents. Just locating the document you want can be a problem. Therefore, it's important to have a system for managing your documents.

It is important to follow a scheme of naming documents so you can readily identify them. If, after creating several documents, you think of a better naming scheme, go ahead and rename the documents. Another important management task is to delete unnecessary documents so you can more easily locate the useful documents.

TIP: You might find it useful to keep related documents on separate floppy disks or in separate directories on your hard disk. For example, you might have a directory of letters, a directory of documents created for a year end report, and a directory of documents for a system design. Using your directories as "file cabinets" will help you find documents easily. You can also organize files under separate subdirectories under the WP51 directory.

This chapter covers speedy file management methods that can help you get started with this important task.

The List Files Screen

The List Files screen can't be beat when it comes to handling document management activities. Go to this screen by pressing F5 (List Files) or by selecting List Files from the **File** menu. A prompt like this appears:

```
Dir C:\WP51\DOC\*.*
```

Type in the drive, path, and file identifier desired. (For example, you could type `A:*.WPP` to display all the files on the disk in drive A that have the .WPP extension.) Press ↵Enter and you are taken to the List Files screen shown in Figure 16.1.

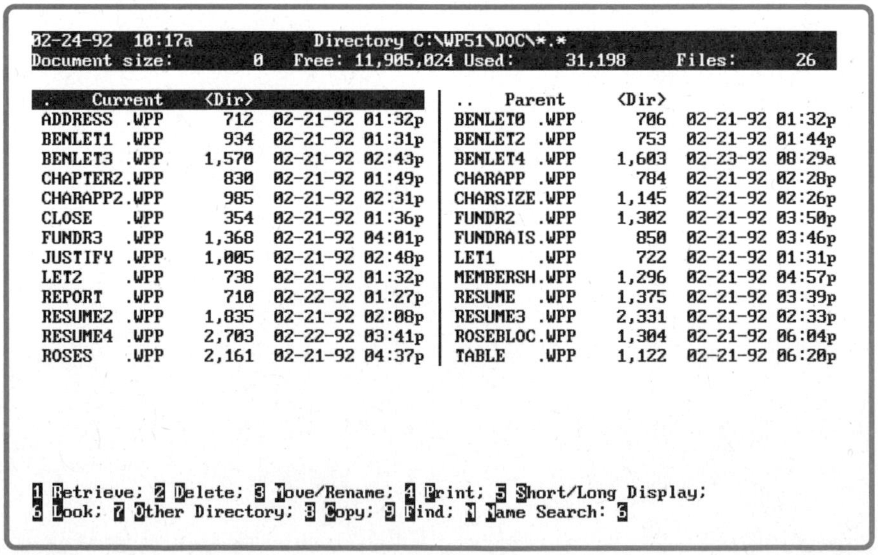

Figure 16.1

List Files screen.

```
 02-24-92  10:17a              Directory C:\WP51\DOC\*.*
 Document size:        0   Free: 11,905,024 Used:     31,198   Files:     26

 .    Current   <Dir>              ..    Parent   <Dir>
 ADDRESS .WPP      712  02-21-92 01:32p  BENLET0 .WPP      706  02-21-92 01:32p
 BENLET1 .WPP      934  02-21-92 01:31p  BENLET2 .WPP      753  02-21-92 01:44p
 BENLET3 .WPP    1,570  02-21-92 02:43p  BENLET4 .WPP    1,603  02-23-92 08:29a
 CHAPTER2.WPP      830  02-21-92 01:49p  CHARAPP .WPP      784  02-21-92 02:28p
 CHARAPP2.WPP      985  02-21-92 02:31p  CHARSIZE.WPP    1,145  02-21-92 02:26p
 CLOSE   .WPP      354  02-21-92 01:36p  FUNDR2  .WPP    1,302  02-21-92 03:50p
 FUNDR3  .WPP    1,368  02-21-92 04:01p  FUNDRAIS.WPP      850  02-21-92 03:46p
 JUSTIFY .WPP    1,005  02-21-92 02:48p  LET1    .WPP      722  02-21-92 01:31p
 LET2    .WPP      738  02-21-92 01:32p  MEMBERSH.WPP    1,296  02-21-92 04:57p
 REPORT  .WPP      710  02-22-92 01:27p  RESUME  .WPP    1,375  02-21-92 03:39p
 RESUME2 .WPP    1,835  02-21-92 02:08p  RESUME3 .WPP    2,331  02-21-92 02:33p
 RESUME4 .WPP    2,703  02-22-92 03:41p  ROSEBLOC.WPP    1,304  02-21-92 06:04p
 ROSES   .WPP    2,161  02-21-92 04:37p  TABLE   .WPP    1,122  02-21-92 06:20p




 1 Retrieve; 2 Delete; 3 Move/Rename; 4 Print; 5 Short/Long Display;
 6 Look; 7 Other Directory; 8 Copy; 9 Find; N Name Search: 6
```

> **TIP:** If you ever type in a path that is not recognized (a message may appear saying the path does not exist), carefully check the punctuation you've used in the path as well as the validity of the directories and file names used. Usually, some typographical error has occurred.

What the List Files Screen Tells You

Starting at the top of the List Files screen, you are given this information:

▲ *Date and time:* If your computer's internal clock is set correctly, you will see the current date and time at the top of the screen. Each document you create or edit will be time-and-date stamped. That way, if you have more than one version of a document, you will be able to tell which is the most recent version.

> **NOTE:** Most computers have a clock that automatically enters the date and time for you. If yours does not, use the operating system date and time commands before using WordPerfect (see your operating system manual for information about these commands.)

▲ *Directory:* This shows the directory for which documents are displayed.

▲ *Document size:* This identifies the size of the document currently highlighted.

▲ *Free and Used:* This shows the amount of unused space (in bytes) on your disk, as well as the amount used in this directory.

> **NOTE:** A byte is approximately equal to one character.

> **CAUTION:** Never allow the free space to dwindle to less than 10% of the total space. If space becomes short, move documents to another disk or delete unneeded documents.

▲ *Files:* This identifies the number of documents displayed.

▲ *The directories* (such as <CURRENT>)*:* The directory you are using appears along with other available directories. To display the files for another directory, highlight it and press ⏎Enter.

▲ *The files:* This listing shows each file name, extension, and size (in bytes), as well as the date and time last saved.

The options you have for manipulating files appear on the bottom two lines of the screen. We covered options 1 **R**etrieve, 6 **L**ook, and 7 **O**ther Directory in Chapter 5. We'll cover the remaining options in this chapter.

Using the List Files Screen

The List Files screen allows you to work with one document or several. If you are working with one document, just highlight it and perform the desired operation.

To work with multiple documents, highlight one of the documents and press the asterisk key (using ⇧Shift-* on most keyboards). An asterisk appears before the file name. Continue to mark as many files as you want. Figure 16.2 shows three files marked with asterisks: BENLET.WPP, BENLET1.WPP, and BENLET2.WPP. The operation you perform will affect all files marked with an asterisk. To eliminate the asterisk from a file name, highlight the document name and press ⇧Shift-* again.

If the number of documents on the List Files screen fills more than one screen, press PgUp or PgDn to move from screen to screen. To leave the List Files screen, press F1 (Cancel) or F7 (Exit).

```
02-24-92  10:20a           Directory C:\WP51\DOC\*.*
Document size:       0   Free: 11,866,112  Used:      2,393      Marked:       3

.    Current   <Dir>                      ..    Parent    <Dir>
ADDRESS .WPP     712  02-21-92 01:32p    *BENLET  .WPP     706  02-21-92 01:32p
BENLET0 .WPP     706  02-21-92 01:32p    *BENLET1 .WPP     934  02-21-92 01:31p
*BENLET2 .WPP    753  02-21-92 01:44p     BENLET3 .WPP   1,570  02-21-92 02:43p
BENLET4 .WPP   1,603  02-23-92 08:29a     CHAPTER2.WPP     830  02-21-92 01:49p
CHARAPP .WPP     784  02-21-92 02:28p     CHARAPP2.WPP     985  02-21-92 02:31p
CHARSIZE.WPP   1,145  02-21-92 02:26p     CLOSE   .WPP     354  02-21-92 01:36p
FUNDR2  .WPP   1,302  02-21-92 03:50p     FUNDR3  .WPP   1,368  02-21-92 04:01p
FUNDRAIS.WPP     850  02-21 92 03:46p     JUSTIFY .WPP   1,005  02-21-92 02:48p
LET1    .WPP     722  02-21-92 01:31p     LET2    .WPP     738  02-21-92 01:32p
MEMBERSH.WPP   1,296  02-21-92 04:57p     REPORT  .WPP     710  02-22-92 01:27p
RESUME  .WPP   1,375  02-21-92 03:39p     RESUME2 .WPP   1,835  02-21-92 02:08p
RESUME3 .WPP   2,331  02-21-92 02:33p     RESUME4 .WPP   2,703  02-22-92 03:41p
ROSEBLOC.WPP   1,304  02-21-92 06:04p     ROSES   .WPP   2,161  02-21-92 04:37p
TABLE   .WPP   1,122  02-21-92 06:20p


1 Retrieve; 2 Delete; 3 Move/Rename; 4 Print; 5 Short/Long Display;
6 Look; 7 Other Directory; 8 Copy; 9 Find; N Name Search: 5
```

Figure 16.2

Three documents marked for work.

— Documents marked with asterisks

Copying Documents

You will want to copy documents to create backups, in case a document becomes damaged or lost. One way to copy a document is to save it under another name or to save it to another disk. Another way to copy documents is to use the List Files screen. The benefits of this procedure are that you can copy a file on disk (instead of having to retrieve it to your screen) and you can copy more than one document in a single operation.

The following Quick Steps identify how to copy one or multiple document files.

Copying One or More Document Files

1. Press `F5` (List Files), or select List Files from the **F**ile menu.

   The current directory is displayed.

2. Change the drive, path, and file information, if desired, and press `↵Enter`.

   The List Files screen appears.

3. If you want to copy more than one file, press `⇧Shift`-`*` to mark each file name with an asterisk. To copy just one file, highlight it. Select 8 - **C**opy.

   Copy messages appear.

4. Enter the drive and path of the disk to which to copy the file, and press `↵Enter`.

   If the files don't already exist, they are copied. A replace message appears for your response if the file(s) are already on the disk (for example: `Replace A:\BENLET.WPP No (Yes)`).

5. If prompted, select Yes to copy over the file.

6. Unmark the file if necessary by pressing `⇧Shift`-`*`.

Estimating How Much You Can Copy to a Diskette

As mentioned, the List Files copy command is often used to create diskette backups of documents. But, how many documents can you copy to a diskette before you get a `disk full` message? With some calculations (involving rounding off numbers), you can easily tell.

First, to see how much space is free on the diskette, use `F5` (List Files), or select List Files from the File menu, and enter the drive of the diskette you will copy to. Jot down this number. Next, estimate the space that the documents you copy will consume (add the file sizes together). Compare this to the free space on the diskette and you'll know how close you're coming to filling the diskette.

Deleting Files

Deleting a document is useful when you are sure you will not want that version of the document again. For example, let's say you've created several different versions of BENLET.WPP for internal review. When one version is selected, you may want to delete the other versions. This not only saves space but saves possible future confusion about which version was used.

> **CAUTION:** When deleting, always proceed carefully. Check and double check the file you want to delete to make sure you will never again want the document. Once a document is deleted, it cannot be recovered through WordPerfect.

The following Quick Steps explain how to delete one or more files.

Deleting One or More Document Files

1. Press F5 (List Files) or select List Files from the File menu.

   The current directory is displayed.

2. Change the drive, path, and file information, if desired, and press ⏎Enter.

   The List Files screen appears.

3. To delete multiple files, mark each with an asterisk by pressing ⇧Shift-*. To delete one file, just highlight it.

4. Select 2 Delete.

   Respond to the delete prompts as they appear.

At Step 4, if you are deleting one file, a prompt like the following appears:

```
Delete C:\WP51\DOC\BENLET.WPP? No (Yes)
```

Make sure this is the document you want to delete. Select Yes to delete the file.

If you are deleting multiple files, each marked with an asterisk, a message like this appears:

```
Delete marked files? No (Yes)
```

This is your chance to verify that you really *do* want to delete all the files marked with an asterisk. Select Yes again to delete these files.

Moving or Renaming Documents

You can move or rename documents through the List Files screen. As you'll see, though these features are handled through the same selection, the results are very different.

When you rename a file, the existing name is replaced with the new name you suggest. Renaming a file is useful when you determine a better way to organize existing files. For example, you may have created these three versions of a document:

```
DEARPT.WPP
DREPORT.WPP
DRT.WPP
```

You could rename these files to suggest the order in which they were created:

```
DERPT1.WPP
DERPT2.WPP
DERPT3.WPP
```

When you move a file, it is removed from the current disk location and placed at a new location you have indicated. For example, you might move a file from one disk to another when the original disk is getting full or if you want to store the file on a disk you use less often.

CAUTION: Don't confuse moving a file with copying a file. When you move, the original location of the file is lost. When you copy, the original location of the file is preserved and a duplicate of the file is made.

TIP: You can only rename files one at a time. You can only move files by marking them with an asterisk.

The following Quick Steps detail how to move or change the names of documents.

Moving or Renaming Documents

1. Press F5 (List Files) or select List Files from the File menu.

   The drive, path, and file information appears.

2. Enter new drive, path, and file information, if necessary. Press ↵Enter.

   The List Files screen appears.

3. Highlight the single file to rename. Or mark the file(s) to move with an asterisk(s) by pressing ⇧Shift-* for each. Select 3 Move/Rename.

   The prompts to rename or move the file(s) appear.

4. Follow the prompts.

   The highlighted file is renamed or the files marked with asterisks are moved.

Creating Directories and Subdirectories

You may use the List Files screen to create a new directory or subdirectory to store the files you have saved (or are about to save).

Press F5 (List Files). The prompt Dir appears followed by the current path. The directory path shown must be the "parent" under which your newly created subdirectory will be placed. If it is not the parent, enter the appropriate path to the parent directory. Figure 16.3 illustrates the following path under which our subdirectory will be created:

```
Dir C:\WP51\*.*
```

Figure 16.3

Path under which subdirectory will be created.

File Edit Search Layout Mark Tools Font Graphics Help   (Press F3 for Help)

Path for subdirectory ——— Dir C:\WP51*.*   (Type = to change default Dir)

At the prompt, enter an equals sign (=) and the name of the new subdirectory. As shown in Figure 16.4 the subdirectory will be named WORK.

After pressing ↵Enter, a prompt like the following appears:

```
Create C:\WP51\WORK? No (Yes)
```

Choose Yes. The subdirectory is created. Look at the List Files screen to confirm the creation of the subdirectory. You can now save documents to this subdirectory.

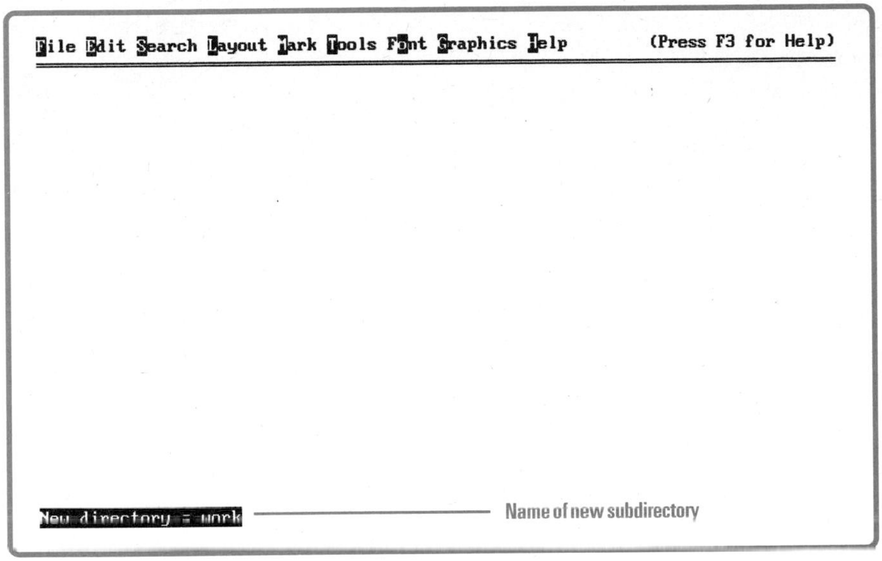

```
 File  Edit  Search  Layout  Mark  Tools  Font  Graphics  Help       (Press F3 for Help)
```

```
New directory = work  ————————————  Name of new subdirectory
```

Figure 16.4

Subdirectory to be named WORK.

To delete a subdirectory, make sure all the files are deleted from the subdirectory. Then, press F5 (List Files), or select List Files from the **File** menu, and go to the parent directory of the subdirectory to delete. Highlight the subdirectory to delete and select 2 Delete. A prompt like the following appears:

```
Delete C:\WP51\WORK? No (Yes)
```

Choose Yes and the subdirectory is deleted.

Finding a File

The ability to find a file by file name or a word in a file is invaluable.

The easiest way to find a file by file name is to press F5 (List Files), or select List Files from the **File** menu, and select

N - Name Search. Begin typing in the letters of the file name and your highlight goes to the file.

This approach is only useful if you know the name of the file. What if you don't know the full name of the file or only know the file contents you seek? You can use the 9 Find option. Find allows you to search by precise file name or word(s), or use an asterisk to stand in place of one or more letters of which you are unsure.

For example, suppose as a convention you use "let" in the file name of letters and .WPP as the extension on all WordPerfect document files. You could search for all letters by searching for this text:

```
*LET.WPP
```

Names like those that follow appear for you to narrow down your selection:

```
BENLET.WPP
JIMLET.WPP
STARLET.WPP
MALLET.WPP
```

Use 9 Find to find a file by full or partial file name or to create a list of files which contains a word or phrase. To proceed, press F5 (List Files), or select List Files from the File menu, and display the files in the directory you want to search. If you want to search only certain files, identify each with an asterisk. Otherwise, all files in the directory will be searched.

Select 9 Find to display the Find menu. Choose among the following options:

1 Name: To search for a file by name.

2 Doc Summary: To search only text on the Document Summaries.

3 First Pg: To search only the first page of the document or the first 4000 characters.

4 Entire Doc: To search the entire contents of each document.

5 Conditions: To add conditions to limit the search. Figure 16.5 shows the Find: Conditions screen that you work from.

6 Undo: To return the file list to its state before the find was performed.

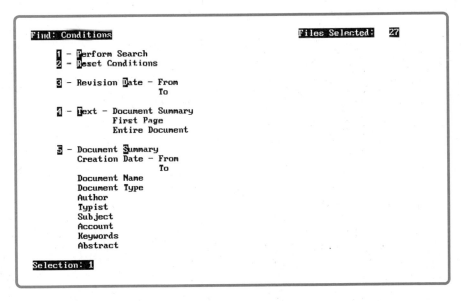

Figure 16.5

Find: Conditions screen used to limit the search performed on documents.

What's Next?

This chapter gives you only a taste of the power of WordPerfect to search through documents. For example, if you use Find to search by name, Document Summary, first page, or entire document, you can use a question mark in the characters to represent a single letter or an asterisk (*) to represent multiple characters which you do not know. Also, you can use punctuation to represent "and" and "or." Look at the following examples to see how this is done:

dog;cat	All files containing the words *dog* and *cat* are found
dog,cat	All files containing the words *dog* or *cat* are found
dog,cat;mouse	All files containing the words *dog* or *cat* and also *mouse* are found
-James	All files that do not contain the word *James* are found
"-James"	All files that contain *-James* are found

If you want to narrow your search to particular dates or text areas, select 5 Conditions from the Find menu. For example, the Find: Conditions screen allows you to enter a Revision Date, From and To range, Text to search on the Document Summary screen, First Page of the document, or Entire Document. Also, the screen allows you to enter text to find in specific fields of the Document Summary screen.

You may also want to learn more about Document Summaries. To create a Document Summary, press ⇧Shift-F8 (Format), 3 Document or select Document from the Layout menu. Select 5 Summary. The Document Summary screen is displayed. Enter any text you may later want to find. Press F7 (Exit) when you are done.

Using a Window

1. Press Ctrl-F3 (Screen) and select 1 - Window, or select Window from the **E**dit menu.

2. Enter the lines or move the arrow keys to identify the size.

3. To close a window, go to the window to keep, then follow the previous Steps 1 and 2. Enter **24** as the lines for the window.

Switching Between Windows

▲ Press Shift-F3 (Switch) or select Switch Document from the **E**dit menu.

Working with Two Documents

Using two documents at one time has a variety of benefits. You can have another document readily available for reference or notes. Or, you copy or move text between documents. This chapter addresses using two documents within WordPerfect.

Why Use Two Documents?

Let's look at an example. Suppose you want to copy the return address from a letter to a new document to start a new letter. Figure 17.1 shows both documents on the screen at once. The screen is split to allow display of each document. The top of the screen contains the existing letter. The bottom of the screen is a "blank" document ready to be copied to. Figure 17.2 illustrates the result after the copy. The return address has been copied to the new document.

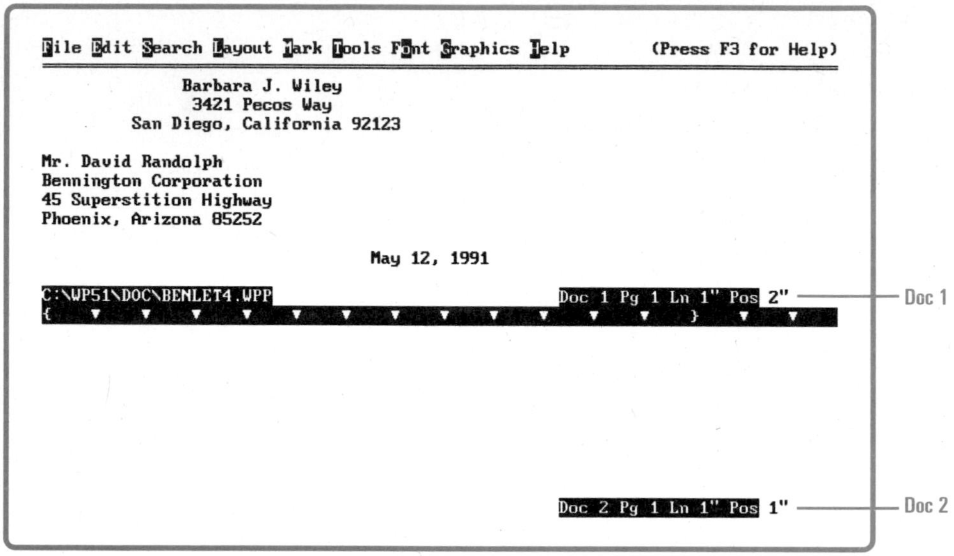

Figure 17.1

Existing letter and blank document before the copy.

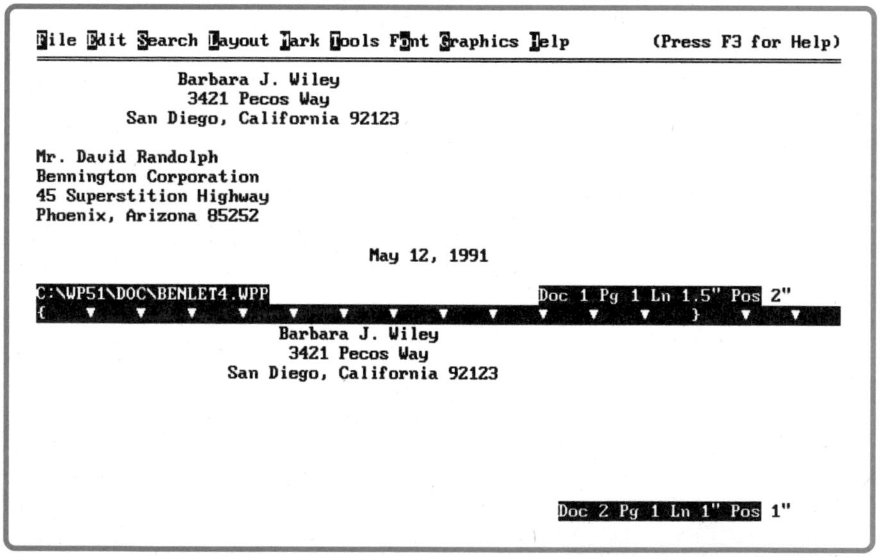

```
File Edit Search Layout Mark Tools Font Graphics Help        (Press F3 for Help)
                    Barbara J. Wiley
                    3421 Pecos Way
                San Diego, California 92123

Mr. David Randolph
Bennington Corporation
45 Superstition Highway
Phoenix, Arizona 85252

                          May 12, 1991

C:\WP51\DOC\BENLET4.WPP                    Doc 1 Pg 1 Ln 1" Pos 2"        ── Doc 1
{    ▼    ▼    ▼    ▼    ▼    ▼    ▼    ▼    ▼    ▼    }    ▼    ▼




                                           Doc 2 Pg 1 Ln 1" Pos 1"        ── Doc 2
```

Figure 17.2

Existing letter and new document after the copy.

```
File Edit Search Layout Mark Tools Font Graphics Help        (Press F3 for Help)
                    Barbara J. Wiley
                    3421 Pecos Way
                San Diego, California 92123

Mr. David Randolph
Bennington Corporation
45 Superstition Highway
Phoenix, Arizona 85252

                          May 12, 1991

C:\WP51\DOC\BENLET4.WPP              Doc 1 Pg 1 Ln 1.5" Pos 2"
{    ▼    ▼    ▼    ▼    ▼    ▼    ▼    ▼    ▼    ▼    }    ▼
                    Barbara J. Wiley
                    3421 Pecos Way
                San Diego, California 92123




                                           Doc 2 Pg 1 Ln 1" Pos 1"
```

You can also move text in the same way. For example, say you decide to move the resumé information from the document called BENLET.WPP into a document you'll call

BENLET-2.WPP. Figure 17.3 shows the beginning of the resumé information in BENLET.WPP (in document 1). Notice that the lower right corner of the status line indicates `Doc 1`. After blocking the appropriate text and then moving it, the text is placed in another full-screen document—document 2. Notice that in Figure 17.4 `Doc 2` appears in the lower right corner. The document has been saved as BENLET-2.WPP.

```
 File Edit Search Layout Mark Tools Font Graphics Help        (Press F3 for Help)
 ─────────────────────────────────────────────────────────────────────────────
                       Barbara J. Wiley
                       3421 Pecos Way
                  San Diego, California 92123

 Mr. David Randolph
 Bennington Corporation
 45 Superstition Highway
 Phoenix, Arizona 85252

                             May 12, 1991

 Dear Mr. Randolph:

      As I discussed,  I am very interested in
 pursuing a career with the Bennington Corpora-
 tion.  I have attached:

           o    My resume with a chronological
                work history as requested
           o    Letters of recommendation
           o    Certificates of achievement

 C:\WP51\DOC\BENLET.WPP                        Doc 1 Pg 1 Ln 1" Pos 2"
```
───── Doc 1

Figure 17.3

BENLET.WPP contents in document 1.

There are two ways to display more than one document on the screen. The first is by using *windows.* Just like a window on a wall splits the wall into segments, windows on a computer screen create small screen portions. You can view documents through these windows. The second way to view two documents at once is through WordPerfect's *Switch* feature. With it, you switch from one full-screen display to another with a special keypress.

Whether you use windows or switch between full-screen displays is really a matter of preference. Use which one is more comfortable for you. You have full WordPerfect editing capabilities with either option.

Figure 17.4

BENLET-2.WPP created by moving BENLET.WPP contents to document 2.

```
File Edit Search Layout Mark Tools Font Graphics Help     (Press F3 for Help)
                        Barbara J. Wiley
                         3421 Pecos Way
                    San Diego, California 92123

Mr. David Randolph
Bennington Corporation
45 Superstition Highway
Phoenix, Arizona 85252

                                                    June 20, 1991

Dear Mr. Randolph:

     I enjoyed speaking with you again last week about how I might
contribute to your organization.  Toward that end, I have included
a schedule of work for the first phase of the project.  This is
what I envision we could accomplish in the first three months.  It
is aggressive but very achievable with the staffing described.

     I'm interested in hearing your reactions to the schedule of
work.  I'll contact you in about a week.

C:\WP51\DOC\BENLET-2.WPP                      Doc 2 Pg 1 Ln 1" Pos 5.05"
```
— Doc 2

TIP: WordPerfect only allows you to use two documents at once. You cannot open more than two windows or switch to a third document.

Windows

To split your screen into two windows, press Ctrl-F3 (Screen), then select 1 - Window. Or select Window from the Edit menu. This prompt appears:

    Number of lines in this window:

Type in a number representing the number of lines desired for the current window. (Entering 11 or 12 will cause the split to be roughly at the halfway point.) Instead of typing the number, you can use the arrow keys to position the bar that separates the windows. After entering a number or positioning the bar, press ⏎Enter. Figure 17.5 illustrates the bar at the starting position. Figure 17.6 shows the result of moving the bar to position 14.

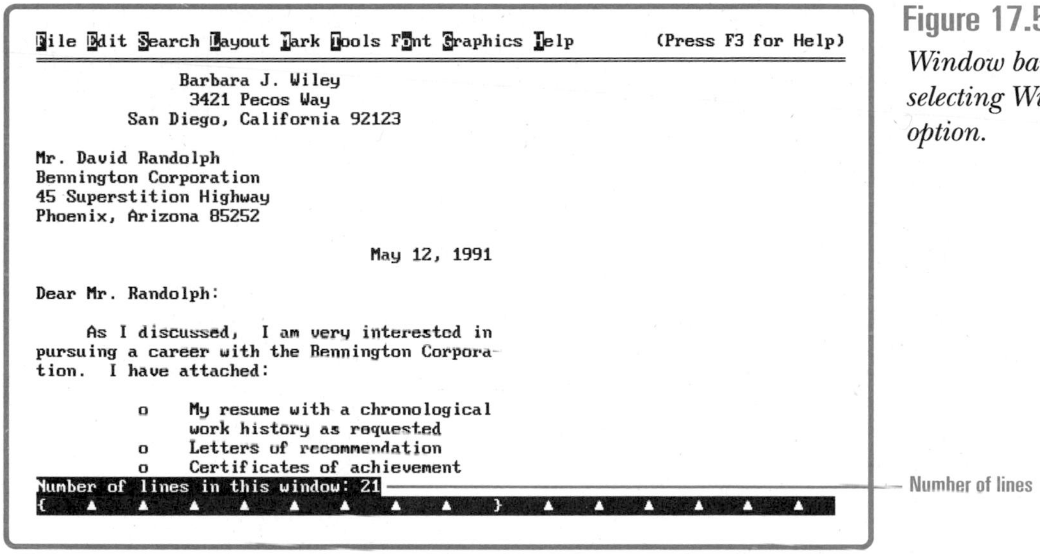

Figure 17.5

Window bar after selecting Window option.

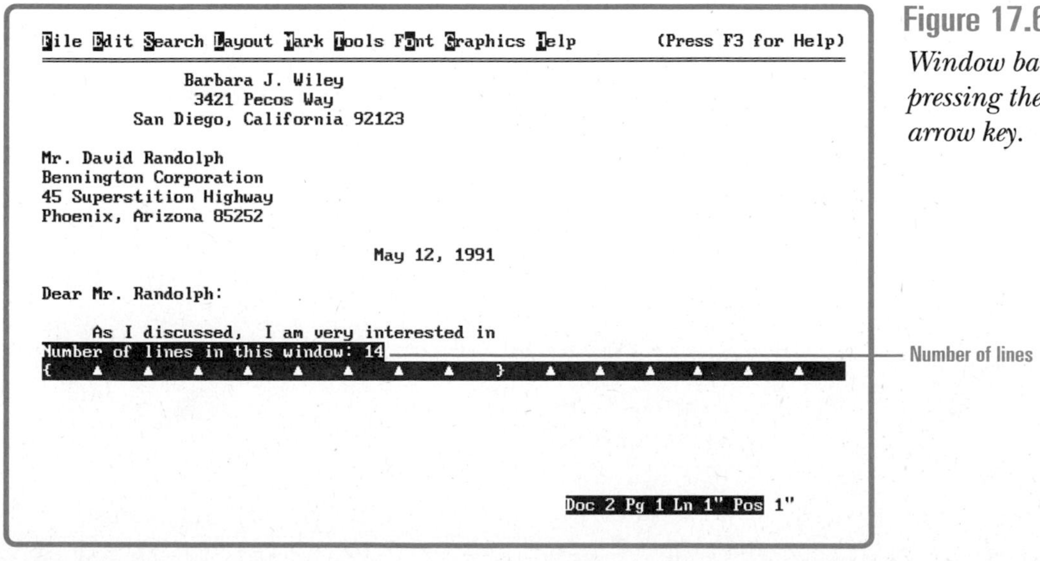

Figure 17.6

Window bar after pressing the down arrow key.

After you have identified the number of lines to be in the window, the screen splits. As shown in the earlier figures, the status-line information for each window appears at the bottom of the first window. The arrows, left bracket, and right bracket in the bar illustrate the active window's tab settings, left margin, and right margin, respectively. To move from one window to the other, press ⬆Shift-F3 (Switch), or select Switch Document from the **E**dit menu.

To return to just one window, press ⬆Shift-F3 (Switch) or select Switch Document from the **E**dit menu to switch to the window you want to keep. Press Ctrl-F3 (Screen) then 1 Window or select Window from the **E**dit menu. Enter 24 for the number of lines (or enter the number of lines your screen displays). Or, use the arrow keys to place the bar at the bottom of the screen. If there is still text in the second document, you may switch to that document (document 2). Also, when you leave WordPerfect, you will be given a chance to save the second document.

The Quick Steps which follow summarize how to open, switch to, and close a window.

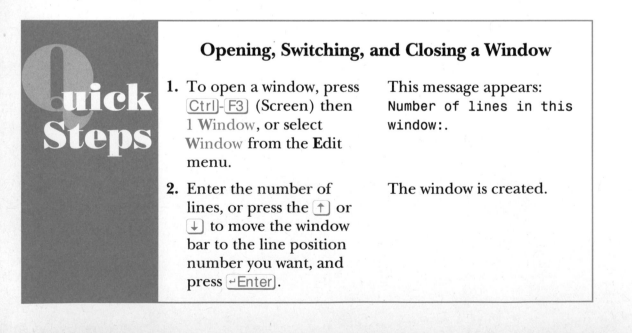

Opening, Switching, and Closing a Window

1. To open a window, press Ctrl-F3 (Screen) then 1 Window, or select Window from the **E**dit menu.

   This message appears:
   Number of lines in this window:.

2. Enter the number of lines, or press the ↑ or ↓ to move the window bar to the line position number you want, and press ⏎Enter.

   The window is created.

3. To move between windows, press ⇧Shift-F3 (Switch) or select Switch Document from the Edit menu.

The cursor moves to the other window. The status bar reflects information for that window.

4. To close a window, place the cursor in the window to keep and follow Steps 1 and 2, entering 24 as the number of lines.

If there is text in the window that disappeared from the screen, it is available by switching to document 2 using Switch (see Step 3).

CAUTION: If you retrieve the same document into both windows and then edit one of the windows, the edits are not automatically applied to the document in the second window. If you make edits that you want to keep, make sure they are made in one document and then that you have that document saved under the appropriate name. The best policy when working with the same document in both windows is to be careful about which document is the "latest and greatest" to save.

The Switch Option

Instead of displaying two windows on the screen at once, you can switch between full-screen displays of two documents. To switch to a new display, press ⇧Shift-F3 (Switch) or select Switch Document from the Edit menu. You are taken to the other full-screen display. Doc 1 or Doc 2 appears in the bottom right corner of the screen, enabling you to distinguish between the two documents. Continue to use ⇧Shift-F3 to move back and forth between the full-screen displays.

To copy or move between displays, identify the text to copy or move, switch to the new display, and complete the copy or move.

To complete activity on one document, use F7 (Exit) or select Exit from the File menu. Complete the Save option for that document.

> **CAUTION:** Remember, if you load the same document in both document displays, however, edits to one display will not "take" in the document in the other display. Make sure when you save that you save the correct document.

Copying and Moving Step by Step

Whether you are working with two full-screen displays or one screen split into two windows, the method to copy or move text is the same. Create the two displays. Then, block the text to copy or move and use Ctrl-F4 (Move) to identify whether to copy or move the block. Once identified, your screen says: Move cursor; press Enter to retrieve. This is when you switch to the other document with ⇧Shift-F3 (Switch). You are now free to press ↵Enter to complete the copy or move. It's just that simple.

What's Next?

If you don't want to use the memory for document 2 that WordPerfect reserves, you can use a special startup option: /n2.

To use this startup option, you will type wp /n2 when you start WordPerfect from DOS. Two other startup options are described next:

wp/*filename* To enter WordPerfect and immediately retrieve the file named (include the path if necessary).

wp/m-*macroname* To enter WordPerfect and immediately execute the macro named (include the path if necessary). See Chapter 18 for more information on macros.

See your *WordPerfect Reference* or an advanced book for more information about these and other startup options.

In This Chapter

Defining a Macro

1. Press Ctrl-F10 (Macro Define) or select Macro and then Define from the Tools menu.
2. Name the macro with eight or fewer letters or press Alt and then a letter that stands for your macro name. Type in a description and press ↵Enter.
3. Enter the keystrokes for the macro.
4. When done, press Ctrl-F10 (Macro Define) or select Macro then Define from the Tools menu.

Executing a Macro

1. Press Alt plus the letter if the macro has this type of name.

   or

   Press Alt-F10 (Macro) or select Macro then Execute from the Tools menu.
2. Enter the name and the macro is played.

Editing a Macro

1. Press Ctrl-F10 (Macro Define) or select Macro then Define from the Tools menu.
2. Enter the name of the existing macro.
3. Select 2 Edit (keystrokes only) or 3 Description (description and keystrokes).
4. Press F7 (Exit) when you are done editing the macro.

Automating with Macros

In this chapter you will learn how to automate your activities to save time and effort. With an investment of just a little time, you'll discover a slick way to make WordPerfect automatically perform tasks specific to your own needs.

Macros: Why and When

A *macro* is a special file you can create with WordPerfect to store your keystrokes and commands. Any time you want to replay the contents of the macro, just call it up and the rest is automatic.

When might you use a macro? There are plenty of opportunities. You may want to create a macro to automatically type in your return address, your name, or other names and addresses you commonly use. Or you may want to use a macro to store formatting codes you commonly use. For example, if you often create letters with 1.5" margins and with justification off, you can enter those commands once in a macro and then replay them in any document.

Another good use of macros is to store your common headers or footers. You can have a macro that stores all the keystrokes required to create a header or footer, or you can have a macro that stores all the keystrokes required to exit the header or footer.

Macros save time. By placing header or footer activities in a macro, you save yourself from trying to remember exactly how you set up the header or footer the last time. Without the macro, you might find yourself looking for old documents—wasting time rummaging through files. In addition, macros save you from extra keyboard activity.

How do you know what macros to create? That's easy. Just watch what you do. Especially pay attention to those activities you perform over and over, those that seem tedious, and those that could be faster or more pleasant if you let WordPerfect do them for you. Since virtually any WordPerfect keystrokes can be in a macro, your limit is your imagination and your mastery of the steps to create and use macros.

Don't Reinvent the Wheel

If you work in an office environment, don't reinvent the wheel. No doubt many people who have created macros are willing to share. Set up some means to pool macros with others in the office. You may want to go so far as to identify common naming conventions and encourage very descriptive descriptions. Create a master list of macros and their descriptions along with where to access the macros. Make this list available to everyone. If you work on a network, this list can be kept up to date in a document to which everyone has access.

Some work environments have one or two "macro masters" who have become very expert at developing timesaving macros and are willing to share their expertise. Find these people and set up a means by which everyone can benefit from their skill.

Defining a Macro

The easy way to get started using macros is to create one by entering keystrokes and recording them as you go. Creating a macro in this way is referred to as "defining" the macro. Let's look at an example. Suppose Barbara Wiley often uses her return address centered on the page (as in the letter shown in Figure 18.1). A macro is a good way to store and replay this type of text.

```
 File Edit Search Layout Mark Tools Font Graphics Help        (Press F3 for Help)
                       Barbara J. Wiley
                        3421 Pecos Way
                  San Diego, California 92123

 Mr. David Randolph
 Bennington Corporation
 45 Superstition Highway
 Phoenix, Arizona 85252

                              May 12, 1991

 Dear Mr. Randolph:

      As I discussed,  I am very interested in
 pursuing a career with the Bennington Corpora-
 tion.  I have attached:

            o    My resume with a chronological
                 work history as requested
            o    Letters of recommendation
            o    Certificates of achievement

 C:\WP51\DOC\BENLET.WPP                        Doc 1 Pg 1 Ln 1" Pos 2"
```

Figure 18.1

Return address centered.

To create the macro, press Ctrl-F10 (Macro Define) or select Macro and then **Define** from the **T**ools menu. This prompt appears in the bottom left corner of the screen:

```
Define macro:
```

You would now name the macro. You enter this name when you want to use the macro. There are two options for naming it. Use the approach with which you feel most comfortable.

Option 1:

Type in eight or fewer letters. (You don't include an extension with macros. WordPerfect automatically adds .WPM to the end, for "WordPerfect Macro.") Press ↵Enter. Using this naming approach allows you to enter a descriptive name. Our example might be called BRETADD for "Barbara's RETurn ADDress."

Option 2:

Hold down the Alt key and type in any letter. The benefit of this naming approach is that you only have to make two keypresses when you later use the macro. For example, you could press Alt and B (for Barbara's return address). The problem with this approach is that you could end up with a lot of macros you can't identify later. Or you could wind up wanting to use the same Alt-letter combination for another macro.

If you accidentally enter a name for a macro that you've already used, a prompt like this appears:

```
BRETADD.WPM Already Exists: 1 Replace; 2 Edit; 3
Description:
```

To quit defining the macro and begin again with a different name, just press F1 (Cancel). If you want to completely replace the macro keystrokes with different keystrokes, select 1 Replace.

(Options 2 and 3 are covered in "Editing a Macro" later in this chapter.) Selecting 1 **Replace** gives you a "second-chance" message like this:

```
Replace C:\WP51\BRETADD.WPM? No (Yes)
```

Choose **No** to return to your document or **Yes** to totally replace the contents of the macro.

After entering the name for the macro you are defining, this prompt appears:

```
Description:
```

This is an opportunity to enter a brief description of the macro. Include information about the contents of the macro or its use. For example, we might use:

```
Description: Barbara's RETurn ADDress, Centered
```

to identify not only what the letters in the macro name stand for but also the fact that the return address is centered. Once you've typed in the description, press `↵Enter`.

The following prompt blinks at the bottom left of the screen to remind you that any keystrokes you enter will be placed in the macro:

```
Macro Def
```

Type in the text and WordPerfect key combinations. You can use most WordPerfect editing capabilities. (You cannot use a mouse, however, to position the cursor within a macro.)

As you enter the keystrokes, you may make a typographical error or press an incorrect command. If you make a mistake that you can correct, first finish the macro keystrokes. Then you can either use the macro with the mistake and its correction (if no harm is done) or you can edit the macro contents (covered later in this chapter). As an example of the former, say you typed in this text when entering a macro:

    San Dieb

To correct, you'd press `◂Backspace` to get to:

    San Die

Then you'd complete the correct keystrokes before continuing:

    San Diego

When the macro is later replayed, the "b", backspace, and "go" would all be replayed. It happens very fast, though, and you could decide not to edit it.

Once the macro text is entered, just press `Ctrl`-`F10` (Macro Define) or select Macro and Define from the Tools menu. The blinking message `Macro Def` goes away to signify that the macro is complete and you are back to regular WordPerfect editing.

The following Quick Steps summarize the process of defining a macro.

Defining a Macro

1. Press `Ctrl`-`F10` (Macro Define) or select Macro then Define from the Tools menu.

This message appears: `Define macro:.`

2. Type in an eight-character (or less) name and press ⏎Enter; or press Alt and any letter.	This message appears: `Description:`.
3. Type in a brief description and press ⏎Enter.	`Macro Def` blinks on the lower corner of the screen.
4. Enter the keystrokes for the macro. When done, press Ctrl-F10 (Macro Define) or select Macro, then Define from the Tools menu.	`Macro Def` disappears.

A good way to display the names of available macros is to press F5 (List Files) or select List Files from the **File** menu. At the `Dir:` directory listing, type in `*.WPM` as the file extension in order to display only macro files. For example:

```
Dir:C\WP51\*.WPM
```

A screen like that in Figure 18.2, displaying only macro files, would appear.

TIP: Macro files are automatically stored on your WP51 directory. You can change this through ⇧Shift-F1 (Setup), 6 - Location of Files.

As you create macros, it can be useful to keep your own list of macro names, descriptions, and uses. That way, you can easily remember the use of each macro.

Figure 18.2

Macro files shown on the list screen.

```
02-26-92  02:15p              Directory C:\WP51\*.WPM
Document size:      347    Free: 11,683,840 Used:        224    Files:    1

    Current    <Dir>              | ..   Parent     <Dir>
 BRETADD .WPM     224  02-26-92 02:14p






 1 Retrieve; 2 Delete; 3 Move/Rename; 4 Print; 5 Short/Long Display;
 6 Look; 7 Other Directory; 8 Copy; 9 Find; N Name Search: 6
```

Executing a Macro

Once you have defined a macro, you can use it. This is called *executing* a macro. (Breathe easy. The work's in the defining, not the execution.)

It is a good practice to execute a new macro right after you've defined it. That way, you can test to see whether it works the way you intended. If it doesn't, you can define it again (select 1 Replace when that option appears) or edit the macro (described later in this chapter).

TIP: It is a good habit to save your document *before* playing a macro. That way, if you have valuable text and a macro that doesn't execute properly, you don't lose the text.

The following Quick Steps show how to execute a macro.

Executing a Macro

1. Press the Alt -*letter* key combination.	The macro keystrokes are executed.
or	
Position the cursor where the macro should execute and press Alt - F10 (Macro), or select Macro, then Execute from the **T**ools menu.	This message appears: `Macro:`.
2. Type in the macro name and press ⏎Enter .	The macro keystrokes are executed.

Quick Steps

Figure 18.3 shows a letter before the BRETADD.WPM macro is executed, and Figure 18.4 shows the letter after the macro is executed. Notice that the text is inserted in existing text. No editing of the document had to be done in this example. Often, however, you may need to add extra lines or spaces after executing a macro to create the proper appearance.

Editing a Macro

When you edit a WordPerfect macro, an editing screen like that shown in Figure 18.5 appears. In this screen, the name of the macro (the file), the macro description, and all the keystrokes appear. Each WordPerfect command appears in braces ({}). For example, the ⌖Shift-F6 (Center) command appears as {Center} and a press of the ↵Enter key appears as {Enter}. Text you have typed in appears as text and spaces are represented by dots or small, underlined circles. Notice in the figure that a typographical error was made and corrected when the macro was defined: San Diego was misspelled as San Dieb, ⌫Backspace was pressed and go was entered.

Figure 18.3

Letter before executing macro.

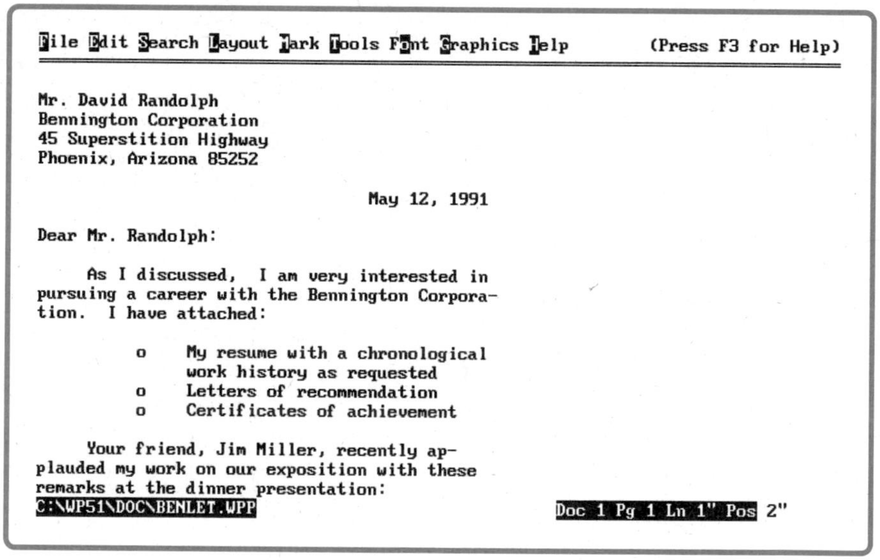

```
 File  Edit  Search  Layout  Mark  Tools  Font  Graphics  Help      (Press F3 for Help)

 Mr. David Randolph
 Bennington Corporation
 45 Superstition Highway
 Phoenix, Arizona 85252

                              May 12, 1991

 Dear Mr. Randolph:

      As I discussed,  I am very interested in
 pursuing a career with the Bennington Corpora-
 tion.  I have attached:

           o    My resume with a chronological
                work history as requested
           o    Letters of recommendation
           o    Certificates of achievement

      Your friend, Jim Miller, recently ap-
 plauded my work on our exposition with these
 remarks at the dinner presentation:
 C:\WP51\DOC\BENLET.WPP                       Doc 1 Pg 1 Ln 1" Pos 2"
```

When you edit a macro, you can correct errors or add new text or keypresses. Just press Ctrl-F10 (Macro Define) or select Macro, then Define from the Tools menu. Enter the name of the existing macro you want to edit, which may be an Alt - *letter* combination (press ↵Enter, if necessary). A message like this is displayed:

BRETADD.WPM Already Exists: 1 Replace; 2 Edit; 3 Description:

To edit the description and the keystrokes, select 3 Description. To make any changes to the description, press ↵Enter, and edit the keystrokes. To edit the keystrokes only, select 2 Edit.

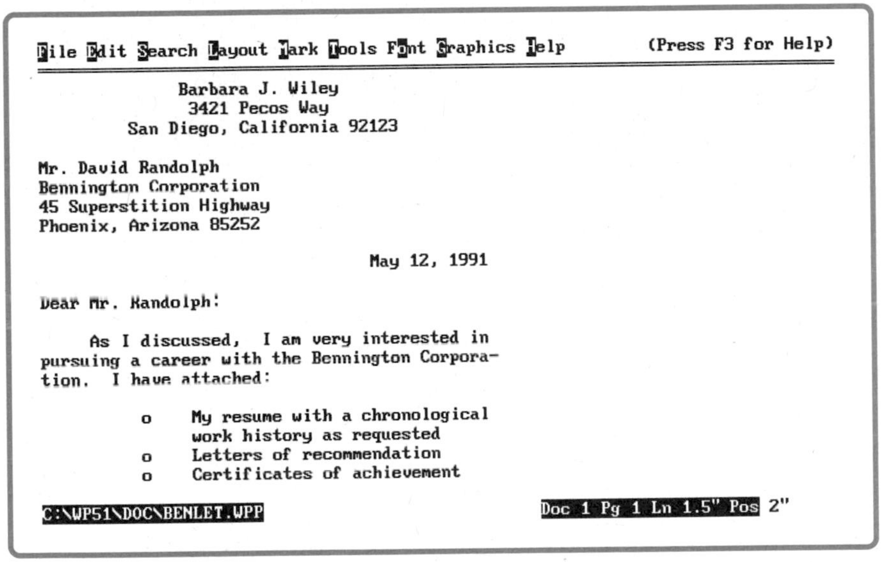

Figure 18.4
Letter after executing macro.

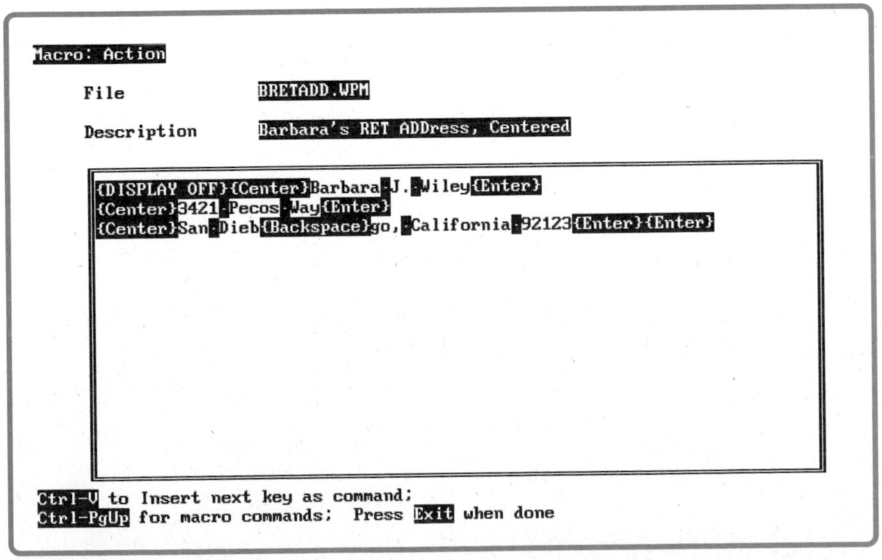

```
File Edit Search Layout Mark Tools Font Graphics Help      (Press F3 for Help)
                    Barbara J. Wiley
                    3421 Pecos Way
              San Diego, California 92123

Mr. David Randolph
Bennington Corporation
45 Superstition Highway
Phoenix, Arizona 85252

                         May 12, 1991

Dear Mr. Randolph:

     As I discussed,  I am very interested in
pursuing a career with the Bennington Corpora-
tion.  I have attached:

          o    My resume with a chronological
               work history as requested
          o    Letters of recommendation
          o    Certificates of achievement

C:\WP51\DOC\BENLET.WPP              Doc 1 Pg 1 Ln 1.5" Pos 2"
```

Figure 18.5
Macro editing screen.

```
Macro: Action

    File                BRETADD.WPM

    Description         Barbara's RET ADDress, Centered

   ┌─────────────────────────────────────────────────────────┐
   │ {DISPLAY OFF}{Center}Barbara J. Wiley{Enter}              │
   │ {Center}3421 Pecos Way{Enter}                            │
   │ {Center}San Dieb{Backspace}go, California 92123{Enter}{Enter} │
   │                                                          │
   │                                                          │
   │                                                          │
   │                                                          │
   │                                                          │
   │                                                          │
   │                                                          │
   └─────────────────────────────────────────────────────────┘

Ctrl-V to Insert next key as command;
Ctrl-PgUp for macro commands;  Press Exit when done
```

When you edit keystrokes, you can use WordPerfect editing commands. Just delete text you don't want and insert the text you want to add. To add a WordPerfect keypress, enter the appropriate WordPerfect keystrokes.

You must be in Command Insert mode to enter these commands:

Enter key

Cursor keys

Macro commands (instructions on how the macro should execute)

Variables (values in the macro that can change under certain conditions)

Control characters (used to determine the appearance of text in messages or to locate messages on the screen)

Keyboard macro names (macro named with the Alt key pressed with a letter)

To go into Command Insert mode, follow the prompt on the editing screen and press Ctrl-V for a single keystroke. The next key you enter is entered as a command rather than regular keystrokes. For example, if you want to enter the {Enter} command, press Ctrl-V then ↵Enter. If you want to enter multiple keystrokes as a command (rather than being entered on the screen when the macro is executed), press Ctrl-F10 before you begin, then Ctrl-F10 when you are done.

In Figure 18.6, the b and {Backspace} have been deleted to correct the typographical error.

During editing, you can press F1 (Cancel) to leave the macro as it was and return to your document. This message appears for your response:

```
Cancel changes? No (Yes)
```

Figure 18.6

*Edited
BRETADD.WPM
macro.*

```
Macro: Action
   File              BRETADD.WPM
   Description       Barbara's RET ADDress, Centered

   {DISPLAY OFF}{Center}Barbara J. Wiley{Enter}
   {Center}3421 Pecos Way{Enter}
   {Center}San Diego, California 92123{Enter}{Enter}




   Ctrl-V to Insert next key as command;
   Ctrl-PgUp for macro commands;  Press Exit when done
```

Choose Yes to cancel any edits and return to your document. Choose No to go back to editing the macro. Once your editing is complete, press F7 (Exit) to save the changes. You are returned to your document.

TIP: After editing a macro, always test it to make sure it executes as you anticipated.

The following Quick Steps summarize the process of editing a macro.

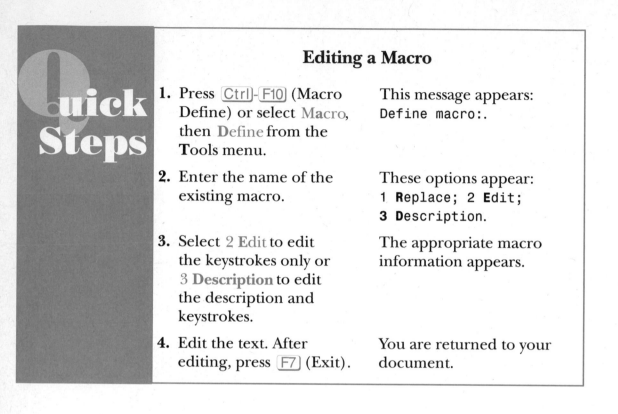

Quick Steps

Editing a Macro

1. Press Ctrl - F10 (Macro Define) or select Macro, then Define from the Tools menu.

   This message appears: Define macro:.

2. Enter the name of the existing macro.

   These options appear: 1 **R**eplace; 2 **E**dit; 3 **D**escription.

3. Select 2 **E**dit to edit the keystrokes only or 3 **D**escription to edit the description and keystrokes.

   The appropriate macro information appears.

4. Edit the text. After editing, press F7 (Exit).

   You are returned to your document.

What's Next?

This chapter has just scratched the surface of the potential of macros. In addition to entering keystrokes and WordPerfect operations, you can include a variety of macro programming commands, expressions, and message display commands. These are the means to add to your macro power beyond typical WordPerfect capabilities.

For example, you could add the WordPerfect programming command {Bell} through the macro editing screen to sound a bell. You could add pauses to enter text from the keyboard, prompts to remind you of actions to take, or use If-Else statements to make choices.

The following is a listing of some of the more commonly used macro commands:

{CHAIN}macroname	Executes the macro named after the current macro is done executing.
{DATE]	Inserts the current date in the document.
{INPUT}message	Displays the message you enter then pauses for the user to enter data.
{PAUSE}	Stops the execution of the macro until ⏎Enter is pressed.
{PAUSE KEY}key	Stops the execution of the macro until the key identified is pressed.
{PROMPT}message	Displays the message on the status line.

These are only a few of the possibilities WordPerfect provides. First, get some experience with the level of macro work described in this chapter. Then consult the *WordPerfect Reference* or an advanced book on WordPerfect to learn more about these sophisticated macro functions.

Creating a Table of Contents and/or Index

1. Mark each entry.
2. Define the Table of Contents and/or Index.
3. Generate the Table of Contents and/or Index.

Marking a Table of Contents or Index Entry

1. Block the text, if necessary, by pressing Alt-F4 (Block) or selecting Block from the Edit menu.
2. Press Alt-F5 (Mark Text) or select the Mark menu and follow the prompts.

Defining a Table of Contents or Index

1. Place your cursor where the table of contents or index should appear.
2. Press Alt-F5 (Mark Text) then 5 Define or select Define from the Mark menu and follow the prompts.

Generating a Table of Contents or Index

1. Press Alt-F5 (Mark Text) then 6 Generate or select Generate from the Mark menu.
2. Select 5 - Generate Tables, Indexes, Cross-References, etc..

Creating an Outline

1. Press Shift-F5 (Date/Outline), then select 4 Outline, or select Outline from the Tools menu. Select 1 On to turn on the Outline feature.
2. Use Enter, Tab, and Shift-Tab to control the outline entry.
3. Press Shift-F5 (Date/Outline) then select 4 Outline, or select Outline from the Tools menu. Select 2 Off to turn off the Outline feature.

Creating Tables of Contents, Indexes, and Outlines

19

WordPerfect has a wealth of tools to make your job easier. Among them is the ability of WordPerfect to automatically generate tables of contents, indexes, and outlines. This chapter details how.

The Benefits of "Automated" Tables of Contents and Indexes

The "old-fashioned" way of creating a table of contents or an index is to identify the text manually in your document after all page numbers have been assigned and then type in each entry along with the page number. If the document is edited and the page numbers change, the table of contents and index have to be updated manually.

However, with WordPerfect, the process of creating tables of contents and indexes is greatly simplified. In the document, you mark the text that is to be included in the table of contents or index. Then generate the table of contents or index automatically. When the document is edited, generate the references again. There's no manual record-keeping of what's in the index and table of contents and no manual updating of the table of contents and index. And there is no chance of errors relative to page numbering.

Creating a Table of Contents or Index

To create a table of contents or index, follow these basic steps:

1. *Mark the text you want to include in the table of contents or index:* This identifies to WordPerfect the entries for the table of contents or index.

2. *Define the characteristics of the table of contents or index:* You can identify the location and appearance of a table of contents and the location for index words.

3. *Generate the table of contents and/or index:* WordPerfect finds each occurrence of the text marked for a table of contents and/or index and creates the references.

> **TIP:** Always plan your table of contents or index before you get started. Have an idea of how detailed you want to get so you are consistent throughout the document. Also consider how many levels you want reflected. For example, the index in this book could have a single level "index" to cover index information or more detailed entry with two levels:
>
> > index
> > > generating
> > > marking and defining

Marking and Defining a Table of Contents

You may create a table of contents with one to five levels. Each additional level is a "sublevel." Figure 19.1 shows part of a table of contents for a document created by Barbara J. Wiley. It has only one level. Figure 19.2 shows a portion of Wiley's table of contents, this time with two levels. Each new sublevel in a table of contents is indented to the next tab stop.

```
                  Developing a Computer System
               By Barbara J. Wiley and Paul G. Otto

Table of Contents

Major Tasks . . . . . . . . . . . . . . . . . . . . . . . . . .    1
Specification . . . . . . . . . . . . . . . . . . . . . . . .    7
Design  . . . . . . . . . . . . . . . . . . . . . . . . . . .   13
Coding  . . . . . . . . . . . . . . . . . . . . . . . . . . .   19
Implementation  . . . . . . . . . . . . . . . . . . . . . .   26
Post Implementation . . . . . . . . . . . . . . . . . . . .   34
```

Figure 19.1

Table of contents with one level.

Figure 19.2

Table of contents with two levels.

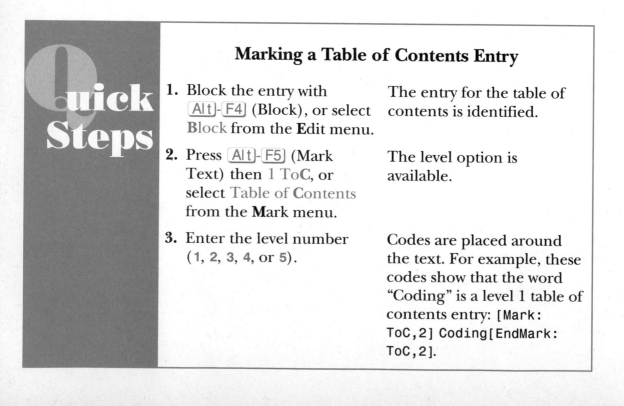

```
                Developing a Computer System
             By Barbara J. Wiley and Paul G. Otto

Table of Contents

Major Tasks . . . . . . . . . . . . . . . . . . . . . . . . . . . .   1
           Specification  . . . . . . . . . . . . . . . . . . . .   2
           Design . . . . . . . . . . . . . . . . . . . . . . . .   3
           Coding . . . . . . . . . . . . . . . . . . . . . . . .   3
           Implementation . . . . . . . . . . . . . . . . . . . .   5
           Post Implementation  . . . . . . . . . . . . . . . . .   6
Specification . . . . . . . . . . . . . . . . . . . . . . . . . .   7
           The Goal . . . . . . . . . . . . . . . . . . . . . . .   8
           User Requirements  . . . . . . . . . . . . . . . . . .   8
           The Role of MIS  . . . . . . . . . . . . . . . . . . .  10
Design  . . . . . . . . . . . . . . . . . . . . . . . . . . . . .  13
           The Goal . . . . . . . . . . . . . . . . . . . . . . .  13
           The Team . . . . . . . . . . . . . . . . . . . . . . .  15
           The Detail System Design Document  . . . . . . . . . .  18
Coding  . . . . . . . . . . . . . . . . . . . . . . . . . . . . .  19
Implementation  . . . . . . . . . . . . . . . . . . . . . . . . .  26
Post Implementation . . . . . . . . . . . . . . . . . . . . . . .  34
```

The following Quick Steps show how to mark an entry for a table of contents.

Quick Steps

Marking a Table of Contents Entry

1. Block the entry with Alt-F4 (Block), or select **Block** from the **E**dit menu.

   The entry for the table of contents is identified.

2. Press Alt-F5 (Mark Text) then 1 ToC, or select Table of Contents from the **M**ark menu.

   The level option is available.

3. Enter the level number (1, 2, 3, 4, or 5).

   Codes are placed around the text. For example, these codes show that the word "Coding" is a level 1 table of contents entry: [Mark: ToC,2] Coding[EndMark: ToC,2].

Once all of the table of contents entries are marked, you must *define* the table of contents.

1. Place your cursor where you want the table of contents to appear. Typically, you will want it at the beginning of the document on its own page. (To create a page, enter a hard page break with Ctrl-↵Enter.) You may also enter a heading, such as "Contents."

2. Press Alt-F5 (Mark Text), select 5 Define, then select 1 - Define Table of Contents. Or select Define, then Table of Contents from the **M**ark menu. The Table of Contents Definition screen appears (see Figure 19.3).

```
┌────────────────────────────────────────────────────┐
│ Table of Contents Definition                        │
│                                                      │
│   1 - Number of Levels        1                      │
│                                                      │
│   2 - Display Last Level in   No                     │
│       Wrapped Format                                 │
│                                                      │
│   3 - Page Numbering - Level 1  Flush right with leader │
│                        Level 2                       │
│                        Level 3                       │
│                        Level 4                       │
│                        Level 5                       │
│                                                      │
│                                                      │
│ Selection: 1                                         │
└────────────────────────────────────────────────────┘
```

Figure 19.3

The Table of Contents Definition screen.

3. Identify the number of levels by selecting 1 - Number of Levels and typing in the number.

4. Leave option 2 - Display Last Level in Wrapped Format at No. (Otherwise the levels wrap around as if they are part of one paragraph.)

5. Select 3 - Page Numbering to choose how page numbers are to be displayed. Examples of the options are:

    None (no page numbers)*:*

    ```
    Major Tasks
    ```

    Page number follows text:

    ```
    Major Tasks 1
    ```

    Page number in parentheses follows text:

    ```
    Major Tasks (1)
    ```

    Page number flush right:

    ```
    Major Tasks                                    1
    ```

    Page number flush right with dot leaders:

    ```
    Major Tasks...............................1
    ```

6. Press F7 (Exit) when you are done. A code like this appears in your document:

    ```
    [Def Mark:TofC,3:5,5,5]
    ```

The code starts with the Definition mark for the table of contents. There are three levels and the page numbering on each level is set to choice 5 (flush right with dot leaders).

Once you have marked the table of contents entries and defined the table of contents, you can generate it, which is discussed in "Generating the Table of Contents and/or Index" later in this chapter. Because you generate both the table of contents and index at the same time, you may want to mark and define an index first.

Marking and Defining an Index

When you create an index, you can use headings and subheadings. Figure 19.4 shows a portion of an index with headings and subheadings. Notice that the subheadings are indented under the associated heading. The tab stops are used for indentation.

To mark a single word as an index entry, place your cursor on that word. To mark several words making up one entry, block the words using Alt-F4 (Block) or by selecting **B**lock from the **E**dit menu. Positioning the cursor marks the text to use to identify the page number. As you will see, you can change the actual wording of the index entry, if you like.

```
Index

ABC Approach . . . . . . . . . . . . . . . . . . . . . . . . . . . 2
Benefits to Users . . . . . . . . . . . . . . . . . . . . . . . . 1
BITTLE Company Experience . . . . . . . . . . . . . . . . . . . . 54
Coding . . . . . . . . . . . . . . . . . . . . . . . . . . . . . 19
      Common Problems and Solutions . . . . . . . . . . . . . . . 24
      Handling DSD Changes . . . . . . . . . . . . . . . . . . . 21
      Managing the Coding Activity . . . . . . . . . . . . . . . 25
      Methods to Code . . . . . . . . . . . . . . . . . . . . . . 22
Cutting Costs . . . . . . . . . . . . . . . . . . . . . . . . . . 42
```

Figure 19.4
Index with headings and subheadings.

Press Alt-F5 (Mark Text) and choose 3 Index, or select Index from the **M**ark menu. This prompt appears:

```
Index heading:
```

The word(s) you've identified appear after the prompt. Press ⏎Enter to use the text as marked or type in your own index entry. (For instance, you may want different capitalization, a different tense, or entirely different text.) Press ⏎Enter. This prompt appears:

```
Subheading:
```

Press F1 (Cancel) if you don't want a subheading. If you want one, either type in a subheading and press ⏎Enter or just accept the one shown by pressing ⏎Enter. Codes are placed in your document around the marked word(s). Here is an example:

```
[Index:Coding;Common Problems and Solutions]
```

In this example, the heading is Coding and the subheading is Common Problems and Solutions.

The following Quick Steps summarize the process of marking an index entry.

Marking an Index Entry

1. Place your cursor on the word or block the words for the entry using Alt-F4 (Block), or select **Block** from the **E**dit menu.

   The page number for the index entry is identified.

2. Press Alt-F5 (Mark Text), then 3 Index, or select Index from the **M**ark menu.

   This prompt appears: Index heading:.

3. Accept the heading or enter a new one. Press ⏎Enter.	This prompt appears: `Subheading:`.
4. Accept the subheading or enter a new one. Press ⏎Enter. Or press F1 (Cancel) to skip the subheading.	Codes appear in your document. The following code indicates the word "Shoes" is an index entry: `[Index:Shoes]`.

There is one other method you can use in identifying words for an index. You can create a *concordance* file, which is a list of words you want in the index. WordPerfect looks for and marks these words in your document. You can check each mark, adding and deleting marks as desired. For more information on using a concordance file, see your WordPerfect Reference.

Once all index entries are marked, define the index. To do this:

1. Place your cursor where you want the index to appear in your document.

2. Press Alt-F5 (Mark Text), select 5 Define, and select 3 - Define Index, or select Define then Index from the Mark menu. This prompt appears:

    `Concordance Filename (Enter=none):`

Press ⏎Enter (this assumes you are not using a concordance file) and the Index Definition screen appears (see Figure 19.5).

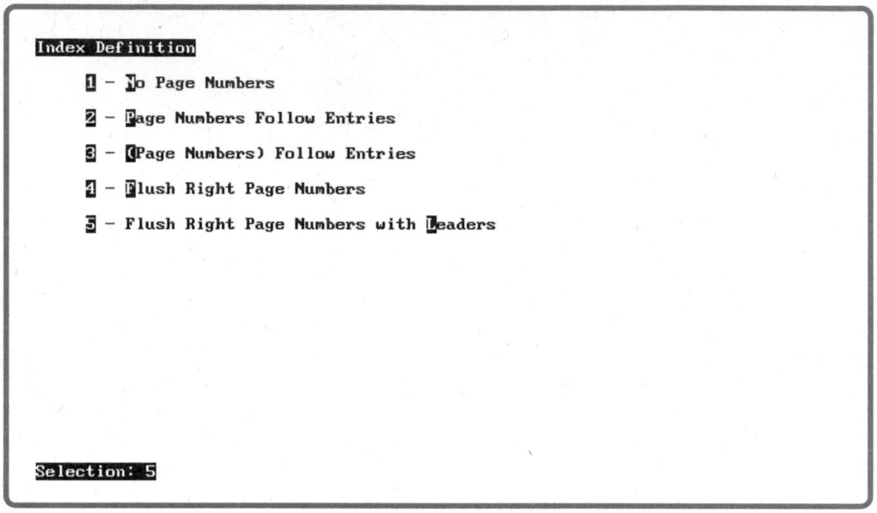

Figure 19.5

Index Definition screen.

```
Index Definition
    1 - To Page Numbers

    2 - Page Numbers Follow Entries

    3 - (Page Numbers) Follow Entries

    4 - Flush Right Page Numbers

    5 - Flush Right Page Numbers with Leaders




Selection: 5
```

The options are the same as with Table of Contents. Once you've selected how the page numbers will appear, a code like this is placed in your document:

```
[Def Mark:Index,5]
```

This identifies where the index will be placed and the type of page numbering. (In this example, option 5 was selected: flush right with dot leaders.)

Generating the Table of Contents and/or Index

To generate the table of contents and/or index:

1. Press Alt-F5 (Mark Text) and select 6 Generate. Or select Generate from the Mark menu. The Mark Text: Generate screen appears.

2. Select 5 - Generate Tables, Indexes, Cross-References, etc.. This prompt appears:

```
Existing tables, lists, and indexes will be
replaced.
Continue? Yes (No)
```

3. To continue, choose Yes. A prompt like this identifies that the work is being done:

```
Generate in Progress. Pass: 1, Page 9
```

When the prompt goes away, the table of contents and index have been generated. The table of contents or index appears after the appropriate [Def Mark:...]. Following the table of contents or index, this code appears:

```
[End Def]
```

CAUTION: Never delete the [Def Mark:...] or [End Def] codes. If you do, WordPerfect will not know where to put the table of contents or index if you generate it again. Only delete these codes if you are deleting the entire table of contents or index.

Once the table of contents or index has been generated, you can edit it like any document text. For example, you may add your own headings, blank lines, or change tab settings to alter the indentation.

The page numbers in the table of contents and index remain the same until you generate them again. As a result, when you edit a document, the page numbers in the table of contents and index do not change automatically. When you are done making changes in the document, use Alt -F5 (Mark Text) and 6 Generate, or select Generate from the Mark menu, and proceed.

> **TIP:** You will usually want to generate your table of contents and index after spell checking but before printing your document. This way, all editing will be complete and the page numbers will be stable. Sometimes, however, it is useful to generate the table of contents and/or index as you work. Doing so provides a reference to see the structure of the document and the location of particular material. You can generate a table of contents and index again and again.

Creative Uses of Tables of Contents and Indexes

Don't let names fool you. You can use Table of Contents and Index functions for applications other than generating tables of contents and indexes. The Table of Contents feature may be used to create any list which places the items in the list in the order they appear in the document. The Index feature places items in alphabetical order and may be used to associate subordinate items to a superior item. Consider their use in putting together any kind of list.

For example, one clever user composed a narrative of her family and used the Index feature of WordPerfect to automatically generate a family tree. (Children were marked as subordinate items to parents.) Open your mind. Create

> vocabulary lists, short narrative summaries, lists of figures or graphics, or any form of list using the Table of Contents and Index features.

Creating Outlines

Outlining is another useful organizing technique WordPerfect makes easy. You can go into outline mode and the text you type will be automatically numbered and indented; you don't have to remember what number or letter comes next or how far to indent. Also, numbers and letters are automatically updated when you edit the outline. Figure 19.6 illustrates part of an outline created using WordPerfect.

```
File Edit Search Layout Mark Tools Font Graphics Help        (Press F3 for Help)

Talk for Data Processing Professional Group          █
By Barbara J. Wiley

I.    Background of presenters
II.   Why computer systems haven't met needs
III.  Benefits of a better approach
IV.   Major tasks
      A.   Specification
           1.    The stated and hidden goals
           2.    Getting user requirements
           3.    Story of BITTLE
           4.    MIS role (new and old)
      B.   Design




Outline                                   Doc 1 Pg 1 Ln 3" Pos 1"
```

Figure 19.6

An outline created with WordPerfect.

To develop an outline, first follow the next Quick Steps to turn on the Outline feature.

Turning on the Outline Feature

Quick Steps

1. Place the cursor where the outline will start.

2. Press ⇧Shift-F5 (Date/Outline) and select 4 Outline, or select Outline from the Tools menu.

3. Choose 1 On to turn on Outline.

   This code appears in your document: [Outline On].

Outline appears in the lower left corner of your screen to remind you that you are in Outline mode. From here until you turn off Outline, text you enter will be in outline form. As you can see, certain keypresses give different results in Outline mode than when you are in regular editing mode.

Press ⏎Enter to have the first-level number inserted. Type in text or, to go to the next level, press Tab↹. To go back a level, press ⇧Shift-Tab↹ (Margin Release). Continue using these keys while you create your outline. Table 19.1 is a summary of the keys to press and the results:

Table 19.1
Outline Mode Keys.

Key to press	Result
⏎Enter	To create a new line at the same level

Key to press	Result
Tab⇥	To go "in" (right) one level
⇧Shift-Tab⇥ (Margin Release)	To go "out" (left) one level

When you insert a level number, a code for paragraph numbering appears in the text:

```
[Para Num: Auto]
```

For example, to recreate the outline in Figure 19.6, you would follow these steps:

1. After the outline title and Barbara J. Wiley's by-line, turn on Outline (as shown in the previous Quick Steps). Press ↵Enter. The first line will automatically be numbered I.

2. Press F4 (Indent) and type in the text. Press ↵Enter at the end of the line. A II appears. Type in the next line, doing the same for lines III and IV. Press ↵Enter at the end of each line.

3. To go to a new level, press Tab⇥. The number V disappears and is replaced with the letter A.

4. Press F4 (Indent), type Specification, press ↵Enter, and Tab⇥ to go to a new level, level 1.

5. From the line marked 1 through the line marked 4, type in a line and press ↵Enter at the end of each line.

6. After line 4, 5 appears. Press ⇧Shift-Tab⇥ to move left one tab setting. The 5 is replaced with the letter B.

> **TIP:** Outlining can feel a little cumbersome at first. Most people new to creating outlines take a few minutes to experiment with the keypresses to get the hang of the actions. Once you become familiar with the results, you'll pick up speed.

When you are done creating the outline, press ⇧Shift-F5 (Date/Outline), then select 4 Outline. Or select Outline from the **T**ools menu. Choose 2 Off to turn off Outline and return to regular editing mode. Outline disappears from the screen and a code [Outline Off] appears in the document.

This description of outlining will get you started. Consult your WordPerfect Reference if you use outlining often and want to learn a few tricks. For example, there are keypresses that move you more than one level at a time and to the most recent occurrence of the same level. Also, you may use the Move/Copy/Delete options to control a level of the outline and all subordinate levels. In addition, you can use the Outline, Define function to change the style of outline numbers, to begin outlining with any number, and to alter the use of the ↵Enter key.

What's Next?

As you strolled through the prompts and menus for creating a table of contents and index, your curiosity may have been raised about several other WordPerfect features.

You can use WordPerfect to create *cross references*. Cross references refer the reader to another page in the document. For example, you can say:

```
See the chart on page 27 for an overview.
```

Or...

```
Page 34 describes the steps in detail.
```

The text you use in the cross reference is up to you. What WordPerfect offers is automatic updating of the page number every time it changes as a result of editing the document.

Another feature is the ability to develop *tables of authorities.* These are used in legal documents to cite statutes, cases, and legal references.

You can also use WordPerfect to create a *master document* in one WordPerfect document file (with or without text). This master document "calls" other documents. The master document can be expanded to include all subdocuments or condensed to include only itself. The benefit of this feature is that you may create small, workable document files and then expand them to one large document file for final editing.

Finally, you may have noticed the references to *redline* and *strikeout.* These features, described in Chapter 8, are useful for editing documents when more than one person is involved in the editing process.

During your exploration of the outlining function, you ran into some other WordPerfect options. The following paragraphs briefly explain those options. See your WordPerfect Reference for a complete description of them if you believe they will be useful in your work. You may also press ⇧Shift-F5 (Date/Outline) then 5 Para Num, or select Paragraph Number from the Tools menu to explore on your own.

▲ WordPerfect allows you to number paragraphs. Use `⇧Shift`-`F5` (Date/Outline) then 5 Para Num, or select Paragraph Number from the **T**ools menu. The numbering scheme is similar to what you have seen with outlining.

▲ Another interesting feature is that WordPerfect will automatically enter the date (actually, the system date entered in your computer). You can use `⇧Shift`-`F5` (Date/Outline) and then one of these options (or select one from the **T**ools menu):

1 Date **T**ext: To enter the date in letters and numbers

2 Date **C**ode: To place a code that will add the current date every time you enter or print the document

3 Date **F**ormat: To change the appearance of the date, add the day, or add the time (for example, November 26, 1992 to Sun Nov 26, 1992)

In This Chapter

Creating a Primary Document

•

Creating a Secondary Document

•

Merging

•

Inserting the Current Date

•

Sorting

Fields and Records in Secondary Documents

▲ Secondary documents contain fields grouped in records.

▲ To end a field, press `F9` (Merge R).

▲ To end a record, press `Shift`-`F9` (Merge Codes) and 2 End Record, or select Merge Codes then End Record from the **T**ools menu.

Fields in Primary Documents

▲ Primary documents contain boilerplate text and field codes.

▲ To identify a field to merge, press `Shift`-`F9` (Merge Codes) and 1 Field, or select Merge Codes then Field from the **T**ools menu. Type in the correct number for the field and press `Enter`.

Merging Primary and Secondary Documents

1. Press `Ctrl`-`F9` (Merge/Sort) and 1 Merge, or select Merge from the **T**ools menu.

2. Enter the name of the primary and secondary documents.

Sorting a List

1. Press `Ctrl`-`F9` (Merge/Sort) and 2 Sort, or select Sort from the **T**ools menu.

2. Identify the input and output files (just press `Enter` at the prompts to sort and save to the screen).

3. Complete the Sort menu and select 1 Perform Action.

Merging Documents and Sorting

WordPerfect allows you to merge the contents of one document with a list of data in another document. The data may comprise any small bits of information, such as names, addresses, telephone numbers, product numbers, sales regions, contributions, booth assignments, office numbers, birth dates, and so on.

Why Merge Documents and Data?

What use is this feature to you? Well, if you ever need to send out form letters or use the same data in multiple documents, the Merge feature will save you a great deal of time and enable you to produce more personalized letters and documents.

For example, you can merge a list of names, addresses, and phone numbers of members of a professional group, a work team, or a scout troop. Then you merge that data with a notice today, a letter tomorrow, or to make a list next week. Or, you could create a document containing raw product data and then pull out the data you need according to the requirements of the immediate document. Virtually any time you have a body of data that you will be using repeatedly, Merge is the way to go.

Elements of a Merge

Each piece of data in a merge is referred to as a *field*. A field may be a first name, last name, phone number, ZIP code any single bit of information. All the related fields are organized into a *record*. For example, all the fields for one person (first name, last name, address, phone number) are organized into a record for that individual.

Three documents are involved in a merge:

▲ *The primary document:* This is the "boilerplate" text that will be used in the merged document. Type it in as regular WordPerfect text. In this document, you also identify what data you want "plugged in." By entering codes for the fields, you tell WordPerfect what to put where.

▲ *The secondary document:* This document contains the data, organized in a way that lets WordPerfect identify what's what. For example, the fields in each record are listed in the same order, and the records are clearly separated. This way, WordPerfect knows what type of field comes first, second, third, and so on. And, WordPerfect knows where one record ends and another begins.

▲ *The merged document:* This is the result of merging the primary document and the secondary document. The data from the secondary document is entered at the appropriate spots according to the instructions in the primary document.

Let's take a look at an example of each type of document. We'll use Barbara Wiley's notice to the members of her professional group as the example. Figure 20.1 shows the primary document. Notice that each field to be inserted during the merge is numbered and appears with a notation on the regular editing screen:

    {FIELD}1~

In the Reveal Codes screen, you'll see:

    [Mrg: FIELD]1~

which reminds you that the field is to be merged.

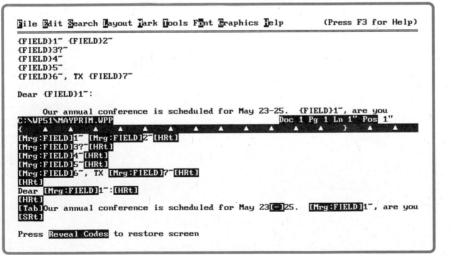

Figure 20.1
Primary document.

The full-screen display of our primary document, shown in Figure 20.2, illustrates that the order of the fields is not important. The numbers of the fields simply let WordPerfect match up with the proper data in the secondary document. Also, fields do not need to be represented an equal number of times in the primary document: field 1 is used three times and field 4 is used twice.

Figure 20.2

Full-screen display of primary document.

```
File Edit Search Layout Mark Tools Font Graphics Help        (Press F3 for Help)

{FIELD}1~ {FIELD}2~
{FIELD}3?~
{FIELD}4~
{FIELD}5~
{FIELD}6~, TX {FIELD}7~

Dear {FIELD}1~:

     Our annual conference is scheduled for May 23-25.  {FIELD}1~, are you
interested in presenting a seminar?  Many successful seminars are
based on "real world" experiences.  How about your experience at
{FIELD}4~?  If you can present a seminar, call me at 253-9900 extension
3050 (day) or 432-9822 (evening).  Thank you.

Sincerely,

Barbara J. Wiley




C:\WP51\MAYPRIM.WPP                              Doc 1 Pg 1 Ln 1" Pos 1"
```

Also notice that field 3 has a question mark after the number (3?) and before the tilde (~). This tells WordPerfect that not every record in the secondary document will have data for field 3. If a record doesn't, field 3 will be skipped, and no blank line will be left.

Now let's take a look at the secondary document. Figure 20.3 shows the full-screen display of several records. Notice that each field (such as first name) is entered on its own line and ends with:

{END FIELD}

The figure also shows that Jennifer Jackson's title is not available. A line is left as a placeholder to alert WordPerfect, but the {END FIELD} code is entered anyway. You can also see that there are more fields in the secondary document than are called for in the primary. The phone numbers, for example, appear in the secondary document but are not used in the primary document. This illustrates that you can use as much or as little data as you wish.

```
 File  Edit  Search  Layout  Mark  Tools  Font  Graphics  Help      (Press F3 for Help)

Jennifer{END FIELD}
Jackson{END FIELD}
{END FIELD}
Williams Manufacturing{END FIELD}
2344 W. Highway 1{END FIELD}
Austin{END FIELD}
78759{END FIELD}
342-8966{END FIELD}
450-9000{END FIELD}
{END RECORD}
=====================================================================
Preston{END FIELD}
Lindermann{END FIELD}
Analyst{END FIELD}
Bottcher Ltd.{END FIELD}
3422 45th Street{END FIELD}
Ft. Worth{END FIELD}
75261{END FIELD}
342-9877{END FIELD}
234-2030{END FIELD}
{END RECORD}
=====================================================================
Field: 1                                    Doc 1 Pg 1 Ln 1" Pos 1"
```

Figure 20.3

Full-screen display of several records in a secondary document.

Take a look at the end of the record for Jennifer Jackson. The notation {END RECORD} signifies to WordPerfect that this record ends and the next record begins. WordPerfect automatically enters a hard page break for you.

Look at the order of the data in each record: the first name is always field 1, the last name is field 2, the title (or placeholder, if not present) is field 3, the company is field 4, and so on. The order in which your fields present data does not matter (for example, the last names could make up the first field). However, all records must have the fields in the same order by type and the same number of field lines. When this merge code is in the primary document:

    {FIELD}1~

the field 1 data is merged (in our example, the first name).

Figure 20.4 shows the codes as shown in the Reveal Codes screen. This code:

    [Mrg:END FIELD]

marks the end of each field. This code:

    [Mgr:END RECORD]

marks the end of each record. Notice that a hard page break [HPg] is also entered after the end of a record.

Figure 20.4

Secondary document Reveal Codes screen.

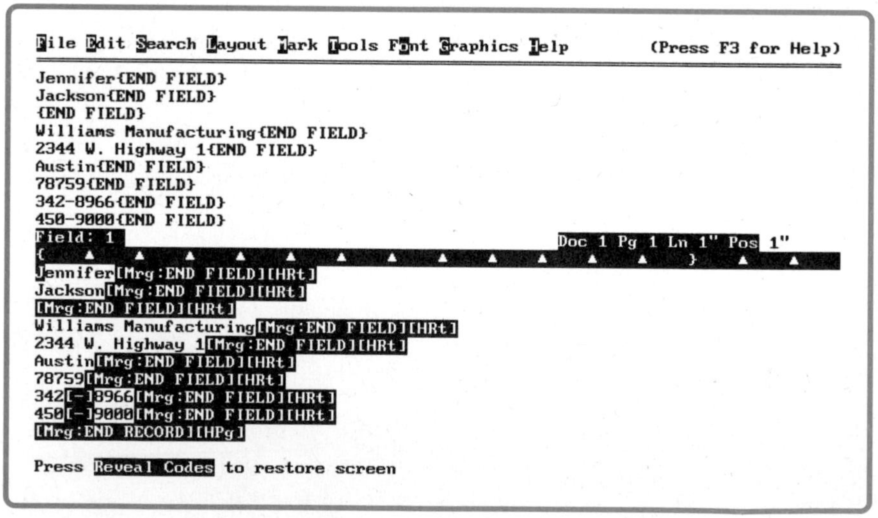

```
 File Edit Search Layout Mark Tools Font Graphics Help        (Press F3 for Help)

 Jennifer{END FIELD}
 Jackson{END FIELD}
 {END FIELD}
 Williams Manufacturing{END FIELD}
 2344 W. Highway 1{END FIELD}
 Austin{END FIELD}
 78759{END FIELD}
 342-8966{END FIELD}
 450-9000{END FIELD}
 Field: 1                                        Doc 1 Pg 1 Ln 1" Pos 1"
 [    ▲    ▲    ▲    ▲    ▲    ▲    ▲    ▲    ▲    ▲    ▲    }    ▲    ▲
 Jennifer[Mrg:END FIELD][HRt]
 Jackson[Mrg:END FIELD][HRt]
 [Mrg:END FIELD][HRt]
 Williams Manufacturing[Mrg:END FIELD][HRt]
 2344 W. Highway 1[Mrg:END FIELD][HRt]
 Austin[Mrg:END FIELD][HRt]
 78759[Mrg:END FIELD][HRt]
 342[-]8966[Mrg:END FIELD][HRt]
 450[-]9000[Mrg:END FIELD][HRt]
 [Mrg:END RECORD][HPg]

 Press Reveal Codes to restore screen
```

Figure 20.5 shows the first document (for Jennifer Jackson) fully merged, and it shows the beginning of the merging of the second document (for Preston Lindermann). The result of the merge, then, is one or more documents with the applicable fields from each record in the secondary document merged into the primary document. You can edit or print the merged document.

```
┌─────────────────────────────────────────────────────────────────────┐
│ File Edit Search Layout Mark Tools Font Graphics Help   (Press F3 for Help) │
│                                                                       │
│ Jennifer Jackson                                                      │
│ Williams Manufacturing                                                │
│ 2344 W. Highway 1                                                     │
│ Austin, TX 78759                                                      │
│                                                                       │
│ Dear Jennifer:                                                        │
│                                                                       │
│     Our annual conference is scheduled for May 23-25.  Jennifer,      │
│ are you interested in presenting a seminar?  Many successful          │
│ seminars are based on "real world" experiences.  How about your       │
│ experience at Williams Manufacturing?  If you can present a           │
│ seminar, call me at 253-9900 extension 3050 (day) or 432-9822         │
│ (evening).  Thank you.                                                │
│                                                                       │
│ Sincerely,                                                            │
│                                                                       │
│ Barbara J. Wiley                                                      │
│                                                                       │
│ ==================================================================== │
│ Preston Lindermann                                                    │
│ Analyst                                                               │
│ Bottcher Ltd.                          Doc 1 Pg 1 Ln 1" Pos 1"        │
└─────────────────────────────────────────────────────────────────────┘
```

Figure 20.5
Merged documents.

Creating a Secondary Document

It's usually a good idea to create the secondary document (the one that lists the data) first. That way, when you create the primary document, you have established the field references in your organization of the secondary document.

Start with a blank WordPerfect screen. Type in the first data field (such as name). When the field is entered, press F9 (Merge R). {END FIELD} appears in your document screen, and

[Mrg:END FIELD] appears in the Reveal Codes screen. Press ↵Enter to start a new line. Type in that second field, then press F9 (Merge R). Remember, if you don't have data for a certain field in a record, press F9 (Merge R) to keep the line as a space holder.

As you work, notice that a prompt like this appears at the bottom of your screen:

```
Field: 1
```

This identifies the number assigned to the field on which your cursor rests. This is the number to use in the primary document to refer to the field.

When you have entered all the fields for one record, press ⇧Shift-F9 (Merge Codes) and select 2 End Record, or select Merge Codes, then End Record from the Tools menu. {END RECORD} appears on the document screen followed by a page break. [Mrg:END RECORD] appears in the Reveal Codes screen along with a [HPg] code for the hard page break. Your cursor is placed past the page break, and this prompt appears instructing you to enter Field 1 for the next record:

```
Field: 1
```

Continue entering fields and records in this manner until all are entered. Make sure to end the last record with {END RECORD}. Then save your document as you would any WordPerfect document.

The following Quick Steps summarize creating a secondary document.

Creating a Secondary Document

1. Enter the first field data and press F9 (Merge R) and then ↵Enter.

   {END FIELD} appears, and you are on a new line to enter another field. The number for the new field appears in the lower left corner of the screen.

2. Enter all the fields for a record following the process in Step 1. On the line after the last field for the record, press ⇧Shift-F9 (Merge Codes) and 2 End Record, or select Merge Codes and End Record from the Tools menu.

   {END RECORD} and a hard page break are entered.

3. Enter the field for the next record. Or, if you are done, save the document like any WordPerfect document.

   After saving the secondary document, you may use it in a merge.

Before leaving the secondary document for good, check the field entries and the end of each record carefully. Answer these questions:

▲ Does each record have the same number of fields?

▲ Are the types of fields in the same order in each record?

▲ Is there an {END FIELD} mark at the end of each field?

▲ Is there an {END RECORD} mark at the end of each record (including the last record)?

▲ Are there unnecessary blank lines or text that should be deleted?

CAUTION: When entering the end field and end record codes, *do not* type in the actual brackets and letter that make up {END FIELD} or {END RECORD}. You must use the appropriate WordPerfect keypresses or menu selections.

Saving Time with Copy

Entering the end field and end record codes can become tedious. Also, some records may include similar information (such as addresses containing common city, state, and ZIP information). To save time and reduce the tedium, use the Copy command.

Enter the sample record. Then, block it with Alt-F4 (Block), or Block from the Edit menu. Then, copy using Ctrl-F4 (Move), then 1 Block, 2 Copy, or by selecting Copy from the Edit menu. Press ↵Enter to complete the copy at the location desired. Copy the text as needed to accommodate your data. Finally, go back and add or delete text in the records to meet your needs. The development of the document is simplified.

Creating a Primary Document

To create a primary document, type in the boilerplate text. When you want to reference a field, press `⇧Shift`-`F9` (Merge Codes) and select 1 Field, or select Merge Codes and then Field from the **T**ools menu. This prompt appears:

```
Enter Field:
```

Type in the number assigned to the field (in the secondary document) and press `↵Enter`. The entry looks like this:

```
{FIELD}1~
```

Again, *do not* type in {FIELD}1~ from your keyboard. If you do, that text will print, and you will not be calling data from the secondary document. You must use the WordPerfect keypresses or menu selections.

Continue to type in the boilerplate text and enter fields as desired. As mentioned earlier, fields need not be entered in order, and you can use all of the fields in the secondary document or only a few. When you are done creating the primary document, save it like any other WordPerfect document.

Using Secondary Documents More Than Once

Don't forget that the information in secondary documents can be used for more than one primary document. For example, you may have a customer list in a secondary document. One primary document might be used to generate a form letter thanking customers for their business. Such a document would be for 8.5" x 11" letterhead.

Continues

Continued

Another primary document could be used to generate envelopes for the form letter. This primary document would include the paper size/type for envelopes. Another primary document might create a postcard-size sales notice. A primary document would be needed to generate mailing labels to be used with the postcard. Need other ideas? How about customized holiday greetings for the customers on the list? As you can see, the use of primary documents is limited only by your imagination.

The following Quick Steps summarize creating a primary document.

Quick Steps

Creating a Primary Document

1. Type in the boilerplate text. When you want to insert a field from the secondary document, press ⇧Shift-F9 (Merge Codes) and select 1 Field, or select Merge Codes and Field from the Tools menu. Type in the number of the field and press ↵Enter.

   A code like this appears in your text: {FIELD}1~.

2. When all text and fields are entered, save the document.

   The document is saved.

Be sure to check your document before saving, asking these questions:

▲ Have you entered each field with the correct number?

▲ Is the punctuation placed appropriately around the field data that will be inserted?

Primary Document and Copy or Macros

If you need to create a primary document that is similar to another primary document, save time by copying all or parts of the first document to create the second. For example, you may have a letter with the address and salutation set up. When you create a new letter, just copy that information to the new document. (Chapter 17 describes how to copy between documents.)

Another timesaving idea is to create macros with often-used field code layouts (such as name and address). This automates the entry of fields.

Using copy or macros to enter primary document field codes not only saves time but reduces the chance of error.

Merging

Once you have completed the primary and secondary documents, you can merge them. Start with a blank WordPerfect screen. Press Ctrl-F9 (Merge/Sort) then 1 Merge, or select Merge from the Tools menu. This prompt appears:

```
Primary file:
```

Type in the name of primary document (include the drive and path, if necessary) and press ⏎Enter. This prompt appears:

```
Secondary file:
```

Type in, as needed, the drive and path, and name of the secondary document. Press ⏎Enter and the merge begins.

TIP: You may use a database or other file (other than one created with WordPerfect) for the secondary file. If this is the case, the file must have "DOS delimiters," which are special characters that separate the fields and records. (See the manual for the database or other package to determine which delimiter characters the program uses.) If you are using a DOS delimited file, when the prompt for the secondary document appears, press Ctrl-F5 (Text In/ Out). The prompt becomes DOS Text delimited file. Enter the name of the DOS text file. The Merge: DOS Text File screen appears. Enter the Field Delimiters and Record Delimiters (press F7 (Exit) after entering each delimiter to continue). When all definitions have been entered, press ⏎Enter and the merge begins.

This prompt tells you that WordPerfect is merging the two documents:

```
*Merging*
```

The documents are merged and appear on your screen. Check to make sure the result is as you expected. Save the

document. You may edit it and print it as you would any
WordPerfect document.

> **TIP:** When you begin using merge, your first results may not
> come out as you wanted. This is pretty normal. Call up the
> secondary document and check each record and field
> carefully. Then look at your primary document and check
> each field carefully. Pay special attention to the fields and
> records where the data did not print appropriately. After
> making corrections, try again.

Inserting the Current Date

WordPerfect has a variety of commands which you can use for
merging. The date command is especially helpful. Place it in
your primary document and the current date will print in place
of the code.

To use the date command, place your cursor in the primary
document where you want the date placed. Press ⇧Shift-F9
(Merge Codes) then 6 More, or select Merge Codes then More
from the Tools menu. The screen shown in Figure 20.6 appears.
Here, {DATE} is highlighted for selection. Once you have selected {DATE}, press ↵Enter. {DATE} appears in your document
and [Mrg:DATE] appears in the Reveal Codes screen. When you
merge the primary document, {DATE} is replaced with the
current date set in your computer.

Merge Codes:
More screen.

```
 File  Edit  Search  Layout  Mark  Tools  Font  Graphics  Help        (Press F3 for Help)


 {FIELD}1~ {FIELD}2~                    ┌─────────────────────────────────────┐
 {FIELD}3?~                             │{CASE CALL}expr~cs1~lb1~...csN~lbN~~  │
 {FIELD}4~                              │{CHAIN MACRO}macroname~        (^G)   │
 {FIELD}5~                              │{CHAIN PRIMARY}filename~              │
 {FIELD}6~, TX {FIELD}7~                │{CHAIN SECONDARY}filename~            │
                                        │{CHAR}var~message~                   │
 Dear {FIELD}1~:                        │{COMMENT}comment~                    │
                                        │{CTON}character~                     │
      Our annual conference is scheduled│{DATE}                         (^D)  │
 interested in presenting a seminar?  Man│{DOCUMENT}filename~                 │
 based on "real world" experiences.  How│{ELSE}                              │
 {FIELD}4~?  If you can present a seminar└─────────────────────────────────────┘
 3050 (day) or 432-9822 (evening).  Thank you.

 Sincerely,

 Barbara J. Wiley



                              (Name Search; Arrows; Enter to Select)
```

Sorting

WordPerfect allows you to sort lists alphabetically or numeri-
cally. This is particularly useful when creating a secondary merge
document. To sort, simply select the text to sort. If you don't
make a selection, the contents of the entire document will be
sorted. For example, Figure 20.7 shows a list to sort.

CAUTION: Before you sort, always save a copy of your
document. That way, if the result of the sort is different than
you imagined, you still have the original document to try
the sort again.

Press Ctrl-F9 (Merge/Sort) then select 2 Sort or select
Sort from the Tools menu. At the Input file to sort: prompt,
press ↵Enter to sort the document on the screen or type in the
name of the file to sort then press ↵Enter. At the Output file

for sort: prompt, press ⏎Enter to replace the document on the screen with the sorted result or enter a file name to sort to. The Sort menu appears in the lower part of the screen (see Figure 20.8).

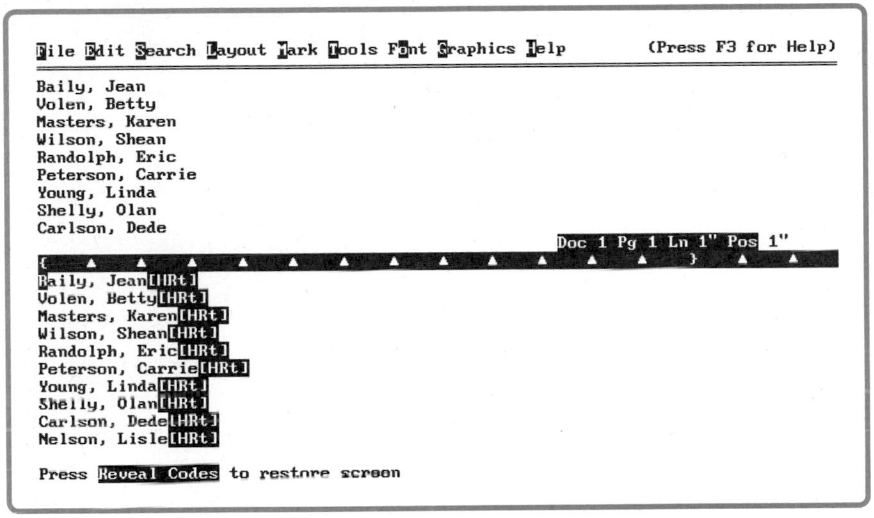

Figure 20.7

A list to sort.

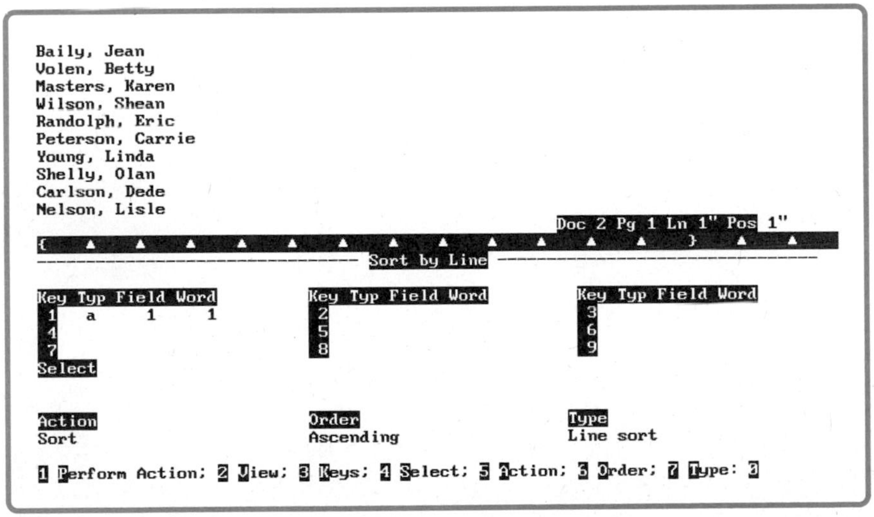

Figure 20.8

The Sort menu.

On the Sort menu, you have several selections. Select 1 Perform Action to begin the sort. Select 2 View to look at the text in the upper half of the screen. When you sort, you won't use 5 Action because you want the value left as Sort. Select 6 Order to change the order to 1 Ascending (A-Z, 1-9) or 2 Descending (Z-A, 9-1). Change the Type if desired by selecting 7 Type and identifying 1 Merge to sort secondary merge records, 2 Line to sort records that are a line in length, or 3 Paragraph to sort records that are a paragraph long.

Once the Action, Order, and Type are defined, you may consider the Keys (set up through selecting 5 Keys). A *key* is the word within the record that you use to sort (for example, last name or city in an address record). You will enter the key Type (either Alphanumeric or Numeric). And then, enter the location of the key by Field and Word. Fields in lines or paragraphs are separated by tabs or indents. Fields in merge records are separated by {END FIELD} codes and those in table rows are separated into cells. Fields are considered to be numbered from left to right. Finally, words within a key are separated by spaces, forward slashes, and hard hyphens (and are also numbered from left to right in the field).

For example, you may have a list of product item numbers, the item description, and size in line records with two fields separated by tabs like this:

54689   Shirt/M

435677   Shirt/XL

435677   Shirt/M

435677   Shirt/S

The first key (key 1) to sort on could be the product item number. To find this key for the sort, WordPerfect needs its Key. That is:

```
Type                              Field Word
(for Numeric)                       1    1
```

The second key (key 2) to sort on is a little more tricky. We want to sort by size. The Key Definition is:

```
Type                              Field Word
(for alphanumeric)                  2    2
```

The field is 2 because the first field in the record in this example is the product number and the second field consists of the product description and size. The Word is 2 because the product description (Shirt) is the first word, followed by a forward slash separating it and the second word, which is the size (the word on which we want to sort).

The result of this sort would be as follows. The first key (the product number) is sorted first. Then, the size is sorted within each product number group.

435677   Shirt/M

435677   Shirt/S

435677   Shirt/XL

54689   Shirt/M

The result of the name sort is shown in Figure 20.9. Notice that the lines were sorted in ascending alphabetical order. No code is placed in the document.

The following Quick Steps summarize how to sort a list.

Sorting a List

1. Press Ctrl-F9 (Merge/ Sort) then 2 Sort, or select Sort from the Tools menu.

   The `Input file to sort:` prompt appears.

2. Press ↵Enter to sort the document on the screen or enter a document name.

   The `Output file to sort:` prompt appears.

3. Press ↵Enter to save to the screen or enter a document name.

   The Sort menu appears.

4. Complete the Sort menu and select 1 Perform Action

   The document is sorted.

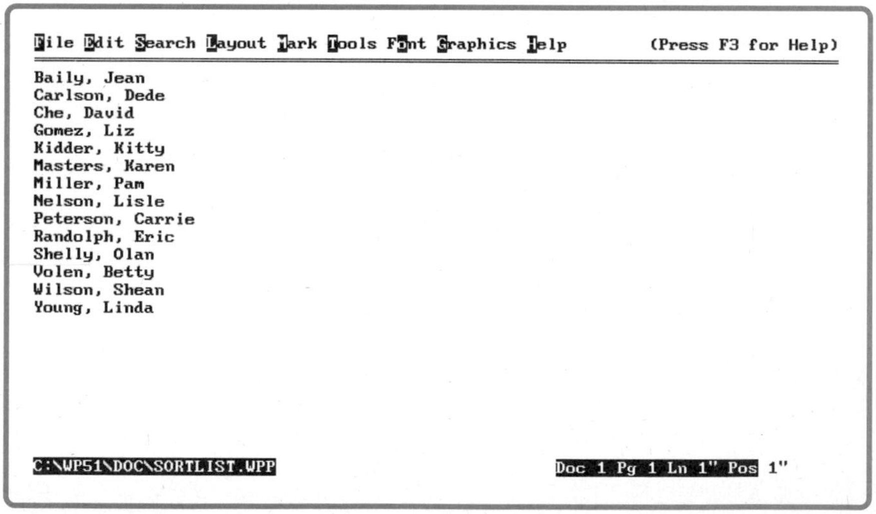

Figure 20.9
A sorted list.

```
 File  Edit  Search  Layout  Mark  Tools  Font  Graphics  Help        (Press F3 for Help)
 Baily, Jean
 Carlson, Dede
 Che, David
 Gomez, Liz
 Kidder, Kitty
 Masters, Karen
 Miller, Pam
 Nelson, Lisle
 Peterson, Carrie
 Randolph, Eric
 Shelly, Olan
 Volen, Betty
 Wilson, Shean
 Young, Linda




 C:\WP51\DOC\SORTLIST.WPP                           Doc 1 Pg 1 Ln 1" Pos 1"
```

What's Next?

We've just touched on the basics of the power of WordPerfect's merge capabilities. WordPerfect's Merge language is almost as rich as its Macro language, and you can do some fairly complex, programming-like operations with it. Master the ones in this chapter first, and then explore other merge features, including:

▲ Assigning field names in place of numbers to make your primary documents more descriptive

▲ Pausing the merge in order to enter data from the keyboard for one-time data needs

▲ Inserting the current date

▲ Starting a macro from the end of a merge to perform another activity

▲ Printing all the records from a secondary document on one page (to create lists of members, for example)

▲ Displaying a message as you merge

▲ Inserting a document file instead of identifying a primary file

▲ Stopping the merge at a certain point (for example, to merge only part of the data in a secondary document)

There are also more sophisticated sort procedures that allow you to select certain records from a document then sort those records. If you use Sort often or on complex documents, you may want to consult a more advanced book to learn how to select then sort.

In This Chapter

Adding or Editing Vertical and Horizontal Lines

1. Press Alt-F9 (Graphics) then 5 Line, or select Line from the **G**raphics menu.
2. Select whether to create or edit a horizontal or vertical line, and continue.

Creating a Figure

1. Press Alt-F9 (Graphics) then 1 Figure or 3 Text Box, or select Figure or Text Box from the **G**raphics menu.
2. Select 1 - Create and complete the screen.

Identifying Options

1. Press Alt-F9 (Graphics) or select the Graphics menu.
2. Select the type of box or figure.
3. Select 4 Options and enter the desired options.

Using Graphics in Your Documents

Whether you have a printer that handles sophisticated graphics or you have a simple printer that produces basic results, there are graphic features you can use in your documents. This chapter will get you up and running. You may want to try out the examples in this chapter on your printer to see the outcome you get.

Adding and Editing Vertical and Horizontal Lines

Just like the slogan from "The Outer Limits" that went, "You control the horizontal. You control the vertical." True for WordPerfect, too.

You may add horizontal or vertical lines in your document for a pleasing effect. The lines may be black or a shade of gray and you can set the width of the lines. For example, the sample resumé shown in the View Document screen in Figure 21.1 is before lines were added, while Figure 21.2 shows the resumé after it was dressed up with horizontal and vertical lines. Even though no fancy fonts are used, the resumé is much more striking with the simple addition of lines.

NOTE: Not all printers handle all line and graph options. You will need to experiment to see what your printer handles.

Figure 21.1

The sample resumé before lines are added.

```
                         Barbara J. Wiley
                          3421 Pecos Way
                     San Diego, California 92123

      Experience:

         1988-present   Programmer    Barney Corporation, 4566
                                      Oakway, Austin, Texas 78759
                                      (512) 253-9900.

                                      Cobol and PL1 in an IBM
                                      environment.

         1985-1988      Operator      Beverly World, PO Box 843,
                                      Austin, Texas 78777
                                      (512) 435-9000.

      Education:

         Bachelor of Science (Computer Science)
         University of Iowa, Iowa City, Iowa.
         Awarded 1984.

      Affiliations:

         Data Processing Professional Group, 1985 to present.




 1 100%  2 200%  3 Full Page  4 Facing Pages: 1          Doc 1 Pg 1
```

CAUTION: Before adding lines or any graphic effects, always save a version of your document before you begin. That way, if the result is not as you anticipated, you can always go back to your "clean" document.

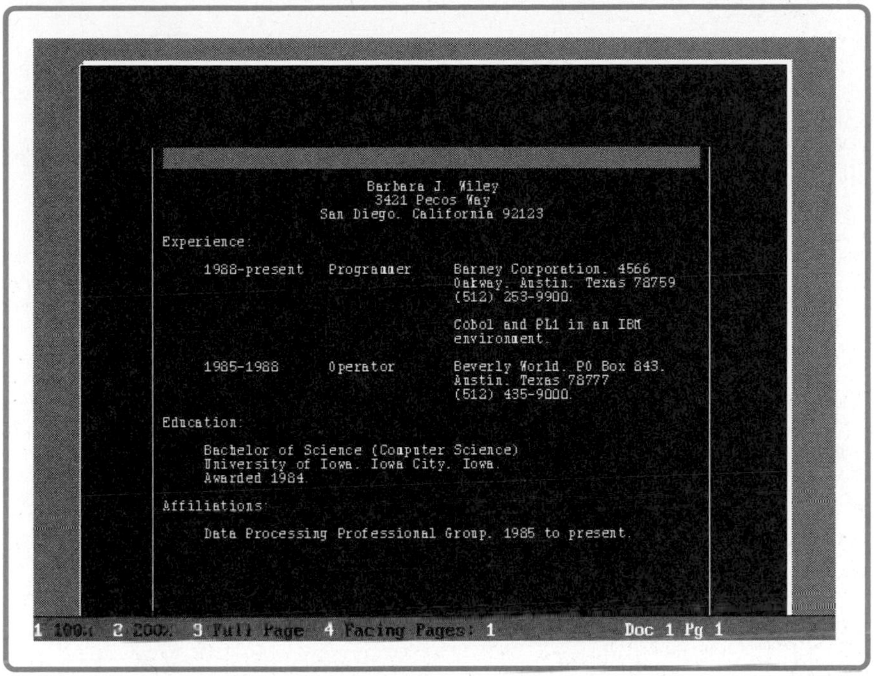

Figure 21.2
*The sample resumé
after lines are added.*

To set up a line, press Alt - F9 (Graphics) then select 5 Line, or select Line from the **G**raphics menu. Select the option to create a horizontal or vertical line. Depending on whether you are adding a horizontal or vertical line, the Graphics: Horizontal Line or Graphics: Vertical Line screen appears. The screens contain the same information (see Figure 21.3 for an example).

On the screen, identify the position of the line by entering the Horizontal Position and Vertical Position of the line from the top and left of the page, respectively. Several Horizontal and Vertical Positions allow you to enter the specific Length of Line in inches. Enter the Width of Line in inches. Finally, enter the Gray Shading as a percentage of black. (Not all printers handle Gray Shading. You may want to test yours.)

The horizontal lines shown in the resumé in Figure 21.2 were set with the Horizontal Position at Full, Vertical Position at Baseline, Width of Line at .25", and Gray Shading at 50%.

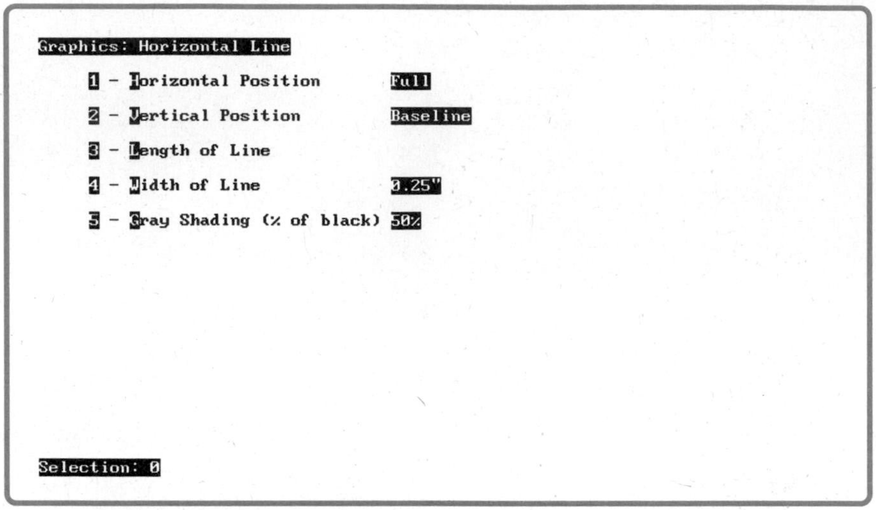

Figure 21.3

*The Graphics:
Horizontal Line
screen.*

```
Graphics: Horizontal Line
    1 - Horizontal Position        Full
    2 - Vertical Position          Baseline
    3 - Length of Line
    4 - Width of Line              0.25"
    5 - Gray Shading (% of black)  50%




Selection: 0
```

The vertical lines in Figure 21.2 were set up with the Horizontal Position (for each vertical line) at Left Margin for one line and Right Margin for the other. For both lines, the Vertical Position is set to Full Page (extending from the top to the bottom margin), the Width of Line set to 0.013", and Gray Shading set at 100% (for black).

The other Horizontal Position options (for horizontal or vertical lines) include Left (against the left margin), Right (against the right margin), Center, Between Columns, and Set Position (to enter a precise measure from the top of the page). Another possible Vertical Position option is to Specify the Position from the top of the page.

When all settings are in place for a single line, press F7 (Exit). A code like the following is placed in your document:

```
[HLine:Baseline,Center,6.5"0.25",50%]
```

It is full of numbers but easy to interpret. It indicates whether the line is horizontal or vertical, the vertical position, the horizontal position, the length of the line, the width of the line, and the gray shading.

TIP: Experiment with lines. To see what your text will look like before printing, don't forget to use View Document. Press ⇧Shift-F7 (Print), or select **P**rint from the **F**ile menu, then 6 - View Document.

To edit a line, place your cursor on or after the code for the line. Press Alt-F9 (Graphics) then 5 Line or select Line from the **G**raphics menu. Choose whether to edit a horizontal or vertical line. (WordPerfect searches backward then forward for the first horizontal or vertical line code.) The Graphics: Horizontal Line or Graphics: Vertical Line screen appears for you to make changes.

The following Quick Steps summarize the procedure for adding lines.

Adding Lines to a Document

1. Press Alt-F9 (Graphics) then select 5 Line or select Line from the **G**raphics menu.

   Options to create a horizontal or vertical line appear.

2. Identify whether to create a horizontal or vertical line.

   The Graphics: Horizontal Line or Graphics: Vertical Line screen appears.

3. Complete the entries and press F7 (Exit).

   A code for the line appears like the following in your document:
   ```
   [HLine:Baseline,
   Center,6.5"0.25",50%].
   ```

Quick Steps

TIP: WordPerfect also has a Line Draw feature which turns your arrow keys into drawing tools. Place your cursor where you want to begin drawing. Press Ctrl-F3 (Screen) then 2 Line Draw or select Line Draw from the **Tools** menu. Just move the arrow keys to begin drawing. To change the style of the line while in Line Draw mode, make a selection 1 through 3. To change the type of line graphic in selection 1, 2, or 3, select 4 Change and pick a new line graphic. To move your cursor without drawing a line (and without leaving Line Draw mode), select 6 Move. To erase a portion of the line, position your cursor and use 5 Erase.

Enclosing and Editing Text in a Box

You can enter text in a box to emphasize it or set it apart. Figure 21.4 shows a simple use of this feature displayed through View Document. (Press ⇧Shift-F7 (Print), or select Print from the **F**ile menu, then 6 - View Document.)

Don't Forget Headers and Footers

A good use of text boxes is in headers or footers. Instead of simple text, a box around the text and/or shading can add interest.

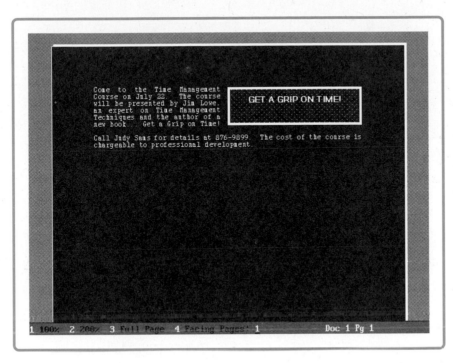

Figure 21.4

Text placed in a box.

To place text in a box:

▲ Enter the options for the box (to set options other than the defaults).

▲ Create the box.

To control options, press Alt-F9 (Graphics), 3 Text Box, then 4 Options. Or, select Text Box then Options from the **G**raphics menu. The Options: Text Box screen shown in Figure 21.5 appears.

Common selections you will want to control are 1 - **B**order Style, 2 - **O**utside Border Spacing (from the border of the box to the text outside the box), 3 - **I**nside Border Spacing (from the border of the box to the text inside the box), 6 - **C**aption Number Style (if you use a caption), and 9 - **G**ray Shading (% of black).

In the example, all four borders are set to Thick Border Style and Gray Shading is set to 10%. All other defaults remain. Press F7 (Exit) when the Options: Text Box screen is complete. A [Txt Opt] code is placed in the document at the cursor location. The Options you set govern any text boxes you create after the code, until you enter new options.

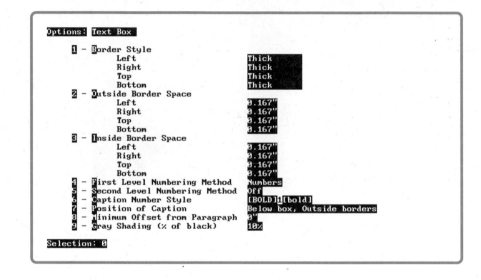

Figure 21.5

The Options: Text Box screen.

To enter text in a new box, press Alt-F9 Graphics, 3 Text Box, and 1 Create, or select Text Box then Create from the Graphics menu. The Definition: Text Box screen appears. Set the options shown in Figure 21.6. These options include:

1 - **F**ilename: To enter a path and filename containing text for the box, if the text is contained in a file.

2 - C**o**ntents: To select the type of box contents.

3 - **C**aption: To enter the text for the caption on the box, if one is desired.

4 - Anchor **T**ype: To identify how you want the box handled when the surrounding text is edited. Select

Paragraph and the box will be kept with the surrounding text, even if you move the text. Select Page and the box will be kept on the specified page. Choose Character for the box to be handled as a character on the line containing the cursor.

5 - **V**ertical Position: If the Anchor Type is Paragraph, type in the distance from the top of the paragraph. If you anchor the box on the page, you may select Full Page display, against the Top or Bottom margins, Center of the page, or Set a Position from the top edge of the page. If you anchored the box to a character, you may place the box so that the box's Top, Center, or Bottom lines move up with the baseline of the text on the line. You may also select Baseline to align the baseline of the box to the baseline of the text in the line.

6 - **H**orizontal Position: If the box is anchored to a paragraph, you may position it against the Left or Right margin. You may Center the box between margins or have the box take up the Full space between margins. If you anchor the box on a page, the options are the same as Paragraph anchoring with the addition of column options (Left, Right, Center, and Full) and you may Set Position. If the box is anchored to a character, you will not set the horizontal position because the box follows the character on the line.

7 - **S**ize: Identify how to set the width and height of the box. You may select Set Width or Set Height and have WordPerfect automatically set the other dimension. You may set both the width and height with Set Both. Or, you may have WordPerfect make both the width and height by selecting Auto Both.

8 - **W**rap Text Around Box: Respond Yes to this option if you want to be able to enter text in your document around the edges of the box.

9 - **E**dit: Select Edit to go to the Box: screen that is shown in Figure 21.7. Type in the text using any of WordPerfect's editing features. As you can see in the Reveal Codes screen in Figure 21.7, text is set up in Helvetica font and centered. Press F7 (Exit) when text has been entered.

Figure 21.6

The Definition: Text Box screen.

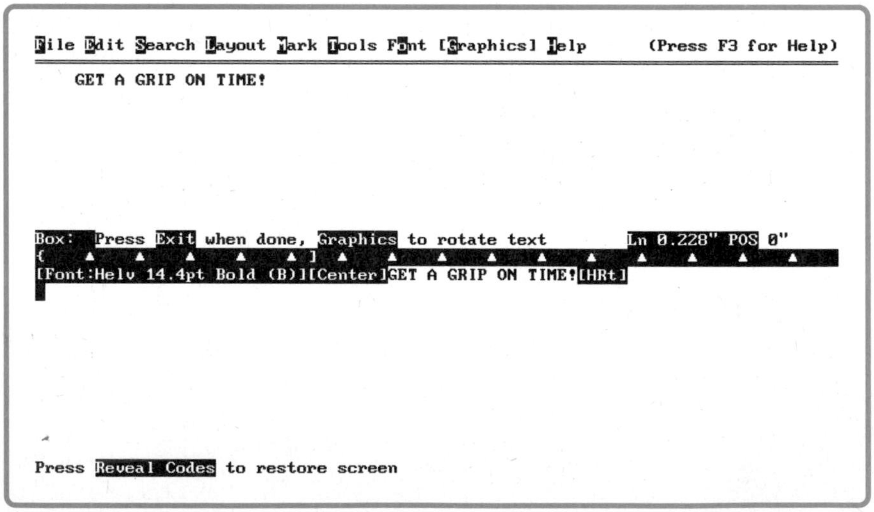

Figure 21.7

The Box: screen with text entered.

Press F7 (Exit) when the Definition: Text Box screen is completed. A code like the following is placed in the document:

```
[Txt Box:1;;]
```

The number in the code is the text box number that WordPerfect assigns. If you have more than one text box in a document, WordPerfect numbers them sequentially.

Figure 21.8 illustrates the completed box displayed through View Document.

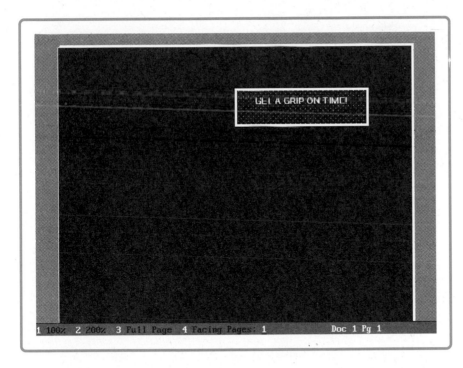

Figure 21.8

The completed text box.

Since we responded Yes to 8 - Wrap Text Around Box (on the Definition: Text Box screen), we can type text around the text box. Figure 21.9 shows the document with text added outside the text box. Notice in the Reveal Codes screen there are no hard returns in the paragraph, which is just left of the graphic. Text just wraps around the text box.

Figure 21.9

*Text wrapped
around the text box.*

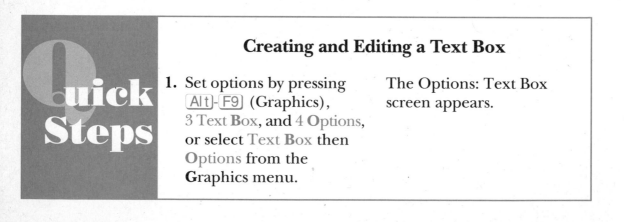

Figure 21.9

*Text wrapped
around the text box.*

To delete a box, delete the code for the box. To edit the
contents of a text box, press [Alt]-[F9] (Graphics), 3 Text Box,
and 2 Edit, or select Text Box then Edit from the **G**raphics
menu. Enter the number of the text box you want to edit and
press [⏎Enter]. Make any changes you like and press [F7] (Exit).

The following Quick Steps summarize how to create and
edit a text box.

Quick Steps

Creating and Editing a Text Box

1. Set options by pressing [Alt]-[F9] (Graphics), 3 Text **Box**, and 4 Options, or select Text Box then Options from the **G**raphics menu.

The Options: Text Box screen appears.

2. Complete the options and press F7 (Exit).

An option code is placed in your document. The code for a Text Box: [Txt Opt].

3. Create a box by pressing Alt-F9 (Graphics), 3 Text Box, and 1 Create, or select Text Box then Create from the Graphics menu.

The Definition: Text Box screen appears.

4. Complete the options and press F7 (Exit).

A text box code like the following is placed in your document: [Text Box:1;BULB.WPG;].

5. To later edit the box, press Alt-F9 (Graphics), 3 Text Box, and 2 Edit, or select Text Box then Edit from the Graphics menu. Enter the box number and press ↵Enter; change the settings and contents and press F7 (Exit).

The box is edited per your instructions.

Adding and Editing Figures

WordPerfect comes with a number of graphic characters which you can insert in flyers, memos, newsletters and so on. You can use these characters in virtually any document that calls for a little pizazz.

While most printers will handle lines and text boxes, not all will print the graphics supplied with WordPerfect. Test your computer to see if this fancy feature will work for you.

Using or Creating Custom Graphics

You may use graphics from third party sources or create your own custom graphics with products like Microsoft Windows Paintbrush. This opens up a wide variety of effects and options. You can be very specific in designing your own letterhead, business cards, birthday cards, invitations, brochures, or advertisements.

Before you buy a graphics product, make sure it is compatible with WordPerfect. You may check your *WordPerfect Reference* for compatible file formats. Or, you may check with the manufacturer of the product you are considering to find out if the product is compatible with WordPerfect.

If you try to use a graphic file that is incompatible, you may have luck using WordPerfect's graphic conversion program to convert the file to WordPerfect graphic format. Check your *WordPerfect Reference* for specific instructions on graphic file conversion.

The basic steps to add a figure are the same as the ones for adding a text box:

▲ Enter the options for the figure (to set options other than the defaults).

▲ Create the figure.

To control options, press Alt-F9 (Graphics), 1 Figure, then 4 Options. Or, select Figure then Options from the **G**raphics menu. The Options: Figure screen shown in Figure 21.10 appears. For the example, all Border Styles were set to Double line. All other defaults remain including the Outside Border Space and Inside Border Space, Minimum Offset from Paragraph (the vertical space from the top of the paragraph to the top of the figure, if the figure is anchored to a paragraph), and Gray Shading. Press F7. Your exit of the screen is complete. A code [Fig Opt] appears in your document. Any figures placed after this code will conform to the options set.

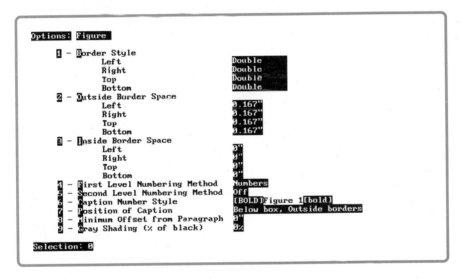

Figure 21.10

Options: Figure screen.

Next, add the figure. Press Alt-F9 (Graphics), 1 Figure, and 1 Create, or select Figure then Create from the **G**raphics menu. The Definition: Figure screen appears. Just like with the Definition: Text Box screen, select 1 - Filename then enter the path and filename of the graphic to place in the figure. If you don't know the filename, you may select 1 - Filename then press F5 (List Files) and continue to search for the file. To find

WordPerfect's graphic files, search for *.WPG files in the WP51 directory. Just list the files for this path: C:\WP51*.WPG.

You may select 9 - Edit to change the appearance of the contents of the figure. When you select 9 - Edit, a screen like that shown in Figure 21.11 appears. The BUTTRFLY.WPG file was selected. You may use this screen to move, scale, rotate, invert, or display the graphic in black and white or color/shaded.

Figure 21.11

Editing WordPerfect's BUTTRFLY.WPG graphic file.

Press [F7] (Exit) as needed to leave the screen to edit the graphic and the Definition: Figure screen. A code for the figure is placed in your document. Figure 21.12 shows the results after text is added.

To see the placement of the graphic on the screen with your text, press [Shift]-[F7] (Print) or select Print from the File menu, and then select 6 - View Document. Figure 21.13 illustrates the View Document screen. Because documents with graphics typically take longer to print, you can save considerable time by

checking and adjusting the look of your document through
View Document before printing.

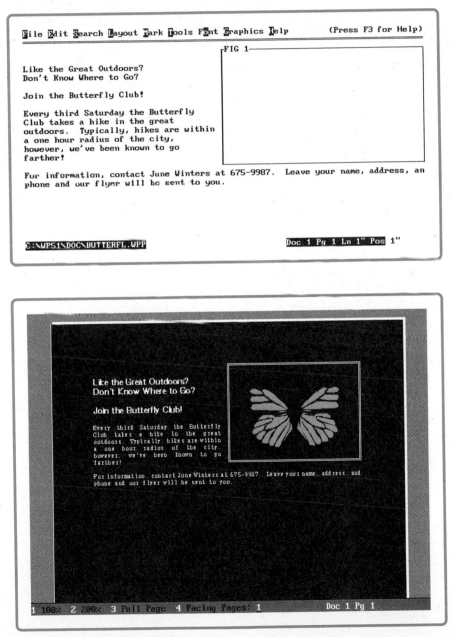

Figure 21.12
The figure with text added.

Figure 21.13
The View Document screen

To get rid of a figure, delete the code for the figure. To edit the figure, press [Alt]-[F9] (Graphics), select 1 Figure then 2 Edit, or select Figure then Edit from the Graphics menu. Enter the number of the figure to edit and press [↵Enter]. The Definition: Figure screen for the figure appears where you may change any settings for that particular figure.

The following Quick Steps detail how to create and edit a figure.

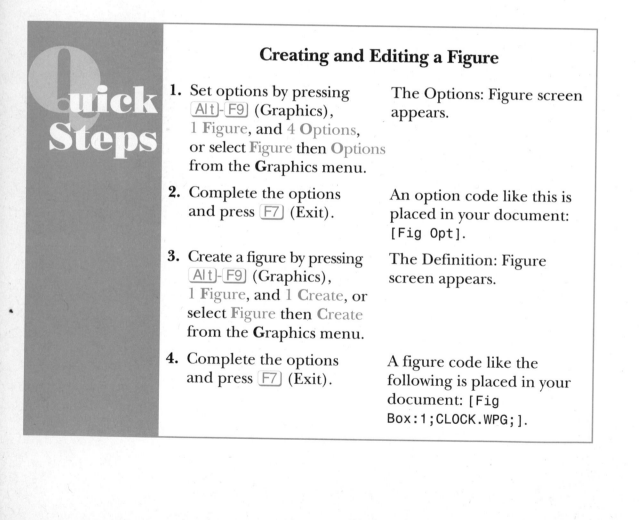

Creating and Editing a Figure

1. Set options by pressing [Alt]-[F9] (Graphics), 1 Figure, and 4 Options, or select Figure then Options from the Graphics menu.

The Options: Figure screen appears.

2. Complete the options and press [F7] (Exit).

An option code like this is placed in your document: [Fig Opt].

3. Create a figure by pressing [Alt]-[F9] (Graphics), 1 Figure, and 1 Create, or select Figure then Create from the Graphics menu.

The Definition: Figure screen appears.

4. Complete the options and press [F7] (Exit).

A figure code like the following is placed in your document: [Fig Box:1;CLOCK.WPG;].

5. To later edit the figure, press Alt -F9 (Graphics), 1 Figure, and 2 Edit, or select Figure then Edit from the **G**raphics menu. Enter the figure number and press ↵Enter ; change the settings and contents and press F7 (Exit).

The figure is edited per your instructions.

What's Next?

This chapter was meant to scratch the surface on graphics and give you some basic skills for getting started. There is much, much more to graphics than can be covered this briefly.

When you become comfortable using the basic approaches in this chapter, read more and experiment more. There are plenty of other looks you can add to spice up your documents. For instance, you can add and control captions for graphics, perform sophisticated editing on figures (enlarging, rotating, mirror imaging, moving, and so on), and place graphics in columns for sophisticated newsletters. You can also create Table Boxes as well as Equation boxes for numbers, mathematical equations, and scientific equations. Additionally, there is a User Box option that allows you to customize your own images.

For example, to create a caption for a graphic, you can create a text box or figure (both described earlier in this chapter). On the Definition: screen, select 3 - Caption. You are taken to a screen where you can enter any caption desired. Press F7 (Exit) when done. You are returned to the Definition: screen and may continue development of the text box or figure.

To learn more (along with the tricks and techniques for what you do know), consult an advanced reference to Word-Perfect.

Creating a Style

1. Press Alt - F8 (Styles), or select Styles from the Layout menu.
2. Select 3 Create and continue.
3. Complete the Styles: Edit screen and press F7 (Exit).

Using a Style

1. Press Alt - F8 (Styles), or select Styles from the Layout menu.
2. Highlight the style and select 1 On.

Style Contents and Control

▲ Styles may include codes, text and graphics.

Creating and Using Styles

If you develop reports, newsletters, or other documents with special font, graphic, or text effects, you will want to learn about Styles. Using styles allows you to save many keystrokes by automating common formatting options.

The What and When of Styles

A *style* is usually thought of as a collection of formatting instructions that you identify based on your own needs. However, you can also include graphics and text, as well as formatting codes, in a style. Then, use the style whenever you want to insert that set of codes, graphics, or text into your document. Styles both save time (because you don't have to continually re-enter the formatting codes) and increase accuracy (because the style is tested, you know it is correct).

When should you create a style? Create a style for any special formatting, text, or graphics that you use over and over. For instance, you may create company reports, develop organization newsletters, or create letters or memos with varying formatting elements. Using styles will speed the more repetitive tasks in developing such documents and free you to concentrate on the more creative aspects of your work.

TIP: You can include in a style any codes, graphics, or text that may be put in a regular WordPerfect document. This includes figures, lines, names, addresses, special fonts, formatting, index or table of contents codes, column on and off settings, and so on.

The example in Figure 22.1 shows a monthly flyer describing company news. It includes five customized styles with different fonts which account for the unusual spacing of text. The document is shown through View Document; press ⌐Shift⌐-⌐F7⌐ (Print) or select Print from the File menu, then select 6 - View Document. The five styles created for this example are:

▲ Flyer heading, which includes the font codes, title of the flyer, and the solid line.

▲ Major heading for company flyer body, which contains font and underline codes.

▲ Minor heading for company flyer body, which contains font and underline codes.

▲ Body of company flyer, which contains font and tab codes.

▲ Article divider for company flyer, which contains the line code.

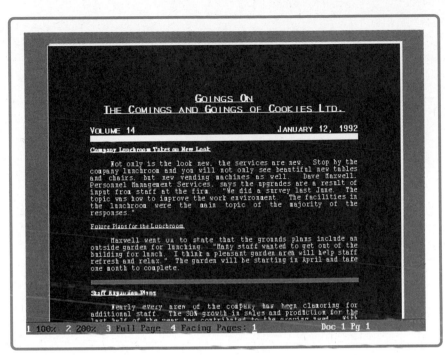

Figure 22.1
*Monthly flyer with
five customized
styles.*

Styles and Graphics

If you find yourself defining graphics options often, you
may want to set up a style for each of the different option
settings you use. This way, you will not have to redefine the
options each time you want to switch. Just insert the new
style and away you go.

Types of Styles

When you create and use a style, the style can be *paired* or *open*.
A *paired style* places two codes in your document. One at the

beginning of the new style and one at the end. An *open style* places a code only at the beginning of the new style. Figure 22.2 shows the paired style codes in place for the flyer.

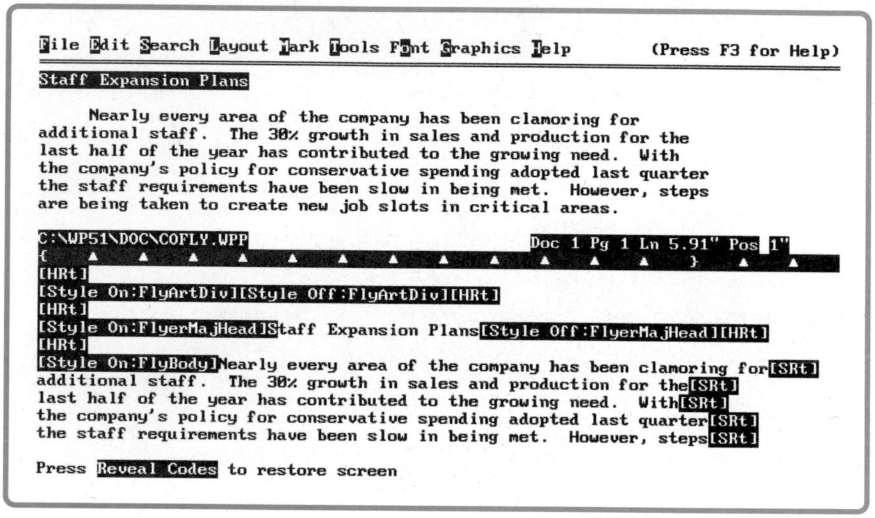

Figure 22.2

Paired style codes.

```
File Edit Search Layout Mark Tools Font Graphics Help        (Press F3 for Help)
Staff Expansion Plans
        Nearly every area of the company has been clamoring for
additional staff.  The 30% growth in sales and production for the
last half of the year has contributed to the growing need.  With
the company's policy for conservative spending adopted last quarter
the staff requirements have been slow in being met.  However, steps
are being taken to create new job slots in critical areas.

C:\WP51\DOC\COFLY.WPP                          Doc 1 Pg 1 Ln 5.91" Pos 1"
{    ▲    ▲    ▲    ▲    ▲    ▲    ▲    ▲    ▲    ▲    }    ▲
[HRt]
[Style On:FlyArtDiv][Style Off:FlyArtDiv][HRt]
[HRt]
[Style On:FlyerMajHead]Staff Expansion Plans[Style Off:FlyerMajHead][HRt]
[HRt]
[Style On:FlyBody]Nearly every area of the company has been clamoring for[SRt]
additional staff.  The 30% growth in sales and production for the[SRt]
last half of the year has contributed to the growing need.  With[SRt]
the company's policy for conservative spending adopted last quarter[SRt]
the staff requirements have been slow in being met.  However, steps[SRt]

Press Reveal Codes to restore screen
```

Notice that these paired style codes mark the location of the divider. No text is placed between the codes.

```
[Style On:FlyArtDiv][Style Off:FlyArtDiv]
```

The following paired style codes contain the text for a major heading. The text is added between the codes.

```
[Style On:FlyerMajHead]Staff Expansion Plans
[Style Off:FlyerMajHead]
```

The body style is represented by these codes with text between the codes:

```
[Style On:FlyBody][Style Off:FlyBody]
```

When you use paired style codes like these and are done with the style, use the arrow keys to move beyond the last code and continue with your work. If you use an open style code, only one code marks the start of the style. To stop using the style, enter a new style or other formatting to change the appearance of the text later in the document.

> **CAUTION:** Whether you use paired or open styles is a matter of preference. If you use paired styles, be careful to move the cursor beyond the last code before starting a new style unless you want to place one style inside another to give the text the effect of both styles.

> **TIP:** If you often use outlining or paragraph numbering, it may be timesaving to create an Outline type of style. That way, when you want to turn outlining or paragraph numbering on or off, you can do so through Styles rather than through Outline. You may also use more sophisticated numbering formats than available through using Alt-F5 (Outline), or selecting Outline from the Tools menu.

Creating a Style

To create a style, press Alt-F8 (Styles), or select Styles from the Layout menu. The Styles screen appears. Select 3 Create. The Styles: Edit screen appears (see Figure 22.3).

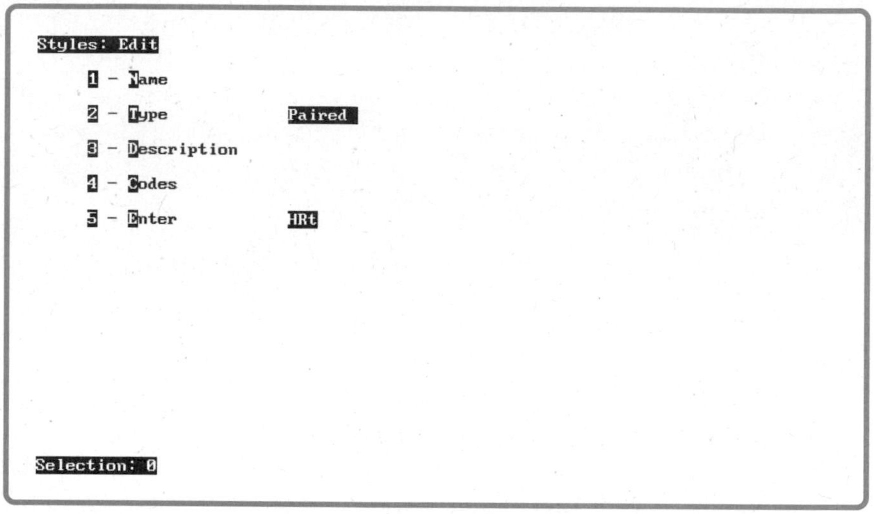

Chapter 22

Figure 22.3
The Styles: Edit screen.

```
Styles: Edit
    1 - Name
    2 - Type          Paired
    3 - Description
    4 - Codes
    5 - Enter         HRt




Selection: 0
```

On this screen, select 1 - Name to enter the name of the style (which will appear in the code). Select 2 - Type to identify whether the style is paired, open, or outline. Enter 3 - Description to type in a descriptive phrase for the style. Enter a description which distinguishes the style from other styles (such as the use or the font type).

Select 4 - Codes to enter the contents of the style. This takes you to the Style: screen shown in Figure 22.4. On the Style: screen you will enter text and codes which will be placed in your document when the style is turned on.

In Figure 22.4, the font is identified, followed by a center code, and then the standard text to be used every time the style is used. A hard return is entered followed by a new font and the code for center justification. Because the figure shows a paired style, you can see the comment. The comment reminds you to place all codes governing the text you will type in before the comment and codes to follow the text you will enter after the comment. (The comment marks the end of the paired style.) For example, press F8 (Underline) before the comment and F8 (Underline) after the comment (or select Appearance then Underline from the Font menu. That way, the text you type in

after turning on the style will be underlined. Use any Word-
Perfect formatting in a style.

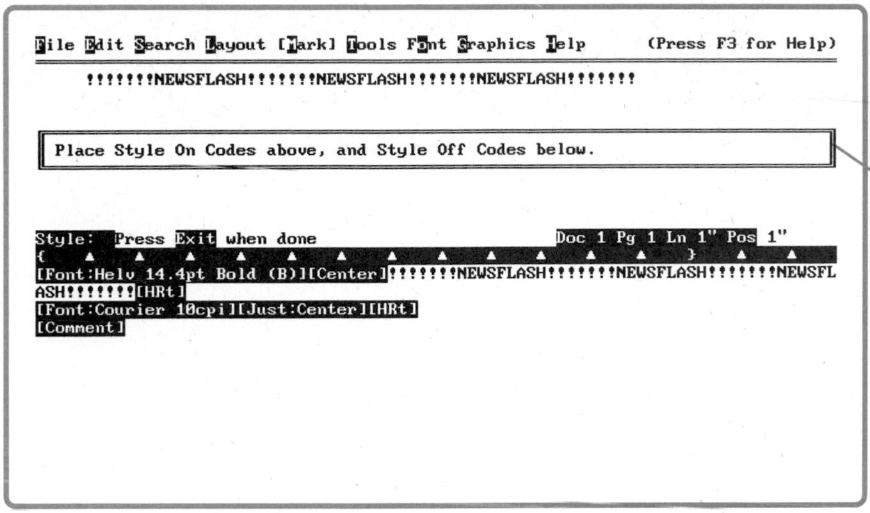

Figure 22.4

*Style: screen for
entering codes and
text for the style.*

Comment

Once you have entered all codes and text on the Style:
screen, press F7 (Exit), or select Exit from the File menu, to
leave the screen. You are returned to the Styles: Edit screen. The
last option is 5-Enter. You may select from three "Enter" options
(which identify what pressing ⏎Enter does for a paired style):

1 **HR**t: When you press ⏎Enter, a hard return is placed in
your document. Because this is the "status quo," it is a
popular setting. With this setting, you need to remember
to move your cursor past the Style Off code when you are
done using the style.

2 **Off**: When you press ⏎Enter, your cursor goes past the
Style Off code. This is helpful if you typically use the style
for a paragraph only. That way, when you press ⏎Enter at
the end of the paragraph, you pass beyond the Style Off
code. Press ⏎Enter again to end the paragraph.

3 **Off/On**: Pressing ⏎Enter moves the cursor past the
Style Off code then inserts another identical Style

On/Off code pair. This is useful if your style includes special formatting up front (such as indenting or a tab or bullet index). Move your cursor out from between paired codes and the use of ⏎Enter returns to normal.

Once you have completed the contents of the style, press F7 (Exit). The style is created. Figure 22.5 shows that this style is now available for use in the Styles screen. Select F7 (Exit) to return to your document.

Figure 22.5

The style is available in the Styles screen.

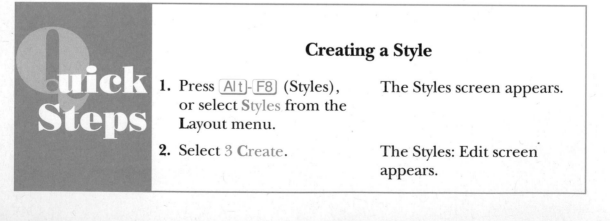

The following Quick Steps summarize how to create a style.

Creating a Style

1. Press Alt-F8 (Styles), or select Styles from the Layout menu.

   The Styles screen appears.

2. Select 3 Create.

   The Styles: Edit screen appears.

3. Complete the 1 - Name, 2 - Type, and 3 - Description fields.	The values appear.
4. Select 4 - Codes.	The Style: screen appears for you to enter the contents of the style.
5. Once all contents are entered select F7 (Exit) or select Exit from the File menu.	The Styles: Edit screen appears.
6. Complete 5 - Enter.	The action for a press of the ⏎Enter key appears.
7. Press F7 (Exit).	The style is created and shown on the Styles screen.
8. Press F7 (Exit).	You are returned to your document.

Using a Style

To use a style, just press Alt-F8 (Styles), or select Styles from the **Layout** menu. The available styles appear on the Styles screen. Highlight the style you want and select 1 **On**. The style code(s) are placed in your document at the cursor. Figure 22.6 shows the result of turning on the NewsFlash style and entering text between the codes in the paired style.

In this example, the cursor was placed on the [Style Onf:FlyNewsF] code. You can see in the code that the formatting, the text, and the font that will be active after the code is shown. You can see more information about a style code by placing your cursor on the code.

Figure 22.6

*The NewsFlash style
with the cursor on
the Style On code.*

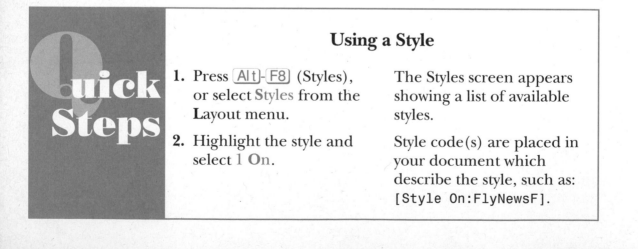

Newsflash style on code ⟶

Any formatting you enter in your document takes priority
over the formatting in the style. That way, if you want to turn off
or add style attributes for a single occurrence, you can do so. For
example, you may have a style that includes a font code and
margin codes but doesn't include underlining of text. You may
add the underline code in the document and use the remaining
codes from the style.

The following Quick Steps detail how to use a style.

**Quick
Steps**

Using a Style

1. Press Alt-F8 (Styles),
   or select Styles from the
   Layout menu.

   The Styles screen appears
   showing a list of available
   styles.

2. Highlight the style and
   select 1 On.

   Style code(s) are placed in
   your document which
   describe the style, such as:
   [Style On:FlyNewsF].

Other Style Options

You may have noticed some other options on the Styles screen. These options allow you to edit, delete, save, or retrieve existing styles.

When you select 4 - Edit, you are taken to the Styles: Edit screen, which allows you to change any element of the selected style. The edits affect any occurrence of that style in your current document. (To affect another document, you must make the document active then retrieve the new, edited style. A description of this retrieve function appears later in this section.)

Save Time by Editing an Existing Style

You may want to create two similar styles. You could enter each setting, code, and text for each style. A faster approach may be to enter the original style in your document, edit the style to make the new style then let WordPerfect re-create the original style. This will save keystrokes and lessen the chance that you will make an error in creating the new style.

First, make sure there is a code in your document for the style you will edit to create the new style. Next, from the Styles screen, highlight that style for editing. Select 4 - Edit. You'll go to the Styles: Edit screen. Change 1 - Name to the name for the new style. When you press ⏎Enter after entering the new name, this message appears:

        Rename Styles in Document? No (Yes)

Respond No because you want to keep the old style to be automatically re-created by WordPerfect.

Continues

Continued

Continue working from the Styles: Edit screen to change any other style settings desired. Press F7 (Exit) when you are done editing the style. The name for the new style appears on the Styles screen. The name of the style you edited is gone. But don't worry. Press F7 (Exit). Move your cursor across the code of the style that was lost during the edit. Press Alt-F8 (Styles) or select Styles from the Layout menu. You can see the original style was recreated by WordPerfect automatically.

If you select 5 Delete, you have three options:

1 **L**eaving Codes: The style is deleted and the style codes are removed from your document, but the codes which made up the style remain. Use this option if you no longer want to use the style but you don't want the formatting of the document altered.

2 **I**ncluding Codes: Deletes the style and all related codes in your document. Use this option if you want all traces of the style formatting removed from your document as well as the style removed.

3 **D**efinition Only: Deletes the style only and all style codes stay in the document. Move the cursor past a style in the document and that style is re-created by WordPerfect according to the information in the document. Try this out if you have many styles created and want to only have the ones in a particular document appear. Delete all definitions, then pass through the document with your cursor. Only those styles in the document are re-created.

Styles are saved with the active document. However, you can save the styles you create for a document to a file then retrieve that style file to use with other documents. This is useful if you have developed some all-purpose styles. To save styles, select 6 Save from the Styles screen. Enter the file name and press ↵Enter . To later retrieve the files to use with an active document, select 7 Retrieve from the Styles screen, enter the file name, and press ↵Enter .

What's Next?

If you use styles a lot, you may want to learn more. For example, you may *nest* styles. This means you can put one paired style within another paired style.

For example, suppose you have two paired styles. You place font style codes in style A and codes for a special box graphic and a hanging indent in style B. From your document, you could select style A, then immediately select style B. The style codes would look like this:

```
[Style On:A][Style On:B][Style Off:B][Style Off:A]
```

Type the text after the two Style On codes and before the two Style Off codes. The text you enter will appear with the font of style A and the graphic and indent of style B.

You will also want to learn about the style library, which is the default list of styles. This list can be recalled any time and you can control the location of the style library. When you use 8 Update from the Styles screen, the style library is returned to the Styles screen. But, be careful when you use the style library! Existing styles with the same names as styles in your document will be overwritten. And, you may lose the styles you've created unless you have saved them to a document.

Consult an advanced WordPerfect text for more information on nesting styles or using the style library.

In This Chapter

Converting Documents to or from WordPerfect Format

1. From the WordPerfect directory (at the C: prompt), type in **convert** and press ⏎Enter.
2. Identify the name of the Input File.
3. Identify the name of the Output File.
4. Select the type of conversion.

Saving an On-Screen Document to DOS or Word Processing Format

1. Press Ctrl-F5 (Text In/Out), or select Text Out from the **F**ile menu.
2. Select the format for the save.

Retrieving a DOS File On-Screen

1. Press Ctrl-F5 (Text In/Out) or select Text In from the **F**ile menu.
2. Select DOS then the retrieve format.

Importing a Spreadsheet On-Screen

1. Press Ctrl-F5 (Text In/Out) then 5 Spreadsheet, or select Text In then Spreadsheet from the **F**ile menu.
2. Select 1 Import and continue to enter the file identifiers.
3. On the Spreadsheet: Import screen, enter the file name, range, and type of layout.
4. Select 4 - Perform Import when the screen is complete.

Linking Spreadsheet Information

1. Press Ctrl-F5 (Text In/Out) then 5 Spreadsheet, or select Text In then Spreadsheet from the **F**ile menu.
2. Continue to create the link by selecting 2 Create Link.
3. On the Spreadsheet: Create Link screen, enter the file name, range, and type of layout.
4. Select 4 - Perform Link when the screen is complete.

Importing to and Exporting from WordPerfect

This chapter addresses how to move information into WordPerfect files (called "importing") and how to change WordPerfect files into other file formats (called "exporting"). Importing text is useful if you have text in another format (such as a spreadsheet) to put in a WordPerfect document. Exporting is handy if you need to share a WordPerfect file with someone using another word processor or if you need to send information over the phone lines via a modem. Even if, at first glance, you believe you may not need these features, read through the chapter anyway. That way, you will be informed of the capabilities of WordPerfect at such time as the features become necessary.

Why Import and Export?

Importing a file into WordPerfect means bringing a file created by another program into a WordPerfect document. *Exporting* means a WordPerfect document file is saved in another form to be used with another program.

Why import or export? It reduces the amount of retyping needed for information exchange. In addition, you can put information into documents that you never would have bothered to include because of all the work involved.

Making Importing and Exporting Easy for Yourself

Many beginning users are intimidated with the perceived difficulty of exporting and importing files. Relax and follow these pointers:

Always make a backup of the file(s) you are using. That way, if you accidentally copy over a file, you still have a backup.

Use the instructions in this book before you begin significant research with other software product manuals. The information here will get you through the most common import and export situations. If you are using less popular software, you may have to check the manual of that software to find out the compatible file formats. You may need to create a file in a common format with the other software. The goal is to find a format that can be "read" by both WordPerfect and your software program. A good bet is an ASCII file or DOS file.

Slow down, read carefully, and think your situation through. New users typically make mistakes by rushing into responding to prompts. WordPerfect will need complete path names to find files to import or export and other details about what you want to do. Work through the steps in a logical fashion. If you don't get the result you want—try again. As long as your files are backed up, no harm is done.

Ways to Import or Export Files

WordPerfect users can import or export files in three different ways:

▲ You may convert a file to or from a WordPerfect format to or from another format. This may be a popular "brand name" word processing file format (such as Microsoft Word). Or, it may be industry standard personal computer formats common to word processing, spreadsheet, and database programs (such as Spreadsheet DIF, ASCII, and Seven-Bit Transfer Format).

▲ You may save a document that appears on-screen to a DOS format, another WordPerfect version format, or a generic word processing format.

▲ You may retrieve a DOS or spreadsheet file on-screen.

Converting Documents

WordPerfect comes with a separate program, called CONVERT, which is run from the DOS prompt rather than from within WordPerfect itself. To convert WordPerfect documents to or from another format, you must know the path and name of the file you want to convert.

Change to the WordPerfect directory. (Hard disk users will typically be at the C:\WP51 prompt.) Then follow the next Quick Steps, which explain how to convert documents to or from WordPerfect format.

Quick Steps

Converting a Document to or from WordPerfect Format

1. From the WordPerfect directory, type **convert** at the prompt and press ⏎Enter.

   Name of Input File? appears.

2. Type the name and path of the Input File and press ⏎Enter.

   Name of Output File? appears.

3. Identify the path and name of the Output File and press ⏎Enter.

   The conversion options are listed, as shown in Figure 23.1.

4. Select the type of conversion. (For example, if the input file is a WordPerfect file, choose 1 WordPerfect to another format.)

   If you choose any option other than 1, the conversion begins. If you choose option 1, the menu in Figure 23.2 is shown, from which you must choose the destination format before conversion can begin.

NOTE: The input file is not changed by this procedure; rather, a copy of it is made and the *copy* is changed.

A message like the following appears and lets you know the conversion is complete:

```
BENLET.WPP Converted to BENLET.ASC
```

```
Name of Input File? benlet.wpp
Name of Output File? benlet.asc


0 EXIT
1 WordPerfect to another format
2 Revisable-Form-Text (IBM DCA Format) to WordPerfect
3 Final-Form-Text (IBM DCA Format) to WordPerfect
4 Navy DIF Standard to WordPerfect
5 WordStar 3.3 to WordPerfect
6 MultiMate Advantage II to WordPerfect
7 Seven-Bit Transfer Format to WordPerfect
8 WordPerfect 4.2 to WordPerfect 5.1
9 Mail Merge to WordPerfect Secondary Merge
A Spreadsheet DIF to WordPerfect Secondary Merge
B Word 4.0 to WordPerfect
C DisplayWrite to WordPerfect

Enter number of Conversion desired
```

Figure 23.1

Conversion options.

```
Name of Input File? benlet.wpp
Name of Output File? benlet.asc


0 EXIT
1 Revisable-Form-Text (IBM DCA Format)
2 Final-Form-Text (IBM DCA Format)
3 Navy DIF Standard
4 WordStar 3.3
5 MultiMate Advantage II
6 Seven-Bit Transfer Format
7 ASCII Text File
8 WordPerfect Secondary Merge to Spreadsheet DIF

Enter number of output file format desired
```

Figure 23.2

Conversion options for a WordPerfect file to a non-WordPerfect file.

TIP: Format names may sound foreign to you. If you are unsure of the format used by a program, consult the manual for the program. It should identify the format that the files are saved in and whether you can convert from that program to other common formats. The program may even convert files directly to the WordPerfect format!

Saving an On–Screen Document

When you are working within WordPerfect, you may want to save a document on your screen to a DOS file format, a file format for another version of WordPerfect, or a generic word processing file format.

To save to a DOS format, make sure the document is saved in regular WordPerfect format. This is a caution in case anything goes wrong with the save. Use the following Quick Steps, which summarize how to save an on-screen document to DOS text format.

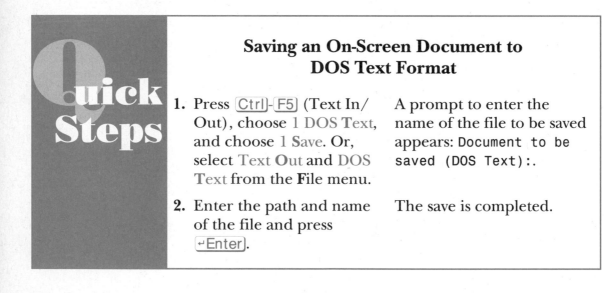

Saving an On-Screen Document to DOS Text Format

1. Press Ctrl-F5 (Text In/ Out), choose 1 DOS Text, and choose 1 Save. Or, select Text Out and DOS Text from the File menu.

   A prompt to enter the name of the file to be saved appears: `Document to be saved (DOS Text):`.

2. Enter the path and name of the file and press ↵Enter.

   The save is completed.

To save a document in another WordPerfect format or a generic word processing format, make sure you have the document saved in regular WordPerfect 5.1 first. Then, follow these next Quick Steps.

uick
Steps

Saving an On-Screen Document to a Word Processing Format

1. Press `Ctrl`-`F5` (Text In/ Out) and 3 Save As, or select Text Out from the File menu.

    The format selections appear.

2. Select the WordPerfect or Generic format desired.

    A prompt to enter the name of the file to be saved to appears: `Document to be saved (Generic WP):`.

3. Enter the path and name of the file and press `⏎Enter`.

    The save is completed.

Retrieving a DOS File On-Screen

You may want to retrieve a DOS file on-screen. This way, you can convert the document to WordPerfect and, potentially, use it in other WordPerfect documents.

TIP: You can retrieve a DOS file into an existing WordPerfect document file. Just bring on-screen the WordPerfect document file you want to retrieve into. Place your cursor in the location to retrieve to. Complete the retrieve (using the steps in the Quick Steps in this section). The name of the current document will still appear in the path prompt on the lower left of the screen.

When you retrieve a DOS file on-screen, you have to choose between two options:

2 **R**etrieve (CR/LF to [HRt]): The carriage return and line feed codes will be formatted as hard returns. This option is less like WordPerfect's format than the one described next.

3 **R**etrieve (CR/LF to [SRt]): The carriage return and line feed codes will be formatted as soft returns. This is the most like WordPerfect's format and may result in the least amount of reformatting.

The following Quick Steps summarize retrieving a DOS file on-screen. (Importing spreadsheets on-screen is covered later in this chapter.)

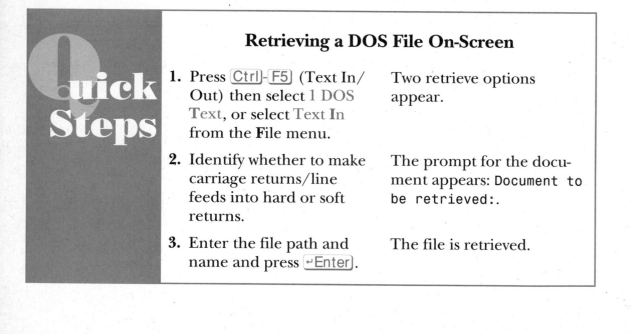

Retrieving a DOS File On-Screen

1. Press Ctrl-F5 (Text In/Out) then select 1 DOS Text, or select Text In from the File menu.

   Two retrieve options appear.

2. Identify whether to make carriage returns/line feeds into hard or soft returns.

   The prompt for the document appears: Document to be retrieved:.

3. Enter the file path and name and press ↵Enter.

   The file is retrieved.

Graphics

WordPerfect supports the graphic files created by most programs, including CGM, DXF (AutoCAD), EPS, GEM, PCX, PIC (Lotus), TIFF, and more. Your WordPerfect Reference lists the types of graphic files that are automatically converted when they are brought into WordPerfect using [Alt]-[F9] (Graphics) or the Graphics menu. (See Chapter 21.) Typically, you don't have to lift (or in this case, press) a finger.

If you have graphic files that are in an unusual format not supported, you can use the Graphics Conversion Program to convert the graphic file(s) to a format WordPerfect supports. (See a WordPerfect reference for more information on how to perform this conversion.)

Bringing in Spreadsheet Data

This chapter already covered how to use WordPerfect's conversion program to convert complete files to or from common spreadsheet formats. Spreadsheet data can also be combined into existing WordPerfect documents. Two Spreadsheet alternatives are available: importing and linking.

Importing spreadsheet data is useful for including a spreadsheet in memos, reports, and letters that will be generated once. *Linking* spreadsheet data means the spreadsheet information can be automatically updated in both files when a change is made in the spreadsheet file. Links are useful for documents that have life over time such as lists and regular reports.

In both cases, you may import or link the whole spreadsheet or a range (a portion) of spreadsheet data.

CAUTION: The Import and Link features were designed to work with the most popular spreadsheets on the market, including most versions of Lotus 1-2-3, Excel, and Quattro Pro. Check with WordPerfect Corporation if your spreadsheet data does not seem to be importing or linking as described. You may have a spreadsheet that is not supported by this feature.

Importing Spreadsheet Information

To import spreadsheet data information into an existing WordPerfect document for one-time use, place your cursor in the WordPerfect document where the spreadsheet data is desired. Figure 23.3 illustrates a memo into which spreadsheet data will be imported.

Figure 23.3

Memo ready for spreadsheet data.

Space for spreadsheet data

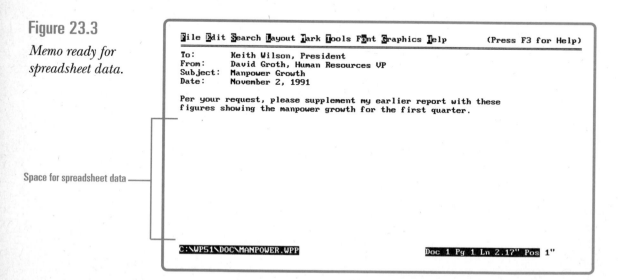

```
 File Edit Search Layout Mark Tools Font Graphics Help      (Press F3 for Help)

 To:       Keith Wilson, President
 From:     David Groth, Human Resources VP
 Subject:  Manpower Growth
 Date:     November 2, 1991

 Per your request, please supplement my earlier report with these
 figures showing the manpower growth for the first quarter.




 C:\WP51\DOC\MANPOWER.WPP                    Doc 1 Pg 1 Ln 2.17" Pos 1"
```

When you import spreadsheet data, you select options on the Spreadsheet: Import screen (an example is shown in Figure 23.4). The options are:

1 - **F**ilename: Enter the path and name of the file to import.

2 - **R**ange: Enter the range of the spreadsheet to import. Cells in a spreadsheet are typically labeled A, B, C, etc., across the top and 1, 2, 3, etc., across the left. Enter a range by identifying the top left cell followed by the cell identifier of the lower right cell. You may put a colon, period, or two periods between the cells in the range. For example, A1:C3, B3.D12, and F6..T22 are all valid ranges. *If you do not enter a range, the entire spreadsheet will be imported.*

3 - **T**ype: Identify whether you want the spreadsheet information imported as a WordPerfect Table or regular WordPerfect Text.

In the Figure 23.4 example, the file name is `C:\123\MANPWR.WK1` (a Lotus 1-2-3 file), the range is cell `A1` through cell `D12`, and the `Text` format will be used.

Figure 23.5 illustrates the import results (using the example facts from Figure 23.4), including the open Reveal Codes screen. Notice that the spreadsheet (imported as text rather than a table) has tabs inserted.

Figure 23.4

The Spreadsheet: Import screen.

```
Spreadsheet: Import
    1 - Filename             C:\123\MANPWR.WK1
    2 - Range                A1..D12
    3 - Type                 Text
    4 - Perform Import




Selection: 0
```

Figure 23.5

Results of import.

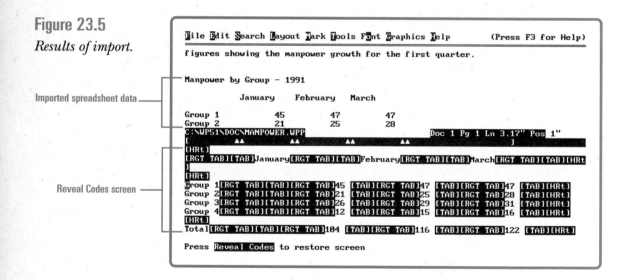

Imported spreadsheet data

Reveal Codes screen

```
File Edit Search Layout Mark Tools Font Graphics Help        (Press F3 for Help)
figures showing the manpower growth for the first quarter.

Manpower by Group - 1991

             January    February   March

Group 1        45         47        47
Group 2        21         25        28
C:\WP51\DOC\MANPOWER.WPP                            Doc 1 Pg 1 Ln 3.17" Pos 1"
[          ▲▲        ▲▲       ▲▲       ▲▲               ]
[HRt]
[RGT TAB][TAB]January[RGT TAB][TAB]February[RGT TAB][TAB]March[RGT TAB][TAB][HRt
]
[HRt]
Group 1[RGT TAB][TAB][RGT TAB]45 [TAB][RGT TAB]47 [RGT TAB][TAB]47 [TAB][HRt]
Group 2[RGT TAB][TAB][RGT TAB]21 [TAB][RGT TAB]25 [RGT TAB][TAB]28 [TAB][HRt]
Group 3[RGT TAB][TAB][RGT TAB]26 [TAB][RGT TAB]29 [RGT TAB][TAB]31 [TAB][HRt]
Group 4[RGT TAB][TAB][RGT TAB]12 [TAB][RGT TAB]15 [RGT TAB][TAB]16 [TAB][HRt]
[HRt]
Total[RGT TAB][TAB][RGT TAB]104 [TAB][RGT TAB]116 [TAB][RGT TAB]122 [TAB][HRt]
Press Reveal Codes to restore screen
```

To import a spreadsheet, use the Quick Steps that follow.

Importing a Spreadsheet

1. Place the cursor where the data will be imported.

   The position for importing the data is identified by the cursor.

2. Press Ctrl-F5 (Text In/Out) then 5 Spreadsheet, or select Text In then Spreadsheet from the File menu.

   The Import option appears.

3. Select 1 Import.

   The Spreadsheet: Import screen appears.

4. Make the necessary selections to enter the path and name of the file, the range of the file to import, and the format type for display of the imported text. Then select 4 - Perform Import.

   The spreadsheet is imported.

Quick Steps

Linking Spreadsheet Data

When you import spreadsheet data into an existing WordPerfect document, the information in your document is not updated when you update the spreadsheet. However, if you link the spreadsheet data, the linked document can be updated when you update the spreadsheet.

Place your cursor where the data should go. (Figure 23.6 illustrates our example document.)

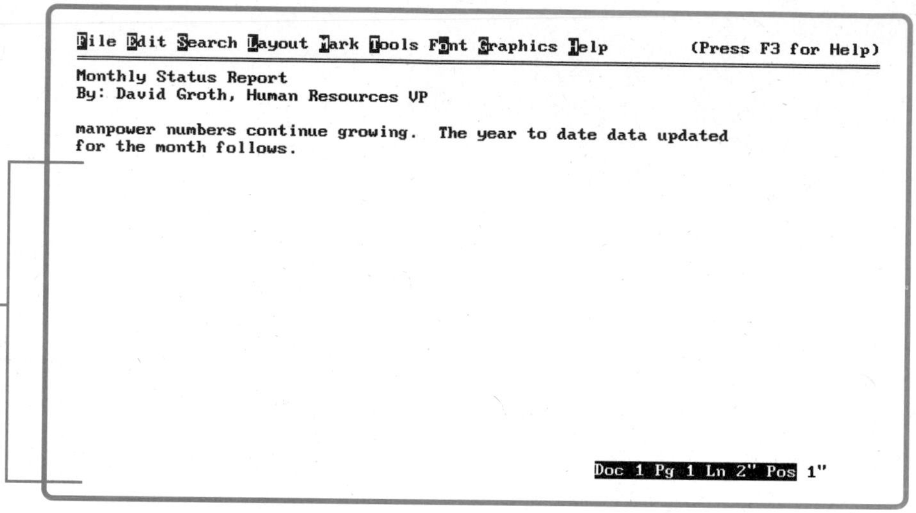

Figure 23.6

Document ready for linking.

```
 File Edit Search Layout Mark Tools Font Graphics Help      (Press F3 for Help)

 Monthly Status Report
 By: David Groth, Human Resources VP

 manpower numbers continue growing.  The year to date data updated
 for the month follows.




                                                    Doc 1 Pg 1 Ln 2" Pos 1"
```

Space for spreadsheet data

To link spreadsheet data, you use the Spreadsheet: Create Link screen options to fill in the following information:

1 - **F**ilename: Enter the path and name of the spreadsheet.

2 - **R**ange: Identify how much of the spreadsheet to link. (The range of the complete spreadsheet will typically be filled in once you enter the path and file name. Change the range if appropriate.)

3 - **T**ype: Choose Table or Text for the type of layout.

In the Figure 23.7 example of a Spreadsheet: Create Link screen, the file name is C:\123\MANPWR2.WK1, the range is cell A1 through F12, and the layout is Text.

The result of the example link (including the Reveal Codes screen) is shown in Figure 23.8.

Figure 23.7

The Spreadsheet: Create Link screen.

```
Spreadsheet: Create Link
    1 - Filename            C:\123\MANPWR2.WK1
    2 - Range               A1..F12
    3 - Type                Text
    4 - Perform Link




Selection: 0
```

Figure 23.8

Document ready for linking.

```
File Edit Search Layout Mark Tools Font Graphics Help      (Press F3 for Help)
for the month follows.

 Link: C:\123\MANPWR2.WK1  A1..F12

Manpower by Group - 1991

        January    February   March    April    May
                                                  Doc 1 Pg 1 Ln 1.67" Pos 1"
{       ▲       ▲      ▲       ▲      ▲      ▲        }    ▲     ▲
By: David Groth, Human Resources VP[HRt]
[HRt]
manpower numbers continue growing.  The year to date data updated[SRt]
for the month follows.[HRt]
[Link:C:\123\MANPWR2.WK1;;A1..F12][Tab Set:Rel; +1",+1.1",+2.1",+2.2",+3.2",+3.3
",+4.3",+4.4",+5.4",+5.5",+6.5",+6.6"][HRt]
Manpower by Group - 1991[RGT TAB][TAB][HRt]
[HRt]
[RGT TAB][TAB]January[RGT TAB][TAB]February[RGT TAB][TAB]March[RGT TAB][TAB]Apri
l[RGT TAB][TAB]May[RGT TAB][DSRt]

Press Reveal Codes to restore screen
```

Beginning of link

Link code

   The beginning of the link is boldly displayed on the screen.
On the Reveal Codes screen, the following code also marks the
beginning of the link. The path and file name are included
along with the range.

```
[Link:C:\123\MANPWR2.WK1;;A1..F12]
```

At the end of the link, another visual display is placed in your document stating *Link End*, and a [Link End] code is shown in the Reveal Codes screen.

To link a spreadsheet, use the following Quick Steps.

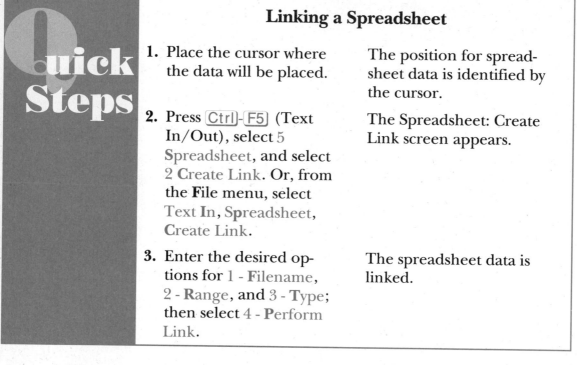

Linking a Spreadsheet

1. Place the cursor where the data will be placed.

   The position for spreadsheet data is identified by the cursor.

2. Press Ctrl-F5 (Text In/Out), select 5 Spreadsheet, and select 2 Create Link. Or, from the File menu, select Text In, Spreadsheet, Create Link.

   The Spreadsheet: Create Link screen appears.

3. Enter the desired options for 1 - Filename, 2 - Range, and 3 - Type; then select 4 - Perform Link.

   The spreadsheet data is linked.

TIP: If you don't like the on-screen display of the link beginning and end, press Ctrl-F5 (Text In/Out), 5 Spreadsheet, and 4 Link Options, or select the File menu, Text In, Spreadsheet, and Link Options. The Link Options: screen appears. Respond No to 2 - Show Link Codes. Also, if you want to delete the link (but not the spreadsheet information), delete either the beginning or ending code in the Reveal Codes screen.

To edit a single link, place your cursor between the beginning and ending link codes. Press Ctrl-F5 (Text In/Out), select 5 Spreadsheet, and select 3 Edit Link. Or, from the File menu, select Text In, Spreadsheet, and Edit Link. The Spreadsheet: Edit Link screen appears. You can change 1 - Filename, 2 - Range, or 3 - Type (Table or Text). Then, select 4 - Perform Link and the spreadsheet is updated.

You can update spreadsheet information manually, or you can have WordPerfect do it automatically any time you change the spreadsheet then reenter the WordPerfect document. To control updating, press Ctrl-F5 (Text In/Out), 5 Spreadsheet, and 4 Link Options. Or, from the File menu, select Text In, Spreadsheet, and Link Options. Use the following options depending on the outcome desired:

1 - Update on **R**etrieve: Set this option to Yes to update the spreadsheet every time the WordPerfect document is retrieved. Set the option to No if you want to manually update the spreadsheet information.

3 - **U**pdate All Links: Select this option to manually update the spreadsheet information in the document on the screen.

What's Next?

If you import or link large spreadsheets, you will run into space problems when you bring a large spreadsheet into a WordPerfect document. If the spreadsheet row is too long, the data displayed as text will wrap around on the line and data in table format will be cut off. Either may give you an undesirable outcome. Your *WordPerfect Reference* describes the maximum columns (32 for Table and 20 for Text format) and gives suggestions on how to handle sizing.

Possible solutions include:

▲ Reduce the column width in the spreadsheet program (if the columns can be made smaller without losing the contents). See the documentation for the spreadsheet program for instructions on how to change the width, resize, or reduce columns.

▲ Change the base font affecting the imported spreadsheet information in WordPerfect. Press Ctrl-F8 (Font) or select Base Font from the Font menu. Select a small font.

▲ Change the margins in WordPerfect by selecting ⇧Shift-F8 (Format) then 1 - Line, or select Line from the Layout menu. Select 7 - Margins and enter small or no left and right margins.

▲ Set up the WordPerfect document for printing in landscape mode ("sideways" on the page). Select ⇧Shift-F8 (Format) then 2 - Page, or select Page from the Layout menu. Select 7 - Paper Size/Type. Select a paper type and orientation listed as Land for landscape (versus Port for portrait) that works with your printer and allows for a long paper length.

Read about these options and hints for handling more complicated import and export tasks in an advanced Word-Perfect text.

Getting Ready to Use WordPerfect

Though you may want to fire up your computer and begin punching keys right now, if you spend just a few moments picking up some basic concepts, you'll avoid confusion later on. Once you have the "big picture," you can fill in the details. This appendix will help you understand how WordPerfect works with your computer, how DOS fits into the picture, and how a WordPerfect document is created.

What is Word Processing?

Word processing is the term used to describe the development of letters, reports, and other documents with a computer. Word processing offers many advantages over handwriting or typing documents. Speed is a primary advantage. Because most people write by hand at about twelve words per minute, you don't have to be a speed demon on a keyboard to improve your efficiency with word processing. Another advantage you gain with word processing is the ease of entry, editing, and printing your work. You replace the cumbersome "cut, paste, and retype" approach with copying, moving, and deleting words instantly. A final, printed copy is only a few keystrokes away. The printed copy is clean and free of erasures and correction fluid.

WordPerfect is one brand of word processor. WordPerfect has been a bestseller for years because of its simplicity and power. At first, you'll probably create small, straightforward documents. But once you get up and running and want to go on to more sophisticated word processing, WordPerfect won't hold you back.

The written works you create using WordPerfect are called *documents.* A document can be any written item you create—a letter, a report, a memo, an expense sheet, a bill, or a list (to name just a few). You can combine elements in one document (such as following a letter with a bill). You decide how many documents you want to create and the contents of each document.

Computer System Components

WordPerfect is available in many versions, each one designed to run on a specific type of computer. This book describes using WordPerfect with an IBM-compatible microcomputer (also known as a personal computer). *IBM compatible* is the standard set by IBM which other (often less expensive) computers match in specifications.

> **NOTE:** Not all IBM-compatible computers are completely compatible, so if you notice a difference in processing from that described in this book, it may be that your computer is not perfectly compatible. If you're concerned about this, ask your computer dealer.

Your computer system includes *hardware* and *software.* Hardware, the "physical" part, is made up of the computer parts you can see and touch, while software consists of the operating system and the programs you run—the "logical" part.

Hardware Components

Your computer is made up of many hardware components, which work together to provide a fully functional unit. Figure A.1 illustrates some common hardware components:

Keyboard: The component that resembles the keys on a typewriter with a few added. You'll "talk" to your computer (and to WordPerfect) through your keyboard. By pressing certain keys you send messages to the computer. You also use the keyboard to type in documents.

Monitor: The component that looks like a television screen. You can see the results of keyboard entries on the monitor. The text you type in also appears. WordPerfect will send you messages on the monitor if it doesn't understand what you have entered or if you need more information to continue. Carefully read the messages when they appear. This is WordPerfect's only means of communicating with you.

Central Processing Unit (CPU): The CPU is typically the most difficult hardware component for a beginner to understand. The wonders of word processing take place within the CPU. Inside is active memory, called random-access memory (RAM). The documents you are using and necessary parts of WordPerfect are stored in RAM as you work. The documents remain in RAM as long as the computer is turned on. When the computer is turned off (or the power is accidentally cut), the documents are lost from RAM. This is why it is so important to save your work regularly as you go. Otherwise, an unexpected power failure could cause you to lose valuable work.

Hard Disks, Floppy Disks, and Disk Drives: When you save your work, it is transferred from RAM to a disk for permanent storage. Once your work is saved on a disk, you can turn off your computer and retrieve the document from the disk when you use WordPerfect again. The disk may be a hard disk, which is fixed in the CPU. Or the disk may be a 5-1/4" or 3-1/2" floppy (flexible) disk. Floppies are removable from a disk drive in the computer. This disk drive is used to copy documents to and from RAM.

Printer (optional): You can use WordPerfect without a printer, but if you do, you can only view your documents on the monitor. You cannot get a hard copy of your work without a printer.

Mouse: You can use a mouse to point to and select WordPerfect options as a substitute for making selections from the keyboard. However, you will still use the keyboard for entering text and for some WordPerfect functions. Many WordPerfect users prefer a mouse because it seems to be easier and faster to use than the keyboard. This choice is a matter of individual taste and skill.

Cables: Hardware components must be linked using cables, supplied by your computer dealer.

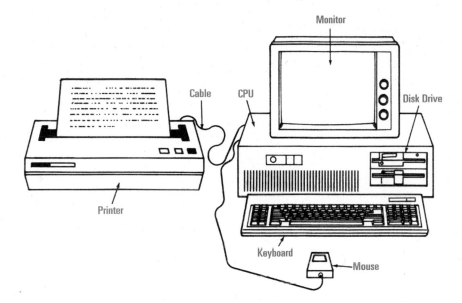

Hardware Care

Hardware is sturdy, but not indestructible. As you use your computer, observe these basic maintenance rules:

▲ Store disks at common office temperatures.

▲ Keep your environment clean and free from dust.

▲ Periodically clean the disk drives.

▲ Use the labels supplied with disks and write on disks with felt-tip pens (not ball-point pens or sharp pencils).

▲ Don't touch the exposed magnetic portion of the disk (housed inside the plastic cover).

▲ Don't spill liquids on the computer or on disks.

▲ Don't expose the disks to magnets.

▲ Always treat the computer with TLC (tender loving care). It is built to last but, like any electronic device, can be jarred or broken if misused.

Software Components

Software refers to a computer program stored on a disk. Different programs have different functions. The software that allows WordPerfect to operate with your computer hardware is called the operating system. In this case, you'll be using DOS, which stands for Disk Operating System.

The WordPerfect program is another kind of software—an application. While the operating system simply keeps the computer up and running, application software helps you perform a task, such as word processing.

Many files make up the WordPerfect application, each one carrying a specific set of instructions to the computer. There are many different types of files, and each file has a unique, descriptive name. Each WordPerfect document that you create can be stored individually on disk too, with its own unique name.

DOS Fundamentals

You do not have to know much about DOS in order to use WordPerfect, but understanding a few basic principles will help you get the most out of your word processing sessions. Two key concepts you should understand are directories and formatting.

Using DOS Directories

A disk can be divided into parts called *directories*. Directories are especially useful on hard disks to keep certain types of files separate so that you can easily find what you need. For example, Figure A.2 shows a diagram representing the directories on a hard disk.

ROOT

DOS   WP51   123

Directories take on the structure of an upside-down tree. The first level is called the *root*, and is represented by a slash. Off the root, typically, is a directory for your operating system, along with a directory for each of your applications. In Figure A.2, the operating system is DOS and the applications installed are WordPerfect (WP51) and Lotus 1-2-3 (123). Notice that the names for the directories, while abbreviated, help identify the software.

When you install WordPerfect, it will automatically make directories for you if you wish. This avoids a lot of hassle for you and is particularly helpful for beginners. Also, when you begin using WordPerfect with a hard disk, you'll probably place your own documents on the same directory as the WordPerfect files and identify them with special naming techniques discussed in this book. Later, if you want to add a directory under WordPerfect and place your documents there, you can.

NOTE: Your DOS manual will explain how to create directories and copy documents between directories.

When you use WordPerfect's directory feature (F5), you may be asked to enter the *path*. The path indicates how to get from where you are to the desired directory. For example, this is the path to a WordPerfect document called MYDOC.WPP:

```
C:\WP51\MYDOC.WPP
```

First, C: identifies the drive. Then, a backslash (\) identifies the root. WP51 shows the software directory and then the name of the document follows. The directory and document names are separated by a backslash.

Formatting Disks

When you buy a floppy disk, it could be used by many types of computers and operating systems. *Formatting* a floppy disk makes that disk ready to be used by your operating system and your computer.

> **NOTE:** An exception to this are preformatted floppy disks. These disks, while more expensive, are ready to use with DOS and do not require formatting.

If you are using a floppy-disk system, you will use floppy disks to hold WordPerfect and your documents. Before installing WordPerfect, you will need at least ten formatted disks. This will allow you to create working backup disks from those supplied by WordPerfect.

If you are using a hard disk or working on a network, you will want to format floppy disks to store additional backup copies of your documents. You don't need these to install WordPerfect, but it's always a good idea to have several extra formatted floppy disks on which you can save your work.

> **CAUTION:** When you format a floppy disk, all the information on the disk is erased. *Never* format a floppy disk if you want to save the information on the disk.

To format a floppy disk using DOS, you must start from the *system prompt* for the drive where DOS resides. (Exit from any application program you are running.) The system prompt is usually the drive letter followed by a colon, slash, or other characters—for example, A>, A:\, C>, or C:\. If the desired letter does not currently appear, just type in the letter of the desired drive and then a colon. Then press the ⏎Enter key. For example, to go to the C drive, you would type:

```
C:
```

and press ⏎Enter.

At the system prompt, type in the command to format the disk. The command is FORMAT, a space, the drive letter where the floppy disk to be formatted will be, and then a colon. For example, you would use the following command from the hard disk C drive to format the floppy disk in drive A.

```
FORMAT A:
```

Press ⏎Enter. DOS will ask you to place the floppy disk to be formatted in the drive that you specified in the command. If there's already a floppy disk in that drive, remove it and insert the disk to be formatted. *Take time to check the drive letter.* Make sure the correct drive is identified. You do not want to accidentally format a disk containing valuable data. And you especially do not want to format your hard disk!

CAUTION: If you format the wrong disk, the contents of that disk will be wiped out. For example, you can accidentally format your hard disk and wipe out all your software and documents. Be careful! Always double check that you are formatting the right disk in the right drive.

CAUTION: At the C drive system prompt, never type **FORMAT** without specifying a drive letter, or DOS will assume that you want to format the current drive—your hard drive.

When you are sure you are formatting the correct disk, press `↵Enter` to begin the format process.

Now you just wait while the computer processes. You can tell it is working by the lights and the sound of the machine. A message similar to `format another disk?` appears when the process is complete. Press `Y` for Yes to format another disk or `N` for No to stop formatting disks.

NOTE: There are two disk densities: double-density and high-density. DOS will normally format a disk at the highest density that the disk drive supports. You can format a double-density disk in a high-density drive by using special command line parameters; see your DOS manual for details.

Using Your Keyboard with WordPerfect

The computer keyboard lets you communicate with WordPerfect. The keys on the keyboard are shown in Figure A.3. Many keyboard keys are the same as those on a typewriter; others are special-use keys that access powerful features or shortcuts.

Figure A.3

Keys on the keyboard.

The following is a description of each group of keys found on the keyboard. Find these on your own keyboard.

▲ The *Letter/Number/Symbol* keys are common to computers and typewriters. Press these to type letters, numbers, and symbols. Press the ⇧Shift key to type capital letters, symbols, or punctuation marks found on the top half of these keys.

▲ The *Function* keys are labeled F1 through F10 (F12 on some computers). They are used to perform special WordPerfect functions. They may be used alone or in conjunction with other keys including Alt, Ctrl, or ⇧Shift. This book uses the convention of using illustrations of keys and placing a hyphen (-) between two key names, such as ⌜⇧Shift⌝-⌜F1⌝, to indicate you are to press the two keys simultaneously (the ⌜⇧Shift⌝ key with the ⌜F1⌝ key in this example).

▲ The *cursor arrow keys* are used to move the cursor. You can use the cursor arrow keys to move across existing text without changing the text. On most computers, pressing the key marked ⌜Num Lock⌝ first will produce the numbers on these keys instead of the arrows.

▲ The *spacebar* is used to enter spaces or blank out text.

▲ The ⌜Home⌝, ⌜PgUp⌝, ⌜End⌝, and ⌜PgDn⌝ keys are used for special WordPerfect movements.

▲ The ⌜Tab⇄⌝, ⌜⬅Backspace⌝, ⌜Ins⌝, and ⌜Del⌝ keys are used for special functions described later in this book.

Creating a WordPerfect Document

Now that you have a broad view of the computer hardware and software, we'll take a look at the overall process you'll use to create a document with WordPerfect. The main chapters in this book cover the details of these major steps.

The first step, of course, is to install WordPerfect on your computer. Installing the program means that the files on the WordPerfect disks are placed on a disk (your hard disk, if you have one) for your daily use. See Appendix B for installation instructions. Installation only needs to be done once.

Once WordPerfect is installed on your computer, you start up the WordPerfect program. Then, you use the *menus* to select what you want to do. Menus are lists of options you have. Figure A.4 shows a WordPerfect menu. Once you become familiar with WordPerfect's function keys, you may want to skip the menus and enter your selections via keystrokes.

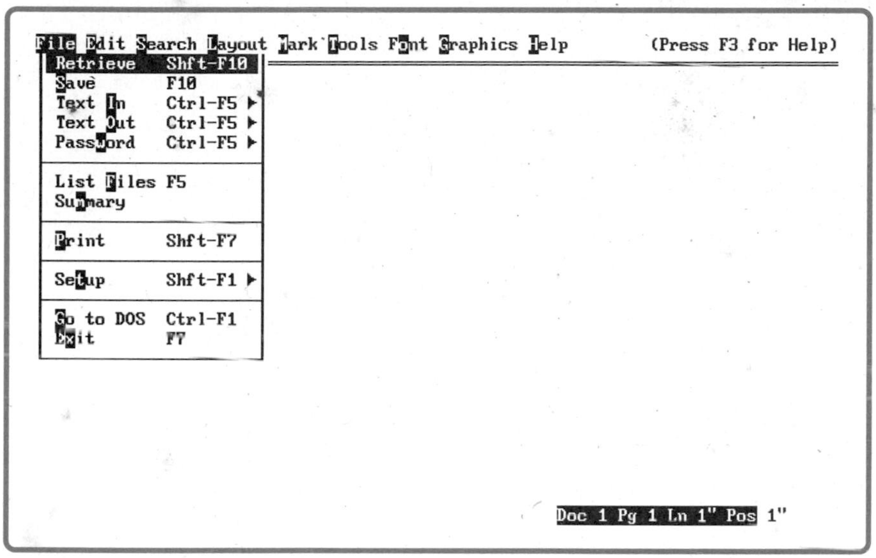

Figure A.4
The File menu.

Then, you type your document. As you work, a small, blinking mark called the *cursor* marks your position on the screen. Figure A.5 shows the cursor under the "t" in the word `typist`. When you use a mouse, the *pointer* appears to mark your location. Figure A.6 shows the mouse pointer indicating "t" in `typist`.

In addition to the text you enter, you may choose certain format options. The word *format* refers to the appearance of your text on the screen and when printed. WordPerfect has a wide variety of format options, including tabs to indent the first line of a paragraph, margins to determine how much white space will surround the printed text, page numbers, and character formats (such as underlines and bold text).

Figure A.5

The keyboard cursor.

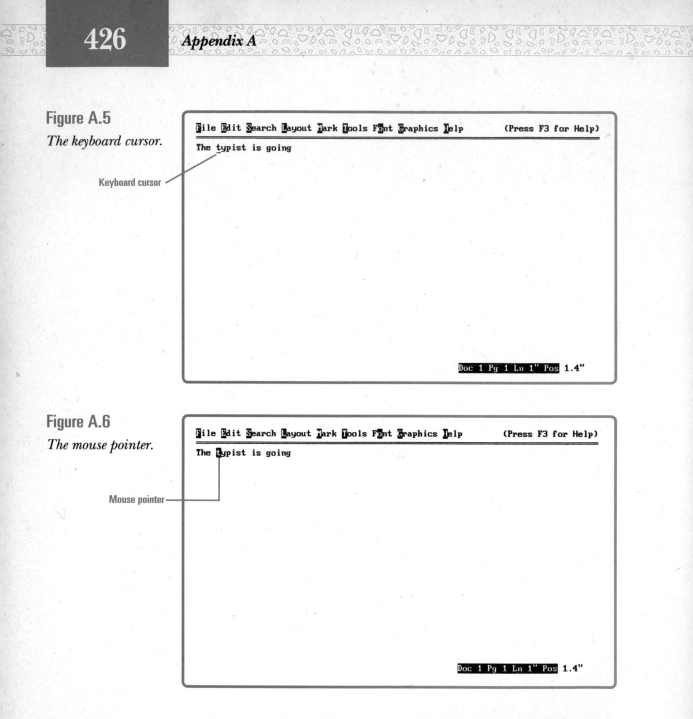

Keyboard cursor

Figure A.6

The mouse pointer.

Mouse pointer

The next step is to save your work. Saving a document copies it from temporary storage in your computer to permanent storage on a disk. Do this regularly as you work to protect your work from a power loss. Always save your work before you leave WordPerfect.

Next, you can spell check your document. Most WordPerfect users wait until they think the document is fully developed before spell checking it. That way, they don't have to spell check the document again because of extensive editing.

Then, you may want to generate special aids such as an index or table of contents. This is the last act to perform on your document because the changes made during editing or spell checking may change the page numbers tied to the aid. Save your work again. (You can never save too often.)

Finally, you print the document. Actually, you can print a draft of your document at any time. Some users like to see a draft as they work just to ensure that the formatting is to their liking.

Exit WordPerfect after you have saved your work and are done using WordPerfect. When you open the WordPerfect program again, the document you've saved is available for retrieval and further editing.

In review, here are the steps you take to create a document once WordPerfect is installed on your computer:

▲ Open the WordPerfect program.

▲ Make selections via the menu.

▲ Type in your document (the cursor marks your spot on the monitor screen).

▲ Enter formatting (such as tabs and margins).

▲ Save the document—often.

▲ Spell check the document.

▲ Generate special aids (such as an index or table of contents).

▲ Save the work again.

▲ Print the document.

▲ Exit WordPerfect. (You can retrieve the saved document later through WordPerfect.)

This book illustrates the many nuances of this overall process of creating a document. The basic process is still the same, however, regardless of how fancy or plain or how long or short your document is. Just invest a little time, follow the process, exercise a smidgen of patience, and you'll be successfully word processing with WordPerfect in no time.

Installing WordPerfect

Before you can use WordPerfect for the first time, you must prepare the program to run on your computer. This is called *installing* WordPerfect, because a working copy of the program is placed on your hard disk (or onto several floppy disks) during the procedure. Installing is a one-time operation; once WordPerfect is available, you can use it again and again.

Because the folks at WordPerfect have you—the first-time user—in mind, the installation process is almost entirely automated. You need only know a little about the type of computer you are using and how to use your keyboard to respond to the screens WordPerfect shows you.

Types of Computers

Regardless of the brand of computer you are using, your installation will fall into one of three categories. WordPerfect will ask you for this information during installation. (Don't worry if you don't know, however, because WordPerfect is able to examine your system during installation and make an educated guess.)

▲ *Hard Disk* (single user): You have a hard disk in the computer with one or more disk drives. WordPerfect will be stored on the hard disk.

▲ *Floppy Disk* (single user): This type of system uses floppy-disk drives only. You do not have a hard disk inside the machine for storing files and documents. WordPerfect resides on a floppy disk as you work.

▲ *Network* (multiple users): Your system hooks several computers into a primary computer. The primary computer is called the *server* and has a hard disk that holds WordPerfect. That copy of WordPerfect is used by all the computers attached to the server.

Network Installation

Installing WordPerfect on a network is usually considered a fairly advanced task. WordPerfect walks you through installing the server, the primary computer with the hard disk to which other computers are attached. It also helps you install the computers, called *workstations*, that are hooked to the server. If you run into problems when you install, don't hesitate to seek help from your dealer or another knowledgeable source.

Entering Commands During Installation

When you install WordPerfect, you will enter commands with your keyboard. Sometimes you will be able to press the keys marked PgUp (Page Up) and PgDn (Page Down) to move through selections and then type in a letter or a number for the selection you desire.

How do you know what to type in? WordPerfect places text on your monitor screen that explains each step. During the installation process (and when using *any* software), carefully read the messages on the screen. Sometimes these messages are called *prompts* since they prompt you on what to do. They typically tell you one or more of the following:

▲ What has happened.

▲ What can happen (the options).

▲ Which selections to choose to do what you want.

▲ Which selections to choose to stop what you are doing.

Also pay attention to the lights on your computer and the noise. When your computer is working, the lights and sound are active. Typically, you must wait until the operation is done before you can proceed.

Starting the Installation

To begin installing WordPerfect, place the WordPerfect disk with the word "Install" on the label in drive A of your computer. Type:

```
A:install
```

and press ⏎Enter

A screen like that shown in Figure B.1 appears. Now is the time to get in the good habit of carefully reading screens. You can see that to continue, you can press Ⓨ for Yes. Anytime you see a letter in bright (bold) text, you can just press it to select the option instead of typing the entire word.

Figure B.1

Installation welcome screen.

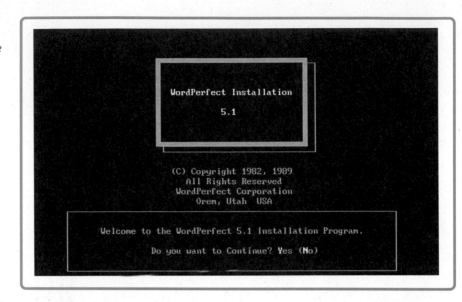

After you have selected Yes to continue, WordPerfect attempts to identify whether you have a color monitor, and whether you have a hard disk or floppy disk system. On the screen you will see WordPerfect's guesses at these—enter the appropriate responses (Yes or No) to confirm or change the information. (If you are not sure, accept the choices that WordPerfect has made.)

After you answer all the questions about your system, you will be taken to the Installation screen shown in Figure B.2. Select an installation option based on your needs. For example, if you are just getting started *and* are not working on a network, select 1 - Basic. If you are performing a special operation (for example, installing on a network), you may want to use another option, but the beginner's best approach is to keep it simple and use Basic.

After making your Installation screen selections, you are walked through a series of screens. WordPerfect tells you when to replace the disk in the drive with another disk. Note the name of the disk WordPerfect requests, find the disk with that label, and—when the drive light is off—place it in the drive.

```
Installation

    1 - Basic        Perform a standard installation to C:\WP51.

    2 - Custom       Perform a customized installation.  (User selected
                     directories.)

    3 - Network      Perform a customized installation onto a network.
                     (To be performed by the network supervisor.)

    4 - Printer      Install a new or updated Printer (.ALL) File.

    5 - Update       Install WordPerfect 5.1 Interim Release program file(s).
                     (Used for updating existing WordPerfect 5.1 software.)

    6 - Copy Disks   Install every file from an installation diskette to a
                     specified location.  (Useful for installing all the
                     Printer (.ALL) Files.)

    7 - Minimal      Install only the files for a standard configuration.

    8 - Exit         Leave Installation Program.

Selection: 4
```

Figure B.2
Installation screen.

CAUTION: Never remove or replace a disk in a drive when the drive light is on, or you might damage the disk.

WordPerfect explains each feature as you install it. If you aren't sure that you want to install a particular feature, go ahead and select Yes to install it. Having features you don't use only takes up some space, but failing to install a feature you later want costs you time and causes confusion when you have to install that feature alone. Plus, until you understand WordPerfect, it is difficult to distinguish which features you won't need. So, installing each feature early in your WordPerfect experience can only help you.

One of the final features you install is the link to your printer. When you get to the printer screen, the operation is a little more complex than just selecting yes or no. The printer screen is shown in Figure B.3.

Figure B.3

Printer screen.

```
   1  Acer LP-76
   2  AEG Olympia Compact RO          * = not on shipping disk.  Type
   3  AEG Olympia ESW 2000              the number next to the printer
   4  AEG Olympia Laserstar 6          for more information.
   5  AEG Olympia Laserstar 6e
   6  AEG Olympia NP 30
   7  AEG Olympia NP 80 SE           IF YOUR PRINTER IS NOT LISTED
   8  AEG Olympia NP 80-24
   9  AEG Olympia NP 136 SE             SUGGESTED EMULATIONS:
  10  AEG Olympia NP 136-24         Dot Matrix - Standard Printer,
  11  AEG Olympia NPC 136-24          Epson FX, IBM Graphics, IBM
  12  AEG Olympia Startype            ProPrinter
  13  AGFA Compugraphic 9400PS      Daisy Wheel - Standard
  14  Alphacom Alphapro 101           Typewriter, Diablo 630,
  15  Alps Allegro 24                 Brother HR15
  16  Alps Allegro 500             Laser - HP LaserJet Series II
  17  Alps ALQ200 (18 pin)         PostScript - Apple LaserWriter
  18  Alps ALQ200 (24 pin)
  19  Alps ALQ224e                 For additional HELP, Press F3
  20  Alps ALQ300 (18 pin)
  21  Alps ALQ300 (24 pin)
  22  Alps ALQ324e

N Name Search; PgDn More Printers; PgUp Previous Screen; F3 Help; F7 Exit;
Selection: 0
```

The printer screen lists all the printers that WordPerfect will work with. First, determine the brand and model of your printer. Then, press `PgUp` and `PgDn` until you see that printer and model. Type in the number to the left of the printer name and press `⏎Enter`. This installs the files for that printer only. Continue following the messages.

If you can't find the brand or model of your printer, you want to select the printer most like your own. Consult your printer dealer or the dealer that sold you WordPerfect.

After selecting your printer, you'll come to a screen that asks you to enter your license number. This is a good idea in case you need to use it when calling WordPerfect Corporation for help. Take the time to find it on the Certification of License card that came with your software and type it in when asked.

Any special messages about your printer appear at the end of the installation process. If your printer is attached, and you want to make a hard copy of the information for later reference, hold down the ⇧Shift key and press the PrtSc (Print Screen) key. To use this function, your printer must be linked to your computer by a cable, be turned on, be on-line (usually an on-line light is lit), and have paper in it.

When installation is done, this message appears:

```
Installation Complete.
```

To be safe, turn off your computer and then start it up again. This way, any changes to the files will take effect.

> **TIP:** If you change printers later, you can use the installation procedure to install a new printer. From the Installation screen, select 4 - Printer. Select the new printer just like you did in Basic installation.

Once WordPerfect is installed, place the original disks from WordPerfect Corporation in a safe, temperate environment. These are your final backup copies so you don't want anything to happen to them.

Special Characters

The letters, numbers, and symbols that you see on your keyboard are not the only characters that you can print with WordPerfect. The following lists show some of the additional characters you can print if you have a graphics printer or have installed fonts that include these characters. When no character appears next to a character number, the character is not supported.

ANSI Character Set

Hold down the Alt key, type 0 (zero), then type the character number, using the *numeric keypad*. Release the Alt key. (The number keys at the top of the keyboard will not work with this feature.)

ASCII value	Character	ASCII value	Character
000	(null)	036	$
001	☺	037	%
002	☻	038	&
003	♥	039	'
004	♦	040	(
005	♣	041	)
006	♠	042	*
007	(beep)	043	+
008	▪	044	,
009	(tab)	045	-
010	(line feed)	046	.
011	(home)	047	/
012	(form feed)	048	0
013	(carriage return)	049	1
014	♫	050	2
015	☼	051	3
016	►	052	4
017	◄	053	5
018	↕	054	6
019	‼	055	7
020	¶	056	8
021	§	057	9
022	▬	058	:
023	↨	059	;
024	↑	060	<
025	↓	061	=
026	→	062	>
027	←	063	?
028	(cursor right)	064	@
029	(cursor left)	065	A
030	(cursor up)	066	B
031	(cursor down)	067	C
032	(space)	068	D
033	!	069	E
034	"	070	F
035	#	071	G

ASCII value	Character	ASCII value	Character
072	H	100	d
073	I	101	e
074	J	102	f
075	K	103	g
076	L	104	h
077	M	105	i
078	N	106	j
079	O	107	k
080	P	108	l
081	Q	109	m
082	R	110	n
083	S	111	o
084	T	112	p
085	U	113	q
086	V	114	r
087	W	115	s
088	X	116	t
089	Y	117	u
090	Z	118	v
091	[	119	w
092	\	120	x
093	]	121	y
094	∧	122	z
095	—	123	{
096	`	124	¦
097	a	125	}
098	b	126	~
099	c	127	⌂

IBM PC Extended Character Set

Hold down the [Alt] key, type 0 (zero), then type the character number, using the *numeric keypad*. Release the [Alt] key.

(The number keys at the top of the keyboard will not work with this feature.)

ASCII value	Character	ASCII value	Character
128	Ç	158	Pt
129	ü	159	ƒ
130	é	160	á
131	â	161	í
132	ä	162	ó
133	à	163	ú
134	å	164	ñ
135	ç	165	Ñ
136	ê	166	ª
137	ë	167	º
138	è	168	¿
139	ï	169	⌐
140	î	170	¬
141	ì	171	½
142	Ä	172	¼
143	Å	173	¡
144	É	174	«
145	æ	175	»
146	Æ	176	░
147	ô	177	▒
148	ö	178	▓
149	ò	179	│
150	û	180	┤
151	ù	181	╡
152	ÿ	182	╢
153	Ö	183	╖
154	Ü	184	╕
155	¢	185	╣
156	£	186	║
157	¥	187	╗

ASCII value	Character	ASCII value	Character
188	⌐	222	▮
189	╜	223	▬
190	╛	224	α
191	┐	225	β
192	└	226	Γ
193	┴	227	π
194	┬	228	Σ
195	├	229	σ
196	─	230	μ
197	┼	231	τ
198	╞	232	Φ
199	╟	233	Θ
200	╚	234	Ω
201	╔	235	δ
202	╩	236	∞
203	╦	237	$\emptyset$
204	╠	238	ϵ
205	═	239	$\cap$
206	╬	240	$\equiv$
207	╧	241	$\pm$
208	╨	242	$\geq$
209	╤	243	$\leq$
210	╥	244	$\lceil$
211	╙	245	$\rfloor$
212	╘	246	$\div$
213	╒	247	$\approx$
214	╓	248	$\circ$
215	╫	249	$\bullet$
216	╪	250	$\cdot$
217	┘	251	$\sqrt{}$
218	┌	252	^{n}
219	█	253	^{2}
220	▄	254	▪
221	▌	255	(blank 'FF')

WordPerfect Characters

WordPerfect includes several special character sets, containing over 1,500 characters. If you do not have these characters in a built-in printer font or soft font, they are printed as graphic characters from the file that comes with WordPerfect. To print these characters, set the Graphic Print Quality setting to High. If either the Graphic or Text Print Quality setting is set to Do Not Print, these characters will not print.

Because there are so many special WordPerfect characters, it is not possible to show them all in this book. Your *WordPerfect Reference* includes a complete list in an appendix. The sets available include:

Character Set	Name of Set	Additional Description
0	(ASCII)	Standard ASCII character set
1	Multinational 1	International characters and diacritical marks
2	Multinational 2	International diacritical marks
3	Box Drawing	Graphic patterns for drawing lines and corners
4	Typographic	Common symbols, fractions, and Symbols graphic characters not available on most keyboards
5	Iconic Symbols	Common graphic icons

Character Set	Name of Set	Additional Description
6	Math/Scientific	
7	Math/Scientific Extension	
8	Greek	
9	Hebrew	
10	Cyrillic	
11	Hiragana and Katakana	
12	User defined	

Index

I

Reader Feedback Card

Thank you for purchasing this book from SAMS FIRST BOOK series. Our intent with this series is to bring you timely, authoritative information that you can reference quickly and easily. You can help us by taking a minute to complete and return this card. We appreciate your comments and will use the information to better serve your needs.

1. Where did you purchase this book?

☐ Chain bookstore (Walden, B. Dalton)   ☐ Direct mail
☐ Independent bookstore   ☐ Book club
☐ Computer/Software store   ☐ School bookstore
☐ Other _____

_____

2. Why did you choose this book? (Check as many as apply.)

☐ Price   ☐ Appearance of book
☐ Author's reputation   ☐ SAMS' reputation
☐ Quick and easy treatment of subject   ☐ Only book available on subject

3. How do you use this book? (Check as many as apply.)

☐ As a supplement to the product manual   ☐ As a reference
☐ In place of the product manual   ☐ At home
☐ For self-instruction   ☐ At work

4. Please rate this book in the categories below. G = Good; N = Needs improvement; U = Category is unimportant.

☐ Price   ☐ Appearance
☐ Amount of information   ☐ Accuracy
☐ Examples   ☐ Quick Steps
☐ Inside cover reference   ☐ Second color
☐ Table of contents   ☐ Index
☐ Tips and cautions   ☐ Illustrations
☐ Length of book
☐ How can we improve this book?_____
☐ _____

5. How many computer books do you normally buy in a year?

☐ 1–5   ☐ 5–10   ☐ More than 10
☐ I rarely purchase more than one book on a subject.
☐ I may purchase a beginning and an advanced book on the same subject.
☐ I may purchase several books on particular subjects.
☐ (such as _____)

6. Have your purchased other SAMS or Hayden books in the past year? _____
If yes, how many _____

7. Would you purchase another book in the FIRST BOOK series? _____

8. What are your primary areas of interest in business software? _____

☐ Word processing (particularly _____)
☐ Spreadsheet (particularly _____)
☐ Database (particularly _____)
☐ Graphics (particularly _____)
☐ Personal finance/accounting (particularly _____)
☐ Other (please specify _____)

Other comments on this book or the SAMS' book line: _____
_____

Name _____
Company _____
Address _____
City _____ State _____ Zip _____
Daytime telephone number _____
Title of this book _____

Fold here

- -

NO POSTAGE
NECESSARY
IF MAILED
IN THE
UNITED STATES

BUSINESS REPLY MAIL
FIRST CLASS   PERMIT NO. 336   CARMEL, IN

POSTAGE WILL BE PAID BY ADDRESSEE

SAMS

11711 N. College Ave.
Suite 141
Carmel, IN 46032-9839

Quick Command Reference (Menu and Keystroke)

Function	Menu Selections	Quick Keys
Base Font in a Document	Font, Base Font, 1	`Ctrl`-`F8`, `4`, `1`
Base Font in Printer File	File, Print, S, 3, 5, 1	`⇧Shift`-`F7`, `S`, `3`, `5`, `1`
Column Off	Layout, Columns, Off	`Alt`-`F7`, `1`, `2`
Column On	Layout, Columns, On	`Alt`-`F7`, `1`, `1`
Column Define	Layout, Columns, Define	`Alt`-`F7`, `1`, `3`
Convert To or From WordPerfect	From WP51 directory, enter Convert	
Create Directory	File, List Files, =	`F5`, =
Delete Directory	File, List Files, (highlight), 2	`F5`, (highlight), `2`
Document Initial Font	Layout, Document, 3, 1	`⇧Shift`-`F8`, `3`, `3`, `1`
Figure Options	Graphics, Figure, Options	`Alt`-`F9`, `1`, `4`
Figure Creation	Graphics, Figure, Create	`Alt`-`F9`, `1`, `1`
Figure Edit	Graphics, Figure, Edit	`Alt`-`F9`, `1`, `2`
Line Creation	Graphics, Line, Create Horizontal or Create Vertical	`Alt`-`F9`, `5`, `1` or `2`
Retrieve DOS File	File, Text In, DOS Text	`Ctrl`-`F5`, `1`
Save to Word Processing Format	File, Text Out, (format)	`Ctrl`-`F5`, `3`
Save to DOS Format	File, Text Out, DOS Text	`Ctrl`-`F5`, `1`
Sort a List	Tools, Sort	`Ctrl`-`F9`, `2`
Spreadsheet Import	File, Text In, Spreadsheet, Import	`Ctrl`-`F5`, `5`, `1`

Function	Menu Selections	Quick Keys
Spreadsheet Link	File, Text In, Spreadsheet, Create Link	Ctrl-F5, 5, 2
Style Create	Layout, Styles, 3	Alt-F8, 3
Style Use	Layout, Styles, 1	Alt-F8, 1
Table Create	Layout, Tables, Create	Alt-F7, 2, 1
Text Box Options	Graphics, Text Box, Options	Alt-F9, 3, 4
Text Box Creation	Graphics, Text Box, Create	Alt-F9, 3, 1
Text Box Edit	Graphics, Text Box, Edit	Alt-F9, 3, 2